CATALOG
OF
Creative
Ministries

CATALOG OF
Creative Ministries

Over 300 Ideas That Work

VIRGIL AND LYNN NELSON

Judson Press® Valley Forge

CATALOG OF CREATIVE MINISTRIES

Copyright © 1983
Judson Press, Valley Forge, PA 19482-0851

Bible quotations in this volume are from the Revised Standard Version of the Bible copyrighted 1946, 1952 © 1971, 1973 by the Division of Christian Education of the National Council of the Churches of Christ in the U.S.A., used by permission, and from *The Holy Bible,* King James Version.

Library of Congress Cataloging in Publication Data

Nelson, Virgil.
  Catalog of creative ministries.

    1. Pastoral theology—Handbooks, manuals, etc.
I. Nelson, Lynn,   II. Title.
BV4011.N37 1983   259′.025′73   83-16219
ISBN 0-8170-1017-3

The name JUDSON PRESS is registered as a trademark in the U.S. Patent Office.
Printed in the U.S.A. ✣

Acknowledgments

Our thanks to the many who have helped with the compilation and completion of this volume:

Contributors: the hundreds of folk who are involved in creative ministry in their communities and in the world;

Correspondence Assistant: Chloe Raitt; *Telephone Researcher:* Earl Hawley;

Provider of Writing Sanctuary and Still Space: Mount Calvary Retreat Center;

Typists: Mary Tebault, Vernon Verdades, Elaine and Linda Sallee, Dan Wakelee, Patty Olson, Timm Peterson, and Helen Dunn;

Illustrations: Timm Peterson;

Reviewers: Lloyd Howard, Larry Dobson, Bob Wallace;

Family: who had to put up with piles of papers in the living room and a preoccupied father and mother for months during the process;

Editor: Harold Twiss for his patience with my trying to meet specific deadlines while coping with the uncertainties of full-time pastoral responsibilities in the parish.

Dedicated to those seeking to be faithful in the kingdom of God everywhere.

Shalom,

Virgil and Lynn Nelson
283 E. Vince St.
Ventura, CA 93001

67647

Contents

Introduction

Purposes for This Book

This book was written in order to—
1. stimulate ideas and reflection about ministry and needs;
2. be a catalyst for use by the Holy Spirit;
3. encourage people to have the faith to "begin small" and trust the results to God;
4. help creative persons ministering in similar areas of need to network with one another.

Focus: "Here Am I! Send Me."

This theme passage from Isaiah 6:1-8 challenges us to accept God's call and forgiveness and then to respond in commitment, discipleship, and service. Being assured of our forgiveness, we can offer ourselves to God to go out among the people of unclean lips with God's Good News of love and forgiveness and the invitation to all people to join God's family.

The primary focus of ministries included in this book is *beyond the walls* of the local congregation. Hence we have not catalogued resources for the "in-house" ministries, such as creative worship, creative methods for teaching church school, or creative youth ministry. We have included references to other resources in some of these areas.

There is an important connection between the "internal" and "external" ministries of the congregation—the people who travel back and forth, in and out, through the entire fabric of our communities. The focus outward comes full circle as people make commitments and are brought into the body of Christ for nurture and discipleship training and are sent forth again.

How to Use This Book

1. Read it straight through during your vacation or whenever you have a convenient block of time.
2. Study the Contents for areas of interest. You will find a number of ideas in each of these areas. These are only samples of the kinds of ministries that are being conducted to meet various needs.
3. Watch for reproductions of book covers throughout this catalog. These key books will get you started in a given area of ministry and lead you on to other resources. All book prices shown are subject to change.
4. Send a *self-addressed stamped envelope* (SASE) to the people listed and request information on a particular aspect of their ministry—or give them a call. For information about any programs or ideas from First Baptist Church of Oak View, California, write to Virgil and Lynn Nelson.
5. Take time to pray, to converse with the Master of creativity, regarding how seeds may be planted in the garden of your life and world.
6. Carry the book to workshops and conferences to show your friends.
7. If all else fails, use the book as a paperweight for that pile of papers on your desk.

Getting Started

If there was ever a time and a need for creative ministry, it is *now* and here in the U.S.A. At every turn we see people hungering. In the wealthy countries people are grasping at cults for spiritual highs and life direction, and many old people are eating cat food. In poor countries people are struggling in darkness.

In the midst of this ever-expanding world of opportunities for ministry as God's people, we see *signs of an ailing church:*
1. Declining formal church membership and church school participation.
2. Pessimism in the training and equipping of professional leadership. Major seminaries have closed or merged with others because we are oversupplied with Protestant clergy and there is less need for schools.
3. Decrease in our commitments to global ministries. When faced with falling budgets, major denominations have chosen to cut budgets for overseas ministry.
4. Narcissistic faith—one which often asks, "What can God/Jesus/my church do for me?" We shop around for a church to fit us rather than asking God where we are called to serve. We have things backwards.

There is need for change. There is need for the creative

winds of God's spirit again to fill and empower not only individual Christians but the entire body of Christ.

All over this land we see glimmers of Christ's light: "I am the Light of the world"; "Behold I do a new thing."

This book is an opportunity for us to celebrate what God is doing already and to be inspired and encouraged in our awareness that God is at work in the midst of this ailing body that is the church. Jesus comes again to us because we have need of a physician!

Creative Ministries: Who Is Creative?

Who is creative? You, the reader. Every reader is special and unique—created in God's image. Therefore, every person is by nature creative.

Before one can be creative, one must be tuned in to the source of all creativity.

Before one can walk a tightrope, one must be centered and balanced within.

Before one can be a peacemaker, one must be at peace.

Before one can share God's love, one must have experienced that love.

Before one can hear God, one must be still.

For many of us, being still is one of our hardest tasks. When the body is finally still, the mind races on and on. Prayer and meditation are the tools we need to place ourselves "in expectancy" before God; they are just beginning to be rediscovered in the Western church. (For resources in this area, see pages 37-38 in this volume.)

What Is Creative Ministry?

Ministry is not creative because it is razzle-dazzle, involves big numbers, or is new and flashy. It is creative because it clearly assesses needs (with the "givens" of a particular situation and its context) and then begins to bring healing of our dis-ease—wholeness out of fragmentation, reconciliation out of separation, and God's *shalom* (peace) out of chaos.

"Many of our programs seem innovative to outsiders because they do not conform to customary ways of doing things. We did not try to be different. People here did not know the 'acceptable way.' They merely organized to get the job done" (Sister Marie Cirillo, Director; Appalachian Community Development Ministry, Clairfield, TN 37715).

As co-creators with God, whose kingdom is to be on earth, we are called to deal both with individuals and with the complex web of structures that are the invisible threads holding our civilization and world togther. When one ministers with individuals, one inevitably ends up in direct conflict with the structures that trap individuals and keep them oppressed and bound.

Creativity Is Situational

It takes creativity to *see* a problem. Then it takes creativity to formulate the problem in such a way that a solution is possible. Finally, it takes creativity to develop and implement a solution for that situation.

Dare to Start Small

Too often we are overwhelmed into inaction by taking something small and do-able and extrapolating it in our minds into a major program which is so grandiose that we say, "I can't do all of that . . . I don't have the time . . . I don't know how."

We need to *start small* in responding to a specific hurt, and we need to *do something*. In the doing, we should turn our actions over to God, even as the boy who gave Jesus his two loaves and five fishes. Other people then may be opened to minister to this same need that God has revealed to us. In miraculous ways, God will multiply whatever it is we give.

DARE TO BEGIN.

Foundations for Creative Ministry

Jesus was born into a world of pain and misery. He was not overcome by the world. He calls us through the winds of his Spirit to overcome the world.

Without spiritual disciplines tying us to Christ, we are like a balloon without a string, lost into the sky with no firm guide. Without the central tie to our Maker, we try to fly on the energy that is available and are soon dashed on the rocks or treetops of exhaustion and despair. With the central "tie point" our balloon can be blown by the winds of God's Spirit or lashed by the icy blasts of life, and still it will be securely fastened to the source of life, energy, and vision.

To begin to understand the creative journey inward and outward, you will find an excellent overview in the book *The Celebration of Discipline: Paths to Spiritual Growth,* by Richard J. Foster, Harper & Row, 1978 ($7.95).

The spiritual disciplines open the door for God to enter. They allow us to place ourselves before God so that God can transform us. This is like the farmer who cannot *make* the grain grow. All the farmer can do is provide the proper conditions for growth. In much the same way, the spiritual disciplines are a way of sowing with the guidance of the Spirit; they are a way of getting us into the ground. They put us where God can work within and transform us.

The path of the spiritual life is "the way of disciplined grace"—grace because it is free, disciplined because there is something for us to do. And yet the path does not produce the change; it only puts us in the place where the change can occur.

If the disciplines ever are turned into "laws," they become a way of death.

Foster divides the disciplines into three categories:

1. The Inward Disciplines: meditation
                                 prayer
                                 fasting
                                 study
2. The Outward Disciplines: simplicity
                                 solitude
                                 submission
                                 service

3. The Corporate Disciplines: confession
                                 worship
                                 guidance
                                 celebration

Each chapter is a unique blend of historical perspective and practical direction, with generous quotation from the Scriptures and the spiritual masters. Specific exercises are suggested, and the text is rich meat for discussion and reflection by individuals and/or groups.

The collected footnotes will lead one to a host of other sources in this vital area.

A second key guidebook for the creative journey inward is *The Other Side of Silence: A Guide to Christian Meditation,* by Morton T. Kelsey, Paulist Press, 1976 ($7.95).

This volume provides a significant overview of the history of Christian meditation with the counterparts in the Eastern disciplines, and it includes a generous portion of specific exercises and tools for meditation. Kelsey has developed a diagram that has been very helpful in conceptualizing the "nature of reality" (see the diagram on the next page as adapted from pages 147 and 170; adapted with permission of Paulist Press © 1976 by the Missionary Society of St. Paul the Apostle in the state of New York).

Entrance into the spiritual world is through the "door opening" between the two kinds of "reality" or "consciousness."

Our Western culture trains us well in the use of the tools needed for working in the world of physical reality, primarily rational thinking, and problem solving (left-brain activities). However, this world is merely the "tip of the iceberg" of reality.

The first awareness of the spiritual world is often in the form of visions or dreams (remember Joseph, Peter, and John). The progressive experience and knowledge of the spiritual world comes from many different levels, represented numerically in the diagram of the spiritual and physical worlds, shown on the next page.

The spiritual disciplines are *tools* for opening the door to the spiritual world and placing ourselves where God can speak to us.

Spiritual forces of GOOD.

⊗ DREAMS

THE DOOR/OPENING BETWEEN THE TWO KINDS OF CONSCIOUSNESS

9.
8.
7.
6.
3.
2.
1.
4.
5.

Spiritual forces of EVIL

THE UNCONSCIOUS (RIGHT BRAIN ACTIVITY)

WAKING CONSCIOUSNESS (LEFT BRAIN ACTIVITY)

▷ REPRESENTS THE PSYCHE.

1. consciousness (waking)
2. memory
3. the personal unconscious
4. the vast stage of the psyche
5. the archetypal unconscious
6. clear communication
7. numinous experience
8. extrasensory perception of the physical world
9. visionary overview

Planning for Creative Ministry

"Where there is no vision, the people perish" (Proverbs 29:18, KJV).

The New Testament provides us with a vision of the creative ministries of the body of Christ practiced 2000 years ago. What can a small or average-size church in America in the 1980s do? The following churches and organizations demonstrate what can be done.

Oakhurst Baptist Church in Decatur, Georgia

Oakhurst Baptist Church (Southern) is committed to crossing the bridge between being concerned and being effectively involved in missions. In attempting to cross this bridge, they have *reversed* the usual approach to mission.

Instead of a committee deciding for the congregation what needs doing, the focus is turned on the membership. Any member impressed with a need can sound a call for the formation of a mission group.

Incredible new energy has been released for world hunger, peace and reconciliation, refugee resettlement, economic justice, training for the unemployed, shelter for homeless men and other ministries.

Here's how it works. An individual who feels impressed with a need . . . first tests his/her impressions with the missions committee and the ministers. This is a clarifying step, never a put down or a put off step.

The person determines that he/she is willing to become the stack pole person around whom a mission group can be formed.

From the Church of the Savior [sic] in Washington, DC, we learned three questions helpful in considering the call. 1) *Is the call incredibly Good News to you?* God doesn't call us to do things out of a sense of guilt or dread, but out of joy or excitement. 2) *Is the call almost impossible to accomplish?* God often calls us to tasks beyond our reach. 3) *Is there a good chance you will fail?* We are reminded that God's love and grace are constant regardless of the outcome or "success" of anything we undertake. Our responsibility is to be faithful to our perception of God's call. If one does that, there is never really a failure.

During a Sunday morning worship, the call is sounded to others who might hear it as "good news." These form a mission group and are encouraged to spend six months to a year studying the need, approaches to meet the need, and how the gospel impacts the area. A biblical understanding of the mission is developed, and in-depth personal time is spent getting to know each other. The group is also encouraged to adopt common spiritual disciplines for an inward journey to sustain the outward journey.

What if no one responds? If so, then we feel either we have not heard the call correctly or the time is not right for that mission. Thus, the call is tested.

What if the group fails? There's a good chance some will—mission groups come and go. Some accomplish their purpose for the moment; others lose their stack pole person, or, for other reasons, don't continue to function. We can celebrate the effort. At least our consciousness was raised concerning the need, and we have seen other groups come later to address the need from another perspective.

How do you control the groups? We do not. That is left to God's Spirit. We seek to free the groups for the work to which they feel called.

(By Walker Knight, chair of the Mission Committee at Oakhurst Baptist Church. Quoted from *Sprouts,* March 1982, with permission.)

The varieties of ministries are evident. One of them, the world-hunger mission group, has had a national impact!

The church is now publishing a full-length magazine, *Seeds,* dealing with the causes of and the Christian responses to world hunger. The commitment is to enable Christians, especially Southern Baptists, to respond to the poor, not just with charity, but with biblical justice. A response of justice demands a mature understanding of the spiritual, political, and economic realities that lie at the root of hunger. *Seeds* is published twelve times a year.

The ministry of *Seeds* and *Sprouts* is maintained by the small missions group within the congregation. It is not operated, directed, or financed by a denomination or any other group. The educational and action impact of the *Seeds* ministry is an example of God's creative miracles using a small core of committed people. Write *Seeds/Sprouts,* Oakhurst Baptist Church, 222 E. Lake Drive, Decatur, GA 30030.

Church of the Saviour, Washington, D.C.

Composed of six faith communities, each with about twenty core members, the Church of the Saviour has initiated and sustained over thirty ministries that creatively serve people for Christ. A brief summary of twenty-two of these ministries is found in Appendix B.

Write to the Church of the Saviour's Bookstore for a list of titles documenting the various aspects of the congregation's growth in ministry. (Bookstore, %Potter's House, 1658 Columbia Road NW, Washington, DC 20009.)

Other Communities of Vision

Other communities of faith are shining examples of God's vision incarnated through the efforts of finite human beings. Studying any one of these can provide new vision.

1. *Koinonia,* located in Americus, GA, is an outgrowth of the life and ministry of Clarence Jordan. (See the December 1979 issue [vol. 8, no. 12] of *Sojourners* magazine for an excellent introduction/overview. Reprints are available.) Write to Koinonia Partners, Rt. 2, Americus, GA 31709-9986, and request a catalog of books/materials.

2. *Sojourners Community,* 1309 L St., NW, Washington, DC 20005.

3. Any one of ten congregations studied in depth in *Growing Churches for a New Age,* by Owen W. Owens, Judson Press, 1981 ($7.95).

To see God's *vision* in our planning we need:

> *Expectancy*—"Thy kingdom come. Thy will be done, on earth as it is in heaven."
>
> *Hope*—"Even greater things than these you will do in my name because I go to the Father" (John 14:12, paraphrased).
>
> *Meditation*—Reflect upon what God wants for men and women, as revealed through Christ and God's faithful servants over the centuries.

These indeed are necessary ingredients to bring to the planning table.

The Process of Planning

A plan becomes a process whereby a vision can take on flesh. During the planning process the seed of an idea—a vision for ministry—can be planted and nourished and helped to grow into a fruitful ministry.

Ministry within a congregation and community needs to be coordinated. The right hand needs to know what the left is doing. For example, the same person should not be approached for major responsibilities by three different committees at the same time. If each person or committee is off "doing its own thing" and the body is attempting to grow in all directions at once, the results may look good statistically but the end result may be total chaos and burnout.

"Growth without focus" in the physical body is a functional definition of cancer. The cells divide and multiply, and yet their purpose genetically and functionally is somehow lost and the organism itself is ultimately devoured.

Planning is one way that growth can be differentiated and focused.

There are a variety of categories for resistance to planning:

1. *"Don't fence me in."* All of life is planned and scheduled. We want one place to do our own thing, but we will be there to do it only if we feel like it.

2. *"Fear of failure."* If we have a plan, it will be used to pass judgment on us and our worth: "We made it; aren't we great?" or "We/you blew it; isn't it awful?" Without a plan, there is no point of reference for reflection or evaluation.

3. *"One day at a time."* Some question the need for planning at all, saying, "Live for today and let tomorrow take care of itself." (See Matthew 6:25-34.) While this is a profound truth, it is only half of a whole. God revealed to Joseph the meaning of the pharaoh's dream (Genesis 41) and used Joseph to plan for the famine that was coming. We are called by God to look ahead and plan for the future; we are also to look behind and see God's mighty acts. But we are to live in neither place—we are here *now*.

4. *"Now that we have a plan, we're finished."* Just because we have the blueprints drawn and approved does not mean the building is built. We are in the work of building God's kingdom, not in the business of drawing up blueprints. A plan only takes on life and fulfills its purpose as it is implemented.

A plan allows commitment to begin moving into action. A plan sets a focus, a goal. It gives us a clear frame of reference that can be modified and adjusted, based on new information and changing circumstances.

Having the structure of a plan allows even more freedom for the Spirit to work in, through, and around it. Plans are but means to an end. We need continuing roots in the spiritual foundations in Christ and the vision of God's kingdom before us.

All of Us Can Plan

"Who me? I don't know how to plan. We need someone else to do it for us. Can't we hire someone to get that done? Don't people get master's degrees in planning and organizational development?"

Planning is nothing special; most of us plan all the time. It is, for the most part, an unconscious process at work in all aspects of our lives. When we get into our auto in order to drive it, planning is happening (and has happened) each step of the way. We planned to bring the key; we plan on the car starting—assuming the battery is charged. If it doesn't

start, we devise plan "B." Assuming that everything works, we drive on—as long as there is gas in the tank. We also plan our route.

We plan constantly, all the time. The question is this: *Do we transfer our planning skills and learning into thinking and planning for the ministries of our congregations?* Too often the answer is no.

Who should do the planning for our congregation if everyone can plan? If we say that everyone is responsible for planning, this often means that no one is consciously doing it. Those with specific leadership responsibilities need to be regularly and consciously involved in planning. Everyone can be invited to enter the process periodically, for example, in an annual all-church planning retreat.

How extensive and detailed do our plans need to be? Plans can become so elaborate and expansive that some people feel a reluctance to do them at all. A 150-page planning-process manual for use over a 10-year period seems overwhelming to many people.

Short of a full-scale thrust, it is possible to include a planning time block in each of several regularly scheduled monthly board or committee meetings. One frustration with this may be the feeling that "things seem to take forever" or "we have been at this for months!"

A couple of special sessions of an intermediate length can produce much more feeling of movement and offer distinct advantages.

We can only begin where we are. For most people that will mean being a "simple tune," something short of a "full symphony." When it comes to the disciplines of planning, we are often "unfinished symphonies," and yet God can use us to make beautiful music.

In preparing to plan, we need to focus specifically on the *people* about whom we are reflecting. In this volume we are focusing on persons in communities beyond our immediate fellowship.

For planning purposes, how can we limit or define our focus on the people beyond our fellowship? One way might

be to establish a "distance" definition—for example, "all of the people within a three-mile radius of our building." Or the focus might be geographical—"everyone west of the expressway." Political or economic entities might provide the limitations of focus—"all people in this city, this county, or this state." Or focus might be determined by a given or common characteristic of the persons we want to reach—"all those who are developmentally disabled" or "all those who have experienced divorce."

(For an extensive listing of possible foci for looking at persons in our community, see Appendix A.)

Planning Models

Half-Hour Planning Session

A. (20 minutes) Divide group into pairs and ask them to reflect on and record their responses to the following questions.
1. How are you feeling about _____ (the defined focus of planning—our church school, our congregation, our possible work with divorced persons—whatever has been chosen)?
2. What strengths do you see in our existing ministry?
3. What weaknesses or problems do you see? What concerns do you have?
4. How can we/I/the congregation/the board better help or support you?

B. (10 minutes) Have the pairs come together in groups of eight people and share their written responses.

C. Collect the written responses from all of the pairs and collate them for future discussion, reflection, priority setting, and planning. Close in prayer together.

One-Hour Planning Session

A. (20 minutes) Individual writing and reflecting on this question: If God told me that I could not fail and God gave me all of the resources I wanted (money/people/ etc.), what would I set out to do in God's name?

B. (20 minutes) Sharing, in groups of eight, responses and feelings about responses.

C. (15 minutes) Groups of eight sharing with entire group or sharing in clusters with complete recording of input from each person/group.

D. (5 minutes) Prayer/song.

Three-Hour Planning Session (expandable)

(Based on *Planning for Campus Ministry*, developed by Rev. John Scherer, Associate Director of Training, Leadership Institute of Spokane, Washington. Used with permission.)

A. (5 minutes) Get acquainted, in twos, by completing the statement "Before this meeting is over, I hope we have. . . ."

B. (15-20 minutes maximum) Use this guided fantasy: "The Helicopter Trip" (imagery adapted). The leader instructs the entire group:

"Get comfortable. Relax with your eyes closed. Imagine that we are out on the church parking lot (or a football field) and we're waiting for a helicopter. Here it comes . . . it lands gently . . . we get in. . . . The pilot takes off and lifts up to 50 feet . . . 100 . . . 200 . . . 500 . . . 1,000. What do you see? We begin to move about the community. What stands out? . . . Where are the centers of activity? Where are the quiet places? We fly over city hall and have the amazing power to see and hear anything going on there. What do you see? hear? . . . Move on to the police department, the planning department, and others."

(Continue, suggesting other structures/people in your community—schools, social service and government agencies, specific groups of people . . . those who are unemployed, those who are undocumented, or those who belong to a particular minority or other group.)

"The pilot brings us back to our parking lot . . . down . . . down. Open your eyes when you are ready. Find a couple of others and write down on newsprint what you 'saw' and 'heard.' The idea is to get a visual collage of all the images you had. Use words, diagrams, sketches, anything. Do not argue or discuss, *just* report."

C. (15-20 minutes maximum) Report as described in the instructions.

D. (15 minutes) Summarize/clarify all issues/concerns on another sheet of newsprint; select two or three as target foci for our possible ministry. The key is significance and accessibility.

E. (15 minutes) Using the issues chosen above, respond on newsprint to three categories: What do we hope people will be able to *think, feel,* and *do* differently when they have been part of this new ministry?

	Think	*Feel*	*Do*
Concern #1.			
Concern #2.			
(etc.)			

F. (15 minutes) Break.

G. (15 minutes each) Respond to the following:
1. Write next to each line listed in D some specific clues as to how you might tell that these things are happening.
2. If we had unlimited resources—money, people, etc.—

what would we do?
3. Prioritize the top five ideas, using the following criteria: (a) highest area of need; (b) feasibility of beginning now with resources we have or can project having; (c) appropriateness and congruency with our mission as Christians in this place. Use the following grid.

Target Group (problem)	Priority	Feasibility	Mission

H. (10 minutes) What excites us most? What gets the creative juices flowing? Record persons' names on the sheet next to the topics in which they are most interested. Move people together who share common concerns.

I. (15 minutes) In small groups, list—
1. what resources will be needed to do this project,
2. what specific things we could do to guarantee the success of this project.

J. (10 minutes) Decide on the division of labor (who? doing what? by when? how?) needed to achieve this ministry.

K. (10 minutes) Report back to total group and close with worship.

Implementation of the plan then rests with the small cluster groups who have created and owned their particular piece of the whole.

Three Two-Hour Planning Sessions

SESSION ONE:

A. Preparation:

Make copies of the following Scripture study material so that each person may have a copy.

Passages for study:
1. Luke 4:16-22
2. Jeremiah 7:1-8
3. Matthew 24:31-46
4. 2 Corinthians 5:17-19
5. Leviticus 19:9-10, 33-34
6. James 2:14-16
7. 1 John 3:10-12
8. Romans 15:13

Read passages out loud to your partner/group; then discuss.
1. What does this passage say?
2. What did the passage mean when it was written?
3. What does it mean in my/our lives now? (How does it apply to us?)

Make copies of the chart on page 20 so that each one will have a copy.

B. Scripture Study: Foundations and Call (45 minutes)

Divide the group into pairs and assign a Scripture passage to each pair. Have each pair read the Scripture and discuss the questions listed. For the final 10–15 minutes, ask the pairs to cluster in groups of 8–12 people. Have each pair read its passage out loud to the group and share briefly the key insights from its discussion.

C. Needs Analysis (using chart on page 20) (30 minutes)

Point out the process of this session, using columns 1-3 and moving from left to right. Indicate that groups are not to discuss needs or try to solve problems at this point; they are merely to record as comprehensive and specific a list as possible.

Ask the following questions to elicit needs: What are the needs/issues/problems in our community? Where is racism/oppression/hunger/injustice/alienation evident? Who specifically are the victims? Where is there need for reconciliation? Who is hurting? How are they hurting (physically, emotionally, spiritually)?

Encourage people to be specific. "We need better schools" is too general. Ask, "How would we know when our schools are better? What would be different when/if they improve?"

Answers to those specifics might be: "Our children could read at grade level; drug abuse would be reduced 75% on campus; there would be better discipline in classroom/on campus"; etc.

D. Dreaming/Wishing (30 minutes)

Note the items that are related and color code these if practical. Pick two critical areas by consensus and write *"wish statements"* for each. Simply share as many "I wish . . ." statements as possible. Wishes assume success and the availability of all resources needed to accomplish the wish.

E. Sharing and Next Steps (15 minutes)
1. Have each group share with the entire group or cluster its list of needs and wishes.
2. In light of all the group reports, be thinking of the *top three* priorities for future work together.
3. Close with prayer in the small groups and sing together as a total group.

SESSION TWO:

Review scriptural foundations. Give an overview of the session, again using the chart on page 20. This session will focus on columns 4 and 5.

A. Setting Priorities (15-30 minutes)

Working with the original newsprint or a written summary of the previous session, ask groups to rank the top three concerns/problems/issues/needs as they see them. If possible, work in the same groups of 8-12 people as before.

B. Reviewing and Expanding the Dreams/Wishes for Those Three Priorities (15 minutes)

C. Brainstorming Objectives (15-30 minutes)

Using the top three priorities chosen, divide the group into three subsections, one for each top-priority need/wish.
1. Brainstorm as many objectives as possible. Objectives complete the statement "To do that we need to . . . ." (Use half the time here.)
2. Have each group pick one of these objectives and brainstorm a list of possible methods by which that objective could be carried out, step by step.

D. Reporting Back by Individual Groups (25 minutes)

Save all working papers for compilation and for a record (for possible future use) of concerns not chosen for the present.
1. Among all possible objectives from small groups, come to consensus on three which seem doable.
2. For each of these three, review the methods suggested and begin to list some brief items with respect to dates, possible people, and resources.
3. List additional methods possible for accomplishing the objectives chosen.

E. Establishing Priorities Among All the Methods Suggested for the Top Three Objectives (10 minutes)

F. Closing: Prayer/Song in Small Groups (5 minutes)

SESSION THREE: (Allot time as needed.)

A. Review scriptural foundations and materials generated thus far in the process.

B. Review priority methods chosen and the focus for this session (three right-hand columns of the chart).

C. Brainstorm additional methods possibilities. Review entire list and recheck priorities. For the top three methods suggested, list—
1. limitations of this method or things which would block it;
2. advantages of this method or things which would help it.

D. For each method, work sequentially through the columns, listing target dates for each item, the ideal time line for implementation of the method, and who is going to do which part of the method and by when.

E. List extensively the resources, equipment supplies, people, funds, etc., that will be needed to implement this method. Securing these is part of the necessary division of labor and, depending upon what is chosen, may result in the need to recycle the entire process with respect to a given resource.

F. Establish a time and date when the entire group is going to review the plans decided upon. Establish who is going

SESSION 1			SESSION 2		SESSION 3		
Theological Foundations and Perspectives	Needs, Issues, Problems	Dreams or Wishes	Possible Objectives	Possible Methods	Target Dates	Who Will Do What By When?	Resources Needed
On which Scriptures, mandates, or principles do we base our concern? (assumptions about the change process; relationship between experience and intellect)	Where are racism, oppression, hunger, or injustice evident? Which persons or organizations need reconciliation? Who is hurting? How are they hurting?	I wish we could. . . . (possible goal statement)	To do that, we need to. . . .	(step by step)	(or time)		(supplies, money, people, etc.)

to keep track of the entire process and its flow.

G. Close with a time of prayer and singing.

The goal of this three-session process is not to solve everything at once but to *get something happening* toward solutions so that momentum and information are generated which can be factored in as the plans are implemented. This information can be included as the group continues to move toward its goal.

Planning Retreat

The first annual planning retreat (May 1982) of the Paradise United Methodist Church (P.O. Box 38, Paradise, CA 95969) was a smashing success, according to Alice Ann Glenn, director of Christian education, primarily because the process was kept simple and was well planned ahead of time.

The entire congregation gave input for the retreat by responding to the following questions in advance:

1. What are your biggest dreams for our congregation?
2. What concerns do you hope will be considered at the planning retreat?
3. I would attend the retreat if—

The format of the day kept closely to the predetermined

timing for action and movement. Goal statements were generated and resources were listed. Participants made lists of hindrances blocking the goals and lists of suggestions for eliminating each hindrance. Specific time and accountability planning was accomplished in subcommittees by area of responsibility. (Child care was arranged for the day, and transportation was shared.)

The accomplishments of the retreat were significant for an 8 A.M.– 4 P.M. day, including transportation time.

All input was saved and typed for ongoing use by committees throughout the year and with the congregation.

Community Tour

The planning models already described have relied heavily upon people's memories of their community. The following approach, going *into* the community for an actual tour, can provide new input for focus. The group divides into twos or threes and goes out to see and discover what is there.

A longer look can come through a ten-step research and interview process for planning ministry developed by Rev. Keith Hubbell of the First Baptist Church, 1100 E. Cameron Ave., West Covina, CA 91790.

A. Introduction and Purpose: What kind of community do you live in? Who are the influential people? What

ROUGH SAMPLE: – HOUSING – VENTURA/AVE.

NEEDS/ISSUE PROBLEM:	WISHES:	POSSIBLE OBJECTIVES, 'TO DO THAT WE NEED TO':	METHODS STEPS:	TARGET DATES, DO WHAT BY WHEN	WHO WILL DO	RESOURCES NEEDED
Some people spend 80% of income on housing	Find ways to help persons + families have adeq. hsg. at fair price	Research housing facts – Hapts, sizes, restrictions, rents – ownership maint.	Secure census data: Library + C. Simmons.	Sept. 1, 82	Karen	Phone
			Secure data from Housing Authority	Sept. 1, 82	Karen	Zerox $15±
Exhorbitent rents + poor maint.		Organization + ed. of tennants re. their responsib's + rights.	Call Richard at SB's Center his study.	Sept. 1, 82	Karen	
Families with children excluded from many rentals	Find ways to help younger fams have source of rentals where ch. ok. / publicize owners violat. law.	Media exposure	Determine property ownership – Assessor's office. → Devise a plan by Sept. 1. Do by Dec. 1.		Joe. Mary Sarah Chris	Travel to co. center
Young families, no hope of ever owning a home	Ways young families can purchase	Establish housing coop on ave.	Create 3 ain for door to poor use. → A. Determine info. needed		Ken	
Run-down, deteriorating homes in ave. area		Explore Habitat for Humanity model for use here.	"Drive by" visual inspection for poor maint.	B. Rough draft by Aug. 1st	Ken + Dan	

areas of pain are there? What can your congregation do to relieve the hurting? How can you discover who is hurting?

B. Ten Steps to Rediscovering Your Community:
1. Research the data about your city; develop its community profile. (For sources/process, see item "C.")
2. Design a tour of your city.
3. Tour the city, taking note of strength/pain areas.
4. Discuss in groups what you saw on the tour.
5. Brainstorm painful issues in the community.
6. Select the specific pain area for which action strategy will be planned. The pertinent question here is not "Can we do anything about it?" but rather "Where does it hurt?"
7. Formulate a goal in response to this pain.
8. Consult with resource persons in church and community in order to gain as much information as possible about the issues.
9. Design a working paper or strategy that outlines the problem, and suggest means whereby the goal addressing the pain can be achieved. Assign people; establish a time line.
10. Evaluate the program for change.

C. Developing a Community Profile: Research your city/community, using the following sources for discovering its strengths and needs.
1. *Census data for 1960, 1970, 1980:* housing and population trends, ethnic background, income, employment, and age groups.
2. *Police department:* personnel, crime rate, areas covered.
3. *Chamber of Commerce:* materials, structure of the chamber, health of business community.
4. *City library:* city history, topical file for local newspaper articles.
5. *Parks and recreation:* programs available.
6. *City hall:* (a) city planners, master plan, map of the city; (b) city clerk, minutes of past 4–6 sessions, structure of city government, names and tenures of officials, description of how decisions are made.
7. *Schools:* school board structure; how decisions are made; attendance projections, ethnic breakdown, and achievement test scores for all schools.
8. *Influential groups* in community: formal/informal.
9. *Daily newspapers:* 10 back issues over last two months.

The Dream Process—Ecumenical Consultations

Rev. Harry Summers and Dr. Arley Kelly have developed an excellent planning process for clusters of congregations within a local community. This process was used in five cities in New Mexico over several years, with significant impact on cooperative ministry at the local level.

At the INITIAL MEETING, state denominational executives are invited to encourage local pastors and laity to enter fully into the entire process. An overview is given of the consultation and the anticipated schedule—over an entire year.

Focal question 1 (small groups): What can we do in this community to make it easier for pastors to live and preach the gospel? This is brainstormed for about an hour, and then each group is asked to pick *one* item of highest importance to share with the entire group. (Remaining items are kept for possible future use.)

After all groups are heard from, the entire group votes to start on the one focus or area of concern that they feel is most important. Hundreds of possibilities are usually generated, involving all aspects of community life—from the need to improve schools, to dealing with alcoholics, to improving relationships between persons of differing cultures, to youth/adult employment.

The SECOND MEETING, occurring during the following month, concentrates on the one focus chosen. The small-group process centers on brainstorming all of the possible ways that that particular need could be addressed and met. The meeting closes with a vote for the best, most doable strategy as a place to begin.

REMAINING MEETINGS, throughout the year, then focus on the implementation, management, and monitoring of the project/program and on its interpretation to the entire community.

The impact of this process has been significant as churches across denominational/theological lines catch a vision of ministry and commit themselves to it.

Rev. Harry Summers, First United Presbyterian Church, 20th and Cactus Streets, Silver City, NM 88061.

Dr. Arley Kelly, Assistant to the General Secretary, National Council of Churches of Christ in the U.S.A., 475 Riverside Drive, New York, NY 10115-0099.

Group-Process Problem Solving

Gregg Churchill has developed an excellent process for the creative generation of ideas, perspectives, new insights, and solutions, called the "Integral Life Leadership Process" (ILLP). The ILLP is a tool for quickly coming to grips with and deliberately developing movement in life/business/family/church situations.

The process provides an easily learned sequence of—
  identifying issues,
  sensing the context and its effect,
  identifying action needs,
  exploring pertinent facts and perception,
  initiating the action-reflection process,
  focusing on the essentials,
  deliberately enlarging one's view of the situation,
  integrating new awareness,
  developing effective decisions,
  completing feedback loops.

While these steps are not new, the arrangement and execution of the steps enable the covenient and effective processing of information in a time- and energy-saving way. Both right-brain and left-brain activities are brought to bear to generate new ideas, and situations may be treated in a developmental, evolutionary fashion. A time-quota system ensures rapid movement through the process and results in rapid exploration and generation of remarkable amounts of data.

"Using the method, I find myself willing to start working on a problem even when I don't know where to begin" (geologist for a major oil company).

". . . an extremely valuable tool in the resolution of family conflicts. It brings focus to the situation while avoiding unnecessary clashes" (pastor, family counselor).

Using the ILLP, a board or committee can in an hour move through a long-term, complex situation; arrive at new, creative insights; and generate alternative action ideas.

Write to Gregg for information about the process and whether he would be willing to lead seminars in your area. Gregg Churchill, 206 N. Signal, Ojai, CA 93023. Tel.: (805) 646-8500.

Planning Resources

1. *Key Steps in Local Church Planning,* by R. Rusbuldt, R. Gladden and N. Green, Judson Press, 1982 ($5.95). The authors of this manual have also written an extensive 248-page book on the planning process, which is overwhelming to many people. This volume is condensed from the larger *Local Church Planning Manual* and includes key steps in the planning process. It is, in its size and format, more doable. With each step is given basic information needed to understand and do it with confidence.

2. *The Parish Planning Resource* is a media resource which includes guide, filmstrips, and transparencies to equip and assist church councils in their planning responsibilities. Augsburg Publishing, 426 S. Fifth Street, Minneapolis, MN 55415. Leader's Manual (code 23-1780), $25. Participant's Pak (code 23-1781), $2.50.

3. *Look Around Us* is a booklet giving a framework for gathering data on the internal/external context of a given congregation. Done in summary style, it is easy to read and effective. Categories include purpose, getting it together, looking at external facts and internal facts, and looking at internal factors and considerations. Available through Lou Acolla, Director for Parish Development, 422 S. Fifth Street, Minneapolis, MN 55415. Tel.: (800) 328-7185.

4. *Retreat Handbook: A-Way to Meaning,* by Virgil and Lynn Nelson, Judson Press, 1976 ($5.95). This volume is a unique combination of ''how to'' materials in the planning of retreats (including retreats for the purpose of planning) and program resource materials.

5. Alban Institute and Center for Parish Development references, see page 27.

Creative People and Networks of Creativity Sharing

There was a time when I was happy if I got one or two great ideas for ministry out of an entire book. Then, back in 1968, I met Dennis Benson and was introduced to the Recycle community of creative Christians who make it a practice of sharing their ideas for free!

It sounds as radical now as it did then; yet the Holy Spirit as the author of all creativity still calls us to give away what has been so generously given to us. While there are commercial imitators of *Recycle*, the Recycle community continues to share God's freely given creativity with others.

Ideas are edited and placed in the newsletter. Those who are interested in a particular item send a self-addressed, stamped envelope (SASE) to the author, who sends a complete description of the specific ministry.

Over 700 of the best ideas from the Recycle newsletter are included in their entirety in two books: *Recycle I* and *Recycle II*, Abingdon Press, 1975 and 1980 ($6.95). Each volume is incredibly well indexed for use according to various aspects of ministry. Sample categories are as follows: celebrating church seasons; experiencing the Bible, with an index of specific Scripture passages; worshiping: Sunday specials; feelings: acceptance, alienation, death; multitudes of media; and "the best" of the book.

Also available from Recycle is the *Hard Times Catalog for Youth Ministry*, Group Books, 1982 ($14.95). It is indexed and cross-indexed to serve the needs of everyone working with youth. (Allow $1.50 for postage and handling.)

Scan is a newsletter forum for the best list of electronic and human resources in print. These resources are "for purchase," as opposed to those in *Recycle*, which are free. Most items/resources are produced by small groups or family/community ministries. *Scan* costs $10 a year.

For *Recycle, Scan*, books, cassettes, and other creative resources, write to Dennis Benson, *Recycle*, Box 12811, Pittsburgh, PA 15241. Tel.: 412-833-7524.

Leadership Sharing:

The American Lutheran Church has asked key leaders to prepare workshops in their fields of expertise. A description of these workshops, with the names of the leaders, is published for use by local congregations looking for input and leadership.

Samples of the workshops include life and mission planning, training of parish (church) secretaries, training for pastors regarding office functions, spiritual-life retreats, and rural church ministry development. There are many others on almost every special issue that faces the church today. (See p. 28 for address.)

Structures for Sharing Professional Leadership

A number of denominations and congregations have begun to experiment with different ways to provide leadership at the pastoral level. Projections for the next ten years are bleak, with the majority of American congregations having less than two hundred members. One study predicted that nearly half of all pastors would be bivocational in the years to come because of continuing economic pressures.

Copastorates, team ministries, yoked churches are all common. Methodists have changed their order of discipline to allow for husbands and wives who are both ordained to divide the pastoral responsibilities within one congregation without obligating the congregation to two salaries.

The Chula Vista First Baptist Church is currently experimenting with copastors, two men dividing responsibilities according to their gifts and talents. Write to the First Baptist Church, 494 "E" Street, Chula Vista, CA 92010.

Modesto First Baptist has become a model for many churches in calling interns from among its members to function in leadership capacities in all aspects of ministry.

Persons receive continuing training and generally begin with twenty hours a week of ministry, often while continuing to work in their former fields of expertise. After a time, many have ended up as full-time professionals in their service with the congregation.

For information on this program and a schedule for orientation/training of interns, congregations interested in exploring this model in their churches should contact Dr. Bill Yeager, First Baptist Church, 1309 12th Street, Modesto, CA 95354.

Sharing Facilities

More and more churches have increased their awareness of the need to be good stewards of their buildings and space.

One good example of a congregation that has opened its doors to the community is Warwick Central Baptist Church (3270 Post Rd., Warwick, RI 92886). The church facilities have been opened to four Alcoholics Anonymous groups, a community action center, two singing groups, Boy Scouts and Girl Scouts, the Junior Women's Club, a foster parents organization, the Red Cross, training sessions for social workers, departments of local government, and many others.

In addition to this sharing, a variety of programs have been initiated as a result of investigating the needs of the community and attempting in the name of Christ to "love our neighbors as ourselves." New programs include a nursery school with a full-day program and a day-care center for elderly and handicapped people, involving fifty people a day. The day-care center has resulted in the construction of a new addition to the building and the employment of paid staff who provide physical therapy, nutrition, health monitoring, occupational therapy, and rehabilitation.

Church leaders say that through the doors of the building come people seeking support and direction in their lives. Church members have the opportunity to meet them and share with them as personal relationships are formed.

Multiethnic Sharing

Temple Church, Los Angeles, is having a unique experience in multicongregational life. Since 1975 its attendance has doubled because of the proliferation of ethnic and foreign-language programs that have developed into self-sustaining congregations, each maintaining its own staff and budget while remaining a part of the same church fellowship and membership.

Presently Hispanic, Korean, Chinese (Cantonese), and English-speaking congregations are part of the Temple Church project, the stated purpose of which is to glorify God in Jesus Christ through the indwelling Holy Spirit by—

1. sharing the Good News of God's redemptive love in Jesus Christ and training as disciples all those who respond (Matthew 28:18-20; Acts 1:8);

2. unifying the worshiping family whose individual members are frequently separated by language, culture, generation, and creed (Deuteronomy 6:6-9; Philippians 2:1-5);
3. building a practicing community of love and understanding between all peoples, taking seriously the message of Jesus Christ (Mark 1:15; John 17:20-23).

The participating congregations of the church adopted a common charter on June 19, 1978. Each congregation elects two representatives to a coordinating council (board), which directs all mutual life of the total body. Committee chairpersons on membership, fellowship, worship, projects, faith, and finance are appointed by the coordinating council. Each congregation elects one of its members to each committee.

Each congregation retains its own by-laws, elects its internal officers, and sets and raises its own budget. Shared space and facilities are paid for through a "shared costs" approach based on a square-foot-per-hour unit charge for facility use. All finances ultimately pass through a central finance committee for tax purposes. Principles of biblical stewardship, good business methods, and individual congregational effort are preserved for the highest benefit of each participating congregation.

This is an incredible adventure into shared ministry and cooperative use of facilities!

Rev. Jim Conklin, Coordinator, Temple Church, 427 W. Fifth Street, Los Angeles, CA 90013. Tel.: (213) 628-7361.

Resources for Pastor-Parish Self-Understanding

Two organizations that have pioneered in the creation of valuable resources for pastors and congregations in understanding, defining, and examining their own roles, functions, and relationships are the Alban Institute and the Center for Parish Development.

Alban Institute

The Alban Institute is committed to the task of equipping the people of God to minister in the church and in the world. This is accomplished through conferences; resource publications; and training for pastors, laity, and leaders of seminaries, denominations, and congregations. It has a multi-denominational membership of individuals, groups, and judicatories.

Resources are helpfully combined by subject and problem focus and are organized in packages of items that relate closely to one another. Some sample packages and some of the included titles are the following:

1. *The Lay Search Committee: On the Call and Care of Pastors, Prime Time for Renewal, Developmental Tasks of the Parish in Search of a Pastor,* and *One Pastor's Search for a Job: Do You Know the Way to San José?*
2. *Ministry of Laity: Religious Pilgrimage, Learning to Share Ministry, Lay Ministry Tool Kit.*
3. *Lay-Clergy Communication: Mystery of Clergy Authority; Confessions of a Board Member; Stress, Power, and Ministry; Lay Person's Guide to Conflict Management.*
4. *Pastors Changing Parishes: The Minister Looks For a Job; Running Through the Thistles; Terminating a Ministerial Relationship with a Parish; New Beginnings: Pastorate Start-Up Workbook.*
5. *Pastors: Stress, Power, and Ministry; Religious Authenticity in the Clergy; Power Analysis of a Congregation.*
6. *Denominational Leaders: Should the Pastor Be Fired? Unique Dynamics of the Small Church; Changing Pastoral Leadership.*

Here are highlights of two of the above.

New Beginnings: Pastorate Start-Up Workbook, by Roy Oswald, Alban Institute, #AL32. This notebook is designed to help clergy working individually or together to deal with the termination of previous pastorates, cope creatively with the stress of transition, and enter the new pastoral position with a clear plan for ministry.

Stress, Power, and Ministry, by John C. Harris, Alban Institute, #AL27, and companion study guide #AL27SG. These are most helpful in examining the specific role of the pastor with respect to lay leadership and function. They provide tools for definition of pastoral style and role, discussion, negotiation of this role with the pastor/laity as changes happen naturally and as special needs are perceived.

The Alban Institute, Mount St. Alban, Washington, DC 20016. Tel.: (202) 244-3588.

Center for Parish Development (CPD)

The Center for Parish Development has a variety of tools for use by the local congregation and its leadership in planning for and managing ministry.

The *Local Church Planning Manual,* published by CPD, is, according to Dr. Lloyd Howard, Associate Executive Minister of the American Baptist Churches of the Pacific Southwest, "The best of the lot when it comes to a tool for local congregational and pastoral planning."

Workshops are held around the country in various aspects of the management of pastoral ministry and church development.

Write: The Center for Parish Development, 1448 E. 53rd Street, Chicago, IL 60615.

Transitions—Resources for Pastor and Congregation

The American Lutheran Churches, under the direction of Rev. Lou Accola, Director of Parish Development, have taken seriously the transitions that happen in the lives of pastors and congregations when staff changes occur.

"Transition awareness events" are held regularly throughout the United States for pastors and laity, and very creative resources have been evolved.

When a Pastor Moves, by Roy M. Oswald, focuses on the pastor and her/his feelings/roles in leaving a parish and starting again in a new parish.

When a Parish Staff Family Moves, by H. M. Berg, is a planning resource manual for the staff family to use, including the children, as the move is decided and planned. Exercises for sharing and reflecting are included for individual and family use. For example, this one called "Old and New Chapters":

I am completing chapter _____ of my life.
  Describe:
I hope to move into chapter _____.
  I will try to make it look like:
  I want to do:
  My goals for the next year are:

The entire family is encouraged to talk about their pilgrimage or life together, as though it were a book. What chapter does each member feel she/he may be in? What do you hope that the next chapter will be for you? for the family?

These resources are available from: Rev. Lou A. Accola, American Lutheran Church, 422 S. Fifth Street, Minneapolis, MN 55415. Tel.: (800) 328-7185.

Congregation of the Covenants—House Church

Throughout the nation there have been a number of experiments in structure that have chosen the label "house church."

The most common denominators for house churches are: (1) they do not have buildings to purchase or maintain; (2) they are small in numerical size; (3) they have a high degree of commitment to giving, ministry, and caring for those persons involved; (4) they are involved beyond themselves in specific ministries in their communities and the world.

In the Congregation of the Covenants in Indianapolis, Indiana, a core of about thirty people trace the existence of their house church to a thirteen-week study of the Gospel of Mark in 1970. Six couples participated in that study, and the following year they organized as an American Baptist house church. Regular Sunday evening worship in homes, study variety for all ages, decision by consensus, and the highest per-capita giving in the Indiana Baptist Convention characterize this fellowship. While the church has no paid pastor, an ordained minister, a seminary-trained person, and a lay minister participate equally in leadership with other members. More than two hundred persons have participated in the ministry over the past ten years.

For information, write to Indianapolis Baptist Association, 1350 N. Delaware Street, Indianapolis, IN 46202.

House-Church Network of Greater Seattle

Three Baptist pastors were the catalysts for the formation of the house-church network—a coalition of five house-church groups composed of twelve to twenty people each. In 1977, Tom Nielson, Curt Smith, and Chuck Elven began their efforts to meet the needs of persons in an area that was already overchurched (with ninety-one congregations). A survey revealed needs among single parents, youth, and older people, as well as a yearning for a sense of community that was not being met by existing churches. The team ministry has been possible because of the shared vision, friendship, and mutual commitment of its leaders, all of whom supplement their incomes with outside jobs.

Participants in the house-church movement do not see themselves as rebels or isolationists. The Seattle group recognizes its interdependence with the larger congregations.

The house churches rely on large churches for special meetings or for space and equipment for training events and for special enrichment programs (for example, musicals during the special seasons of the year). The small congregations serve a special function as "halfway houses" for those who burn out in the traditional church.

A key to the survival of house churches is the focus beyond the needs of the group per se. "When house churches lose connection with something bigger than themselves, they die," comments Curt Smith. A commitment to mission is necessary. That commitment has been demonstrated in support of Cambodian refugees sponsored by the network, in substantial giving to missions projects, in collecting food for food banks, and in helping the elderly with home repairs.

For information: Rev. Tom Nielson, House-Church Network, 12501 N.E. 137th Place, Kirkland, WA 98033.

Households/Communities Within and Alongside Congregations

Living Together in a World Falling Apart, A Handbook on Christian Community, by Dave and Neta Jackson, Creation House, 1974 ($1.95). The Jacksons visited a dozen Christian communities around the United States and, after spending time with them, wrote this in-depth volume on five of them.

A sequel volume, *Coming Together: All Those Communities and What They're Up To,* was published in 1977 by Brethren Press. It is a follow-up based on revisiting most of the communities. It documents progress and changes and includes new and valuable insights into the ongoing dynamics of God's work through such groups of people within and beside local congregations.

Shared Ministry—Through Area Councils of Churches

The Grand Rapids Area Center of Ecumenism (GRACE) is creatively involved in a broad spectrum of ministry. Its overarching purpose is "to witness to the unity of the people of God under the Lordship of Jesus Christ by: (1) increasing the effectiveness of God's people; (2) promoting an ecumenical approach to human need; and (3) leading churches to deeper fellowship with each other."

The center is involved in ongoing ministries in criminal justice, hunger and poverty, education, minority concerns, and institutional chaplaincy. Samples of a few of the creative ministries that have grown out of standing task forces and affiliated ministries include the following:

A. *Revolving Security-Deposit Fund*—providing assistance to the working poor by guaranteeing their security deposit to landlords. To qualify, one family member must be employed full-time and total family income must not exceed poverty guidelines. Applicant must have lived in the area for at least twelve months, have a satisfactory reference from previous landlords, agree to verification of income, and sign for verification of the terms of the security for the deposit loan.

B. *Widowed-Person Service*—assisting churches in educating the community to the needs of the widowed. Encourages local congregations to reach out to help individuals through the grief process and to support them with practical information as they face the maze of legal and life decisions following the death of a spouse.

C. *Minority Concerns*—creating educational and action opportunities in bringing agencies together to deal with the issues of racism and minority relations in the city.

For information: Rev. Vernon Hoffman, Director, GRACE, 9 Federal Square Bldg., Grand Rapids, MI 49503.

Shared Ministry—Through Nonprofit Organizations

Project Understanding of Ventura, California, is the vehicle for shared ministry by nine congregations. Formed in 1974 around the issue of racism, the focus has expanded to include oppression, hunger, and justice.

Education and action programs are aimed at "building bridges not walls" and include workshops and training sessions on the issues of racism and oppression from a biblical perspective, multicultural events for the entire community, and direct service programs.

Hunger-related needs have led groups to start an emergency food pantry (see p. 77); a food salvage/gleaning program called Food-Share (see p. 78); a county-wide hunger coalition committed to hunger education/advocacy/action in efforts to bring about an end to local and global hunger; and groundwork for a bulk-food purchasing cooperative.

Efforts have been made to work with various county grand juries and other organizations in assessing the needs of the county and planning specific programs with respect to minority persons and women. For instance, housing for farm workers is an ongoing need and has led to involvement with ninety farm-worker families facing eviction.

For information on these and other programs, write: Project Understanding, P.O. Box AE, Ventura, CA 93002.

Creative Resources and Support Structures for Clergy

A number of books and organizations exist to help pastors and lay leaders serve more effectively in ministry and leadership.

1. To help pastors in examining their own priorities and those of their congregations, one of the best resources is *MBO for Non-profit Organizations*, by Dale McConkey, American Management Association, 1975.

   While only one specific chapter deals with religious organizations as one kind of nonprofit organization, the entire book is very helpful in its application to the religious institution and its unique problems and functions.

2. A less technical book that is directed entirely at local congregation leadership is *Creative Church Administration*, by Lyle E. Schaller and Charles A. Tidwell, Abingdon Press, 1975.

   Lyle Schaller draws upon his years of experience as a Christian consultant to local congregations in planning and management of ministry in this valuable volume.

3. *Legal Aspects of Church Management, FECO Edition*, March 1980, is an excellent handbook dealing with the following issues: Internal Revenue Service regulations, state and Social Security taxes, nonprofit status, lobbying, unemployment insurance, corporate charters, profitmaking, and others.

   In this book, information about the legal issues and history of legal rulings is clearly presented, providing a basis for discussion with expert accounting or legal people. It is published by the Financial Executives of Christian Organizations (FECO), P.O. Box 4651, Diamond Bar, CA 91765 ($10—quantity discount available). FECO also publishes a regular bulletin with updated information on legal aspects of church management. Write to find out the cost and the frequency of bulletin publication.

Pastoral Self-Assessment

Rev. William G. McAttee has created a fantastic self-analysis tool for pastors and professionals in ministry as part of his Doctor of Ministry work.

Time/Energy and Effectiveness, A Self-Assessment and Planning Guide for Professional Staff in Voluntary Church Organizations, by William McAttee, 1976. 2029 Dellwood Drive, Lexington, KY 40503.

This manual and process were designed for the person who is always going to slow down "when I get the time."

Bill has done an excellent job of creating a process for categorizing and rating the regular activities of a pastor's day into energy units. These energy units are then budgeted according to pastoral priorities. For each area of functioning, a user is encouraged to establish ranges of energy needed to function effectively and then begin the process of caring for himself or herself by sticking with the plan which has been established.

The process is set up for use over a five-week period. First, one assesses the energy units and then records them on a simple log sheet which Bill has prepared. These form the basis for calculating a weekly total. Each week then has five reflective questions for self-examination and decision regarding the next week.

This manual is a carefully designed, useful, and relatively simple tool for personal awareness, reflection and self-generated change. It lends itself very well to group use among staff/colleagues in a community who can support one another in efforts to change.

Pastoral Time Management

Alan Lakein's book *How to Get Control of Your Time and Your Life* (Signet, paper, 1974) is well worth its minimal cost. Although it is small, it is packed with practical suggestions on taking charge of your life and functioning in all quarters.

Just to wet your whistle, here are some of the items/ideas: "A-goals"; not confusing goals and activities; getting more done by doing nothing; defining tasks as "A," "B," and "C" with respect to importance; why the "A's" are harder; the 80-20 rule; asking the question "What is the best use of my time right now?"; the Swiss-cheese method for determining when you are procrastinating; doing your best and considering it a success.

These topics, I hope, will lead you to purchase and use this tremendous volume.

Pastoral Phone Calls

As a pastor who lives eight miles from the area where most of the congregation lives, I have found it extremely helpful to use the phone for many visits. In this way I conserve energy by recognizing the uncertainties of the schedules of some church members.

In an hour during the evening I can contact five to seven people for a short conversation. Often chosen are those who have not been to worship for a time and those who have returned from the hospital or have been ill. I try not to do business in these calls but to make them an opportunity for a brief life check-up with those in the congregation.

These calls in no way take the place of face-to-face visits, but they are one way to maintain contact and to save time and energy at the same time (Virgil Nelson).

Ministers' Life Resources

"Ministers face enough problems. Money shouldn't be one of them." Toward that end, Ministers' Life Resources publishes a number of items to help pastors plan for their financial future, including: *Clergy Tax Tips*, quarterly, $5 a year; *Church and Clergy Finance*, twice a year, $14 a year. Write for sample copies and descriptions of valuable tape resources as well as stress/burnout materials described in detail on p. 88.

Ministers' Life Resources, 3100 W. Lake Street, Minneapolis MN 55416. Tel.: (612) 927-7131.

Creative Tools for Ministry

There are a variety of tools available for a local congregation to use in creative ways. Their applicability is determined by their focus.

Retreats

A time away from the normal routine can provide an opportunity for personal spiritual growth, training in evangelism, training for church school teachers or other leaders, or planning for discipleship or community outreach ministry.

Retreats are a time for doing, educating, being, experiencing, studying the Bible, growing, refreshing, relaxing, working hard, sleeping, staying up, feasting, fasting, laughing, crying, grieving, healing.

For congregations seeking guidance in the planning of special retreat experiences, one useful tool is the *Retreat Handbook: A Way to Meaning,* by Virgil and Lynn Nelson, Judson Press, 1976.

Simulation Games

Great is the teaching power of simulated situations. Most publishers now include a number of simulation games in the resources they offer.

Dr. Myron R. Chartier, director of doctoral programs and professor of ministry at Eastern Baptist Theological Seminary, is an expert on the creation and use of simulation games.

A fantastic summary of his learnings and perspective as they have evolved through the years is included in the *1981 Annual Handbook for Group Facilitators,* published by University Associates, 8517 Production Avenue, Box 2624 C, San Diego, CA 92126.

The article details a framework for planning the use of simulation games; understanding the variables that are involved; defining the roles, activities, and resources involved; and evaluating the results. The planning framework is such that it can be used as a checklist guide in the creation of games. The article also includes an extensive list of resources for simulations: associations, directories, books, and journals.

One volume specifically addressed to the process of creating simulation games is *Gaming, the Fine Art of Creating Simulation/Learning Games for Religious Education,* by Dennis Benson, Abingdon Press, 1971. This exciting resource includes twelve actual games. More important, it gives an empowering spirit and process for creating your own games. The book is out of print but is available from Dennis Benson, P.O. Box 12811, Pittsburgh, PA 15241.

Storytelling

God's word of life and love and truth comes to us in story form in the written word of the Scriptures as well as the stories of other people's lives.

Speaking in Stories, by William R. White, Augsburg Press, 1982, is a great volume aimed at helping Christian storytellers learn to tell stories, find story ideas, and make stories interesting. Three chapters are included on the history and art of storytelling, and the book also has many stories ready for telling: Bible stories, folktales, legends, fables, parables, and Christmas stories.

William White draws on over fifteen years as a teacher, pastor, and summer camp director. He is pastor of Immanuel Church, Mt. Pleasant, Michigan, and leads workshops nationally on storytelling.

All of us can use help in creating new ways to share stories about how God has been at work in our lives.

Humor
Clowns, Puppets, Mime

The whole world of ministry is exploding with clowns, puppets, dance, and mime. Hundreds of ministries in these fields have begun in local congregations and through cooperation between persons of several congregations.

Resources and information in all of these fields are now being shared through:

Clown, Mime, Puppet, and Dance Ministries (CMPD)
Rev. Tom Nankervis, Director
Box 24023, Nashville, TN 37202.

This organization sponsors four or five national workshops each year for those participating in these creative

ministries. At one workshop in Chicago over five hundred participants shared their creativity for nine days.

CMPD publishes a magazine for clown ministries called *Red Rubber Noses*. It is a networking point for a number of other organizations now clustered through the efforts of CMPD. These include ISAAC: The Institute for Support of Amusing Anecdotes in Church; Cast-Off Productions, directed by Rev. Bill Burdick; and others.

Two introductory films that will give a feel for clown ministry are *A Clown Is Born,* and *A Mark of a Clown.* Both of these are available through many denomination film libraries, as well as Mass Media Ministries, 2116 N. Charles St., Baltimore, MD 21218.

The excellent filmstrip *Introduction to Clown Ministry* is well worth using to whet people's appetites for what can be accomplished through the use of humor in all aspects of ministry.

CMPD also has information on other media resources in these exciting areas of ministry. Write for resources and contacts in your specific area of interest.

Character Creations

Karen Claydown (Emma, Emmaus–the Clowns)
Character Creations, 5144 San Simeon,
Santa Barbara, CA 93111. Tel.: (805) 964-9284
Karen Claydown describes herself as a professional clown. Her ministry within the religious community is unique and exciting. Her activity includes instructing and creating with a troupe of high-school-age seminarians at St. Anthony Seminary in Santa Barbara. The troupe has written material

and performed in churches, in convalescent hospitals, in train stations, on the street, and at social service agencies.

Karen also shares her talents in performances in the church, as well as in shopping malls and educational or party settings. She sees herself as a "fool for Christ" and develops her themes on the truths of the Scriptures. Her schedule includes retreats, workshops, and lots of fun as she meets and shares with a host of different people.

The potential for "speaking" to the public is incredible. People will stop in shopping malls or on the street to watch a clown act. Some of Karen's friends created a short segment that spoke very powerfully to the issue of the arms race and its consequences for humanity. Two clowns, each with a wheelbarrow, began a silent race to fill their barrows with guns and various weapons and then ran down the shopping mall to a ribbon finish line. The winner was presented with a large, specially gift-wrapped box, which was opened with pomp and circumstance to reveal —*ashes*. A time of silence followed; the box was closed; and the act began again—all in the space of about two minutes.

Hundreds saw and heard the prophetic message that day.

Cartoons

1. *The Parables of Peanuts,* by Robert L. Short, Harper & Row, 1968. A sequel to *The Gospel According to "Peanuts"* (John Knox Press, 1965), this book is equally classic in its examination of secular cartoon material from a theological perspective. The categories for reflection are broad and varied, and both books include hundreds of actual "Peanuts" cartoons as specific examples.

   Parables is divided into chapters such as "Interpreting the Signs of the Times"; "Savior—Who Needs a Savior?"; "Where Your Bank Is, There Will Your Heart Be Also"; "You Shall God Your Neighbor as Yourself"; and many other exciting chapters.

2. A more recent similar volume, equally useful for small group discussion, media presentations, sermons, and the like, is *The Gospel According to Andy Capp,* by D. P. McGeachy, 3rd (John Knox Press, 1973). Filled with cartoons from the internationally popular comic strip, this volume uncovers the spiritual dimension in Andy's behavior. Through our identification with Andy, we can gain new insight into ourselves and the scriptural truths of the gospel.

3. *The Mad Morality,* by Vernard Eller, Brethren Press, 1979 ($3.79). This excellent volume uses excerpts from *Mad Magazine* to provoke serious reflection on the meaning of the Ten Commandments in our day.

4. *Feiffer: Jules Feiffer's America from Eisenhower to*

Reagan, edited by Steven Heller, Knopf, 1982, 254 pages ($12.95).

5. Book collections of "Doonesbury" cartoons, edited by G. B. Trudeau; Holt, Rinehart, and Winston ($2.95 each). Nine books in all.

6. Make up your own cartoon characters and scripts, using existing strips. Delete the captions and make up your own. Challenge your folk to create an in-house comic strip, featuring the antics of your people.

Satire

1. *The Wittenburg Door* (periodical) from Youth Specialities, 1224 Greenfield Drive, El Cajon, CA 92021.

   Characterized by some as a "Christian *Mad Magazine,*" this spicy volume draws either intense criticism or intense support. *The Door* is funny, sometimes irreverent, satirical, stimulating, provoking. Not everyone likes it, but maybe you will.

2. *Cotton Patch Gospel* (record album), Harry Chapin, Chapin Productions, 1982 ($8.95). Available from Koinonia Partners, Route 2, Americus, GA 31709-9986.

   A fresh retelling of the Jesus story in the music and context of Georgia.

Creative Financing

One of the blocks to beginning a new ministry can often be related to finances. When this problem is coupled with the natural hesitation to become involved in a major program, the result can be immobilization and inaction.

Many of the housing ministries described in the community concerns section of this book began with a vision and a commitment to build one house for one family. When that work began, other people caught the vision, other resources became available, and the project grew.

One small way to begin is to establish a rotating deposit fund for people seeking to rent an apartment. The fund can be established with a modest number of small gifts. This has been done in the Oak View First Baptist Church, which has only fifty-five members.

When programs with large budgets and staffs are initiated, there is a danger that they will die if funding is cut off and there is not enough local support. That is not to say we should not take advantage of available state, city, and federal funds, but programs need to be built so that if outside funding is terminated, decisions about priorities have been made so that some parts of the programs can continue.

There is money "out there" for creative projects. After reaching agreement about the specific needs for a program, you can begin to inquire about possible sources of funds.

Libraries and appropriate public agencies are good sources of information. These sources can also provide guidance in writing up applications and coordinating the process of seeking grants.

An important factor is to keep the proposals very practical. At Oak View First Baptist Church, over a three-year period three small grants for a seniors' program were obtained from Federal Titles II and III-C Funds, administered by the area agency on aging. These grants included (1) an initial start-up fund of $3,500 for building improvements and kitchen equipment, matched by $9,000 in donated labor; (2) $12,400 for the purchase of a 15-passenger van for transporting seniors in the community, provided that local funds covered the operation of the van; and (3) $2,500 for carpeting, painting, and window sealing of the building, matched by over $1,000 in donated labor and material.

In order to develop creative financing we must have a clear sense of need, a willingness to ask, and a commitment to administer the operation all the way through. Whatever resources are found can be multiplied if we turn them and our energies over to God.

Christians in the Media

A whole book could be written regarding creative Christian use of the media. With respect to outreach, most of the programs on television and radio assume that the viewer is already a Christian person or at least open to religion.

This assumption is clearly evident with the usual formats: broadcasts of Sunday morning worship services, straight Bible-study lectures, talk shows with heavy religious language. The viewer who is flipping channels can immediately identify these kinds of programs and will move on.

In past years, thousands of creative programs aimed at listener needs have flown from the creative mind of Dennis Benson and those people with whom he has been a catalyst in brainstorming exciting new ways to use the airwaves. His older but still relevant book, *Electric Evangelism* (see p. 34), is a good starting place for examining the assumptions of the church regarding the airwaves.

Local congregational creativity can often find expression through the local cable television station. It is often possible to take creative ideas to it and secure the help of the station in the production of locally originated programming. There is also more and more access to good video equipment. One can make quality tapes and take a sample to the station for viewing. The very act of making the tape can be an outreach event through which dialog can be begun with people.

Portable Video Equipment

The mystique of TV is still with us, and anyone carrying

a portable TV camera can attract a crowd. Did you ever watch video news reporters on the street or in a shopping mall? Why not take a portable TV camera and do on-the-street interviews/opinion polls on specific reflective questions related to the meaning and purpose of life?

You and your group could brainstorm a whole list of questions. Books like *Values and Faith: Value Clarifying Exercises for Family and Church Groups* (page 69) will also stimulate your thinking. After a number of responses have been recorded, you could edit them for airing on a local cable channel in any one of a number of different formats.

Some possible reflective questions and focus ideas are:
1. Why do you go to work each day?
2. If you had only one day to live, what would you do with your time?
3. Feature an interview with one senior for each program. Let it be a sharing of wisdom about life, with stimulus questions such as "What have you learned?" or "What has been the most difficult part of the aging process for you?" Show different aspects of the person's life/hobbies/faith.

Resources Available for Cable TV

1. *Cable TV and the Local Church* was created by the cable TV subcommittee of Christian Associates of Southwest Pennsylvania, 1800 Investment Bldg., 239 Fourth Avenue, Pittsburgh, PA 15222. It gives the beginner a basic overview and a place to start, along with resources for further exploration.
2. *A Short Course in Cable,* by Jennifer Stearns, Office of Communication, 105 Madison Avenue, New York, NY 10016 (1981). Ask for a list of other cable TV resources.
3. *Cable and VTR Communications Packet,* United Methodist Communications, 1525 McGavock Street, Nashville, TN 37203. Single copy is free.
4. *The Video Pencil: Cable Communications for Church and Community,* by Gene Jaberg and Louis G. Wargo, Jr. (University Press, 1980) can be used as a companion manual to *Using Nonbroadcast Video in the Church* (see page 35). It provides extensive theological perspective for using video, and it describes ministries currently using the access channel of local cable systems. Several model scripts for program creations are included. University Press of America, 4721 Boston Way, Lanham, MD 20801 ($7.95).
5. *Electric Evangelism: How to Spread the Word Through Radio and TV,* by Dennis Benson, Abingdon Press, 1973. Theological basis and practical step-by-step creation processes for radio, TV production. Out of print, available from Dennis Benson, Box 12811, Pittsburgh, PA 15241.

Media Impact

A special shared ministry of the Southern California Ecumenical Council is Ecumedia, aimed at impacting the electronic and print media with the major social justice concerns of the Protestant religious communities. Past projects have included efforts to eliminate hunger in Los Angeles County, including influencing script writers and producers in the TV and film industries and producing actual programming for radio and TV.

For information, contact Ecumedia, 4270 W. Sixth Street, Suite 221, Los Angeles, CA 90020. Tel.: (213) 381-6334.

The Communications Division of the San Diego Ecumenical Conference is active in the production of *Focus-Five,* a daily five-minute program of religious information, raising levels of awareness of Judeo-Christian values, and addressing social issues in the San Diego area from an ecumenical viewpoint.

The production team is composed of clergy and lay persons from numerous Protestant and Catholic churches. *Focus-Five* was nominated for an Emmy Award in 1982.

San Diego Ecumenical Conference, Communications Program, 1875 Second Avenue, San Diego, CA 92101.

Religious Public Relations Handbook for Local Congregations of All Denominations

Published by the Religious Public Relations Council, Inc., Room 1031, 475 Riverside Drive, New York, NY 10115-0099 (1982 edition). Available also in Spanish.

This basic introductory manual is helpful to local congregational persons in planning for creative use of local media in ministry: newspaper—press relations; cable TV and radio; newsletters; special events; use of displays, signs, and exhibits; and specific how-to-do instructions and guidance.

Provides a good place to start and leads to many other creative resources.

Paulist Productions

A great source of films and video cassettes, often originally produced for TV use, including the *Insight* series. The purpose of these films is to share the Good News of God's love for all children in the human family. Programs and materials are aimed at crisis points in people's lives and at sharing the wonder of God's love and creation.

Paulist Productions, P.O. Box 1057, Pacific Palisades, CA 90272. Write for a catalog.

Media Use Within the Congregation

For the creative use of media within the life of the congregation, these three books will help you to get started.

1. *Gadgets, Gimmicks and Grace,* by Edward N. McNulty, Abbey Press, 1976 ($3.50). Order from Visual Parables, First Presbyterian Church, Westfield, NY 14787. Add $1.50 for shipping and handling. Ask for catalog of Visual Parables media resources.

   This book provides a theological basis for understanding the use of different media in the church and hundreds of ways that media can be created on threadbare budgets. Processes for making slides, creating multimedia programs, and building rear-screen projection screens are among the practical items shared.

2. *Festival,* by Lyman Coleman and Ken Curtis, Serendipity Books, Word Books, 1973.

   This book outlines a group process for the production of top-quality 8mm. sound movies. The process takes small groups from sharing their faith and its meaning to writing a script and producing a film. The process is transferable to other media, making this a basic volume for use with any group, even if only two people are interested in media production.

3. *Using Nonbroadcast Video in the Church,* by Daniel W. Holland, *et al.,* Judson Press, 1980.

   This exciting volume provides hundreds of ideas on the use of video by a local congregation in its ministry within the church and as an outreach into the community.

   With the continuing drop in the price of this equipment and its ready availability in most congregations (Have you dared to ask who has video equipment? You may be surprised!), the potential for use is more of a reality than you might think.

Under the leadership of Rev. Edwin Heuer, the congregation of the First Baptist Church, Hyattsville, Maryland, has ventured deeply into the use of a whole range of media within its life and ministry. Primary children use "show and tell" Bible stories, and older elementary children are using computer games. Junior and senior highs often have full-length films or excerpts from them as part of their church school classes and youth group sessions (for example, *Jesus of Nazareth*). Portable video recorders have been used to document and report on all aspects of church life, including youth and adult retreats and special programs. Creative Bible-study classes have interpreted Scripture passages through making video skits/scripts and recording them to share with others. Shut-ins share in the worship services, and special events such as infant dedications, baptisms, and weddings can be recorded on videotape.

The church board of education has an audiovisual chairperson, who works with a very active subcommittee in the development of resources, in laying out the production schedule, and in the actual production process.

Rev. Ed Heuer, First Baptist Church of Hyattsville, 5906 Shepherd Lane, Seabrook, MD 20801.

Shared Ministry Through Computers

Is your congregation too small to afford a computer? How about joining together with another one nearby and sharing the cost of purchase and operation? Why not have a number of congregations go together to purchase good equipment and tie in, each one with its own terminal and printer?

Short of these dreams is the possibility of finding someone in your congregation who owns a personal computer. First Baptist Church of Oak View is fortunate to have a member with his own computer Radio Shack TRS-80℠. He has taken a basic bookkeeping program, Visi-Calc℠, and adapted it for use in keeping the church financial records. At the end of each month, all the calculations and tabulations are done and printed out quickly for easy copying for the board.

Using Personal Computers in the Church, by Kenneth Bedell, Judson Press, 1982, gives a good summary of computer operation and use by the church for financial, secretarial, and educational purposes. The book includes case studies, sample systems, and even some specific computer programs. More important, a checklist of questions to ask prior to any use/purchase of computers is included for those considering this step.

Rev. Merrill S. Cook, of the Federated Church in Masonville, N.Y., is also experimenting with programs for use on the Radio Shack TRS-80℠. P.O. Box 990, Masonville, NY 13804-0279.

Those with access to Apple℠ computers may contact G.R.A.P.E. (Group for Religious Apple Programming Exchange) P.O. Box 203, Port Orchard, WA 98366.

A Library Party!

The Bethesda Missionary Temple, 716 E. Nevada, Detroit, MI 48234, had an idea that can be readily adapted to meet almost any need. Their pressing need was for library books for the church and the school.

A "Library Shower Party" was organized for which the "entrance ticket" was one book (or the money to cover the cost of one book) chosen from a preprinted list of needed books.

This same idea could be used in many ways. Whatever your church needs—articles, money, or ideas—becomes the entrance ticket. Can you imagine toilet paper? hymnbooks? an associate pastor? canned food to share with the needy? tires for the church bus?

Buttons and Badges

Symbols and slogans and their creation and production can be a powerful part of the process of building a group and owning the goals and program it has created.

One tool for creative use in this whole process is a button maker. Creating and making your own buttons can be a new way to spark and use the imagination and creativity of the group.

One source is Badge-Amount, starter kit and supplies. Write for a catalog and current prices: Civic Industrial Park, Box 618, LaSalle, IL 61301.

Discipleship

A disciple is one who follows someone else. Discipline has come to mean punishment in its common usage, and yet that is a dramatic perversion of its true meaning. Jesus did not punish people into the kingdom; he called and loved them into it.

Like babies, new followers start with the milk of faith. For the author of Hebrews (5:12-15), milk represented our basic needs: our assurance of salvation, our call, our repentance, our instruction in baptism, and the hope of resurrection. Solid food is the goal of maturity and was described as the fruit of the Spirit: love, joy, peace, patience, kindness, goodness, faithfulness, gentleness, and self-control (Galatians 5:22).

Discipleship is both personal—each person taking charge of his or her own process of spiritual feeding—and corporate—the responsibility of the Body of Christ to call and support its individual members in their spiritual journeys.

J. Foster, and *The Other Side of Silence: A Guide to Christian Meditation,* by Morton T. Kelsey, are reviewed earlier in "Foundations for Creative Ministry" (see page 13).

Books

1. *Creative Ministry,* by Henri J. Nouwen, Doubleday, Image, 1978 ($2.45). Nouwen's intention is to make clear

The journey begins with our response to God's call and our commitment to Christ, a process that moves us inward and outward. Resources for the personal and the corporate journeys follow.

Resources for Individual Discipleship

Summaries of the two basic starters books, *The Celebration of Discipline: Paths to Spiritual Growth,* by Richard

the *spiritual basis for ministry.* He uses John 15:13 as a theme. In the words of Jesus, "A person can have no greater love than to lay down his life for his friends." This passage makes clear the meaning of all ministry.

Are we willing to pick up the towel and wash one another's feet, or are we interested in power? The acts of teaching, preaching, organizing individual pastoral care, and celebrating go far beyond the level of professional expertise precisely because in them we are asked to lay down our lives for our friends, and even our enemies!

2. *Spiritual Disciplines for Everyday Living,* by Ronald V. Wells, 1982, Character Research Press, 266 State St., Schenectady, NY 12305 ($8.95). An appropriate theme for this volume might well be "Hasten unto God; hasten into the world." Eight ideas/disciplines are examined to expose the central issue, to present selections from the "family documents" of the devotional classics, and to pose questions for reflection and action. The eight include: interrelatedness, creative solitude, the practice of the presence of God, humility, love, attachment and detachment, joy, and how we hasten to God and into the world.

3. *The Adventure Inward: Christian Growth Through Personal Journal Writing,* by Morton T. Kelsey, Augsburg, 1980. Aimed specifically at Christians, this book covers the "whys" and "hows" of journal writing. Kelsey gives a theological and historical overview, looks into some of the possible pitfalls, offers specific suggestions for hearing and understanding our dreams as "God speaking to us," and has extensive ideas for how to use our imaginations in journal writing to help us hear God's messages for our daily lives. As we seek God's creative birth in our lives and ministries, it is helpful to keep a personal record (journal) of how we perceive God's action in our lives.

4. *Honey from a Rock: 10 Gates of Jewish Mysticism,* by Lawrence Kushner, Harper & Row, 1977. Ten "gates" to religious transcendence are shared by Rabbi Kushner, drawing upon the rich tradition of the Jewish mystics and on the Old Testament Scriptures. This book is poetic and refreshing.

Monasteries and Retreat Centers

To find silence, sometimes one must "go away." Contact the Catholic churches in your area and inquire regarding retreat houses and monasteries and their openness to "outsiders." Many Protestant denominations also have retreat centers and monasteries that are open to all people seeking opportunities for a quiet time away from other concerns.

One such group is the Order of the Holy Cross, West Park, NY 12493. The order is a monastic community for men in the Episcopal (Anglican) Church and was founded in 1884 by the Rev. James Huntington as a contemporary expression of the religious life. Nine monasteries, retreat houses, or priories are maintained worldwide. Write for addresses and information about these facilities. Tel.: (212) 862-6143.

The order also offers individuals the opportunity to be disciplined in spiritual growth through associate member groups.

Corporate Discipleship

In many congregations the membership requirements and processes are minimal. Is it any wonder that Christians in general are often unfaithful in their commitments, ignorant in their theology, and hard to motivate in service of Christ?

Membership Training

New-Member Training for Discipleship

Rev. Bill Mellinger and Rev. Robert Brouwer, First Baptist Church, 200 N. Second Avenue, Covina, CA 91723.

Six two-hour sessions make up the structure of the membership classes for this congregation. The first hour is spent in inductive Bible study, and the second hour in small group experiences that involve folk who are already members of the congregation.

Discipleship groups continue on two tracks, one for those who are new Christians and another for those who are older in the faith.

Dine-In Club

Rev. Al Van Selow (First Baptist Church, 426 S. Mill Rd., Ventura, CA 93003) has encouraged a dine-in club in which newer members are matched with "old-timers." Interested participants indicate their desire to participate and commit themselves to sharing one meal a month for three months. Three families are grouped, and they rotate among homes.

Yearlong Discipleship

Rev. David Dunn has developed resource materials for a yearlong discipleship program. The class is small, usually seven to twelve persons who commit themselves to one and one-half hours of involvement each week. The goals are support, study, and personal growth.

The first four months deal with the "how tos" of Christian faith: how to pray, how to study Scriptures, how to be a witness, how to be a good steward, etc. The second four months are spent in practical discipleship, following a personal meeting of the pastor with each person and his or her family to discern possible ministries. The third and fourth sections are a combination of more in-depth doctrinal studies and practical individual and family ministry.

Rev. David Dunn, First Baptist Church, RD #8, Gettysburg, PA 17325.

New-Christian and New-Member Follow-Up

In Bethany Baptist Church, Montclair, California, those who make a profession of faith in Christ are counseled by a lay person, one-on-one, to help them be clear about their commitment to follow Christ and what it means in their lives.

An appointment is made with one of the church staff persons who meets with them individually to provide any further clarification necessary and to invite their participation in a six-week class for those interested in church membership.

A "placement officer" meets with each new member to take a "spiritual gift inventory" of each person joining—registering his or her special interests, experiences, skills, and talents for use in ministry in the body.

Discipleship continues as each new member is linked in a thirteen-week discipleship program, one-on-one with an older member, using specific Bible study and sharing resources. Further discipleship courses are available on a group basis following the thirteen-week series.

Rev. Paul Cox, Bethany Baptist Church, 9950 Monte Vista Avenue, Montclair, CA 91763.

New-Member Assimilation

The process of assimilating new members needs to be one that is consciously decided by a local congregation. All too often this process is left to chance, and statistics reported by one congregation in Ventura are all too likely to be true nationwide: "Over 50 percent of all new members showed no activity in the congregation after the first six months."

One study has shown that new people usually do not feel at home in a congregation until they can call eight people by their first names, and until *they* are known and can be named by eight people.

For specific insights and help in planning for the process of assimilation, see *Assimilating New Members,* by Lyle Schaller, Creative Leadership Series, Abingdon Press, 1978 ($4.95).

Inactive-Member Reclamation

A creative answer to the problem of inactive members is proposed, after years of parish ministry, by Rev. William Cline in the booklet *Growing as a Caring Community,* Department of Evangelism, National Ministries, American Baptist Churches, P.O. Box 851, Valley Forge, PA 19482-0851 ($1.25).

The process is designed to be implemented by lay persons in the church. Its cornerstone is training in visitation-listening evangelism that assumes that being listened to is one of the major ways in which people feel cared for.

In the training, the assumption is that people are inactive for many reasons and that, in most cases, no one has bothered to hear them out regarding their concerns and then lovingly encourage them to make decisions regarding their own futures in the congregation.

The book is designed for use in a five-session training process for laity: (1) facing fear and anxiety, (2) doing evangelism naturally, (3) learning to care through listening, (4) preparing for visitation, and (5) using the membership data form.

Sessions vary in suggested length from 45 minutes to 15 minutes, and are designated to be used in a single-day format—from 9 A.M. to 3:30 P.M.

At the heart of the home visit is a simple membership data form for use in discussion and sharing with the person/family being visited.

The form is reproduced here in miniature.

Membership Data Form

Name _____ Birthday _____

Address _____ Home Phone _____

Occupation _____ Business Phone __

Age Group: Child ___ Jr. High ___ Sr. High ___ College ___

Young Adult ___ 30 Plus ___ 50 Plus ___

1. When did you first become aware of God in your life? _____

2. Who were the important people who helped you to discover the reality of God in your life? _____

3. Have you always been related to this congregation or have you been a member somewhere else? ___ Where? _____

4. When did you first become a member of this congregation? _____

5. What was your age group when you became a member?
   Child ___ Youth ___ Young Adult ___ Adult ___

6. If you did not grow up in this church, how did you first come to visit this congregation? _____

7. What factors about this church influenced your decision to join?
   Fellowship/friendliness ___ Pastor ___ Friends ___ Spiritual Vitality ___

8. How has this congregation met or failed to meet your expectations? _____

9. What first caused you to withdraw from active membership? (Where applicable) _____

10. Is there any way in which our congregation could improve its ministry to you (and your family)? _____

11. How do you feel you personally could help this church minister more effectively? _____

12. How do you feel now about your membership in this church? _____

Training for Visitation of Inactive Members

Through the cooperative efforts of GRACE (Grand Rapids Area Center for Ecumenism), regular workshops are offered to train participants in nine depth-listening skills for a caring ministry to active and inactive church members.

1. One-third of the average congregation is made up of persons who were once active but have now become inactive. 2. Extensive research shows why people leave, how to stop the drop-out cycle, and ways of getting those who left to return. 3. Personal *visitation*. A personal visitation program is the only effective method for reclaiming these persons.

For information write Dr. Savage, c/o GRACE, 9 Federal Square Building, Grand Rapids, MI 49503.

Ongoing Discipling of the Flock

Learning/Spiritual Growth for New and Older Christians

Guidebook for Victorious Christian Living, by Rev. Russel A. Jones, Judson Press, 1983 ($5.95). This workbook offers twenty-six chapters of bedrock material for effective Christian understanding and growth. Appropriate for new members' classes, church school classes, and especially for one-on-one discipling. Session foci include: the Bible, the nature of God, man, overcoming sin, Jesus Christ, the Holy Spirit, the new birth, grace, the church—its message and mission, the Christian life, and the eternal future. Each session includes background, in-depth Bible study, and a reflective "check yourself" test.

Write Rev. Russel A. Jones, Director of Evangelism/Discipleship, American Baptist Churches of the Pacific Southwest, 970 Village Oaks Drive, Covina, CA 91724, for Leader's Guide.

How Jesus Trained Leaders

This long-standing work by Dr. W. Maxfield Garrott, Southern Baptist missionary in Japan, is an excellent resource for person-to-person training. Each of the sixteen pages is crammed with material for thought and action.

Four key principles are used as the framework exemplified by Jesus in his relationships:

1. The principle of *concentration*—a few thoroughly trained workers are more effective than many superficially trained.

2. The principle of *personality*—character training is essential for Christian leaders.

3. The principle of *contact*—daily presence in all aspects of life is like the contact print made by a photographer from film.

4. The principle of *reality*—the most potent instrument of character training is personal association, in the day-to-day, real world.

Available from National Ministries, American Baptist Churches, P.O. Box 851, Valley Forge, PA 19482-0851. ($1 each).

Serendipity

Serendipity Foundation: Free University/Lay Academy in Christian Discipleship, Box 1012, Littleton, CO 80160. Tel.: (303) 798-1313.

Serendipity: "The accidental coming together of old things—the surprise visitation of the holy into the 'ordinaries' of life."

Lyman Coleman has developed a variety of resource tools for use with groups of all ages in coming to grips with the truths of God's word and their application in our individual lives and in the life of our fellowship.

The most recent Discipleship Series is divided into two broad categories, (1) the Foundations Series (for all ages), and (2) a special Youth Series.

The Foundations Series includes nine separate study books:
1. *Self Profile: The Me Nobody Knows*
2. *Spiritual Basics: New Life in Christ*
3. *Body Building: Where Two or Three Are Gathered*
4. *Coping: Oh, God, I'm Struggling*
5. *My Calling: Here I Am, Lord*
6. *Moral Issues: If Christ Is Lord*
7. *Holistic Health: He Touched Me*
8. *Holy Spirit: Come, Holy Spirit*
9. *Life-style: 'Tis a Gift to Be Simple*

The Youth Series includes:
1. *Dear Me: On My Identity*
2. *Go For It: On Becoming a Christian*
3. *Hot Button: On Morality*
4. *Torn Between: On My Lifestyle*
5. *Belonging: On Deep Friendship*
6. *All the Way: On Discipleship*
7. *Hassles: On Relationships*
8. *Up Front: On Tough Issues*
9. *Heavy Stuff: On What I Believe*

Encyclopedia of Serendipity, by Lyman Coleman, Serendipity Foundation, Box 1012, Littleton, CO 80160 ($11.95). This volume is one of the most comprehensive listings of small-group exercises and sharing ideas ever compiled.

Drawing upon years of experience in leading sharing groups, growth groups, and discipleship groups, Lyman Coleman has compiled his best into this volume.

Yokefellows: Small Growth Groups

A Yokefellow group is a group of about 12 people who meet regularly to share their feelings about themselves and God in a safe environment. It is *not* a social group, a discussion group, a confrontation group, a prayer fellowship, or a Bible study.

A Yokefellow-group covenant typically is:

1. To meet together weekly for three months. At the end of this time, covenants may be renewed or ended.
2. To practice personal disciplines:
   a. Prayer, especially for one another
   b. Regular Bible and devotional reading
   c. Regular giving of a portion of one's income for ministry
   d. Regular worship
   e. Use of time, especially in one's daily vocation
   f. Reading and study
   g. Group attendance and participation
3. To communicate in the group honoring the following procedures:
   a. Each speaks personally rather than in the abstract.
   b. Feelings rather than thoughts are shared. One speaks of no one's problems other than one's own.
   c. The group stays on the subject.
   d. Everyone has an opportunity to participate, but no one is forced to participate.
   e. There are no arguments, no advice given, and no judgments made.
   f. Everything said in the group is held in strict confidence.

Some personal testimonies from members of the Cambridge Drive Baptist Church groups (550 Cambridge Drive, Goleta, CA 93017):

> Until my Yokefellow experience I had never admitted my fears. Once I admitted them, they lost their power over me.
> In Yokefellows, with God's help, I have turned myself around. My outlook on life has changed from negative to positive, and my constant depression has been broken. I have become free to be myself without fear of rejection or condemnation. I found permission to laugh and cry. And, best of all, I found a chance to give to others in need.

Yokefellows, Inc., Dr. Cecil Osborne, Director, 19 Park Road, Burlingame, CA 94010. Tel.: (415) 342-6089.

Bethel Bible Series

This series is for adult study of the Scriptures. In this course, a pastor or church staff person is trained to be a trainer of a solid core of persons who commit themselves to two years of leadership time as small-group Bible-study leaders. The first period is training for them, which is followed by a general enrollment of the congregation in the entire course series.

Two years is the projected time for completion of the entire study. Weekly home-study sheets are included with each lesson, and the materials give an in-depth study of both Old Testament and New Testament books and themes.

Information regarding leadership training schedules and fees can be obtained by writing: Adult C. E. Foundation, Box 5305, Madison, WI 53705. Tel.: (608) 849-5933.

Liberation-of-Life Discipleship Exercises

Liberation of Life: Growth Exercises in Meditation and Action is an excellent book created by Harvey and Lois Seifert, Upper Room, 1977 ($3.95). It is a book of spiritual exercises designed specifically for a combination of individual and group use over a six-week period of time. Group size can be two persons or more.

Each week has a separate focus: (1) Surprises in Wholeness; (2) The Secret of Devotional Vitality; (3) Meditation, Its Meaning and Method; (4) Experiencing the Constant Presence of God; (5) Devotional Action as Consumers; and (6) A Devotional Approach to Daily Work.

Each week's focus includes an introduction and is then divided into daily activities; among these are passages of Scripture to be studied, reflective questions to be answered, values and choices to be made, priorities to be set, and numerous meditative/silencing/centering exercises to be participated in.

Ample suggestions for group meetings and their flow are included at the close of each section.

Lay Ministry

University Associates

8517 Production Ave., Box 2624C, San Diego, CA 92126. Write for a catalog of hundreds of books in areas of time management, organizational development, personal growth, minority relations, and communication.

Rainbow Days Lay Training

Dottie Hedgepeth, Presbytery of Santa Barbara, 6067 Shirrell Way, Goleta, CA 93117.

Ever feel as though you are out in the desert when it comes to opportunities for training/discipling of laity?

The people of Santa Barbara, Ventura, San Luis Obispo, and Kern Counties felt left out of the metropolitan Los Angeles area and its opportunities. Rather than sit and mope, they came together under the able direction of Dottie Hedgepeth and the Santa Barbara Presbytery and organized what has become an annual January event: *Rainbow Days*.

Leadership from almost every denomination is recruited to lead workshops in different areas of expertise. Each year's potpourri of offerings has included over one hundred workshops, offered from Friday morning until Saturday evening, with most workshops being offered twice.

Workshop titles have included: Tender Loving Care for

Volunteers; Puppets in Christian Education; Christians in a World of Many Faiths; Understanding Teens; Children's Workshop; Building Christian Community Through Small Groups; Organizing Educational Resources in the Local Church; Songs, Games and Fingerplays; The Reformation of Our Worship; Building Effective Ministry in Smaller Churches; Meditation and Prayer: A Christian Perspective; Christmas Films for Children and Families; Introduction of Clown Ministries Celebrating Easter, Lent, and Seasons of the Church Year; Rich Christians in an Age of Hunger; Your Music Ministry; Running Effective Meetings, to name just a few.

Stephen Ministries

One-on-one support ministry during times of crisis is the focus of the Stephen Ministry, a program of training laity to function with the pastor in providing nurture and care for members and others in need in the community.

While Stephen Ministries grew out of the Lutheran church, it is open to any denomination or group and has had Catholic, Episcopal, Baptist, Mormon, and Seventh-Day Adventist participants.

One staff person from a congregation receives a week-long intensive training and is then equipped to train a core group of laity, who meet once a week for two hours for a year.

Curriculum resources and training manuals have been developed which help the group to be aware of their scriptural roots and to improve their listening skills. For example, three of the early sessions during the year include: "Feelings, Yours, Mine, and Ours," "The Art of Listening," and "Tele-care, the Next Best Thing to Being There."

Trinity Lutheran Church, 196 N. Ashwood, Ventura, CA 93003, has participated in this program of ministry for several years under the direction of Rev. Stan Gjervik and Rev. Luther Tolo. "The results in changed lives have been fantastic, both for those in the group and those who are being helped."

Write for information regarding training schedules, fees, and resources to Stephen Ministries, Pastoral Care Team Missions, 7120 Lindell Blvd., St. Louis, MO 63130.

Family Shepherding

The Church of Jesus Christ of Latter-Day Saints (LDS) congregations are clearly organized for "Family Home Teaching." Lay leaders are trained and assigned a specific number of families for watch-care.

This means a once-a-month visit with the family as a spiritual check-up to see how the family is doing and to provide support and encouragement if there are specific needs or problems. The visit also includes a time of study and sharing in the Scriptures together.

For information on this process, contact the local stake of the LDS church in your area.

Lay Shepherding

"I myself will be the shepherd of my sheep, and I will make them lie down, says the Lord GOD. I will seek the lost, and I will bring back the strayed, and I will bind up the crippled, and I will strengthen the weak, and the fat and the strong I will watch over; I will feed them in justice" (Ezekiel 34:15-16, RSV).

This is a theme passage for the book *Lay Shepherding: A Guide for Visiting the Sick, the Aged, the Troubled and the Bereaved* by Rudolph E. Grantham, Judson, 1980 ($3.95). Here is a practical manual for pastors and lay-shepherding groups, which includes a wealth of suggestions and training exercises to help participants become more sensitive to the special needs of those who are sick, hospitalized, bereaved, or facing special crises in their lives.

Rudolph Grantham draws upon his years of experience as the Director of the Department of Pastoral Care of the Candler General Hospital, Savannah, Georgia. Each lesson plan includes discussion questions, possible areas for additional study, and role playing.

Lay Ministry of Pastoral Care

Twenty-five couples and some single adults in the Neffsville Mennonite Church have been trained in pastoral care. Each is assigned eight to twelve family units within a geographical area. Ministry includes giving special care in times of illness, hospitalization, bereavement, weddings, anniversaries, births, birthdays, and graduations. Personal home visits, phoning, and sending cards are all regular activities. Informal group meetings of all those in an area are also arranged, such as picnics, potlucks, and brief outings.

"The results of the first year have been tremendous," according to Pastor Bontrager. "It is exciting to be part of a congregation where almost one thousand different contacts are made each year by lay people as they care for one another."

Rev. G. Edwin Bontrager, Neffsville Mennonite Church, 2371 Lititz Pike, Lancaster, PA 17601. Tel.: (717) 569-0012.

Center for Ministry of the Laity (CMTL)

The Andover Newton Laity Project was a five-year action-research project sponsored by six cooperating churches seeking to recapture the early vision of Christianity that *every Christian,* having been given different gifts, is called and empowered to share in Christ's ministry in the world (Romans 12:6).

While the project formally ended in December 1982, it has evolved into the "Center for Ministry of the Laity." Resources available include:

- Empowering laity for fuller ministry;
- Covenanting for support and ministry;
- Identifying gifts and arenas;
- Listing resources for the journey.

Write to: Rev. Richard Broholm, Director, CMTL, 210 Herrick Rd., Newton Centre, MA 02159.

Identification of Gifts and Talents

Rev. Richard Broholm, director of the Laity Project (Andover Newton Theological Seminary), has developed two complementary processes for discovering personal gifts and for the seeing how the gifts/talents of individuals within a group complement one another. Excerpts of the two processes follow. (Summarized, adapted, and reprinted by permission, Andover Newton Theological School © 1979 The Laity Project.)

PROCESS A: PERSONAL IDENTIFICATION OF GIFTS/TALENTS:

1. List thirty things you have enjoyed/valued doing during your entire life, including childhood.

2. Pick the five you most valued/enjoyed and list these.

3. Look over the following list of talents and put a small check by each talent that was important in doing the five things you most enjoyed/valued.

4. Review your *top five*, one at a time. *For each of them*, go over the talent list items you have checked. Of those checked, select the *two* most important talents for that single accomplishment. (Place two additional checks by the most important and one additional check by the second most important.) Repeat this process for all five accomplishments, one at a time.

5. Add the total number of check marks for each talent on the talent list. Write the talents in order, beginning with the one with the most checks. You have now identified your God-given talents/gifts.

Talent List for Use in Identification of Gifts

conceptualize, interpret	design, envision
coordinate, organize	create, invent
analyze, diagnose	do precision work
research, investigate	accept, advise
compile, classify	counsel, guide
compute, estimate	negotiate, arbitrate
audit, do bookkeeping	reconcile
copy, record	instruct, teach
compare, observe	supervise, manage
construct, repair	motivate, lead
artistic presentation	inspire
evaluate, inspect	perform, demonstrate
inventory, catalog	facilitate, moderate
maintain, caretaking	persuade, sell
operate, drive, use tools	communicate, talk
collect, arrange	write
display	serve, wait on others
encourage	listen, support
other talents:	

PROCESS B: IDENTIFICATION OF ARENA ISSUES FOR MINISTRY:

Having identified all the gifts and talents of individuals in your group, it is time to look at the overview of your group with respect to how the gifts/talents, interests, concerns of individuals complement one another.

Using a large sheet of newsprint, have each person make a duplicate of the circle diagram which is located on this page. Ask each person to write in ring #1 the names of persons, things, activities, organizations, issues that are of priority interest or concern to him or her as an individual.

In ring #2, have each person write brief wishes he or she has for those priority interests/concerns. In ring #3, list talents or gifts that might apply. What are other talents that are needed? Who do you know who might possess them?

CLOSING, SHARING, AND COMPILING:

Using a large master circle reproduced on the wall, have

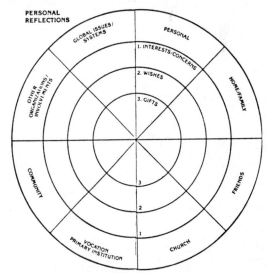

each person record his or her individual discoveries from *both* processes. Allow time for small groups to share their discoveries and feelings.

Reflect on the compiled results as a total group, looking

for areas of concentrated interest and for parts of the circle with blank space. Use these reflections to help with input for making decisions regarding potential group ministry.

Church of the Saviour Mission Groups

The mission group and its individual members are committed to both an inward journey and an outward journey.

A. The *Inward Journey*

1. *Growth in the life of meditation and contemplation* rooted in the Scriptures. The book *Search for Silence,* by Elizabeth O'Connor (Word Books, 1972), unfolds the vision of this dimension of the group life, and includes specific exercises for individuals and groups.

PERSONAL DISCIPLINES OF THE SPIRITUAL LIFE: Individuals in the group are committed to specific minimal disciplines which are clearly spelled out and embraced at each level of membership. These are not goals. They form the "base line" of commitment at each level. Each person is expected to work out his/her own personal maximum.

ACCOUNTABILITY: Each group defines an accountability process regarding the disciplines embraced. Some groups have a written weekly report.

As a sample:

a. How the disciplines have helped me grow, as well as any failures in keeping them.

b. How God has addressed me through the Scripture.

c. Crucial problems or peak experiences of my life for the week.

2. *Growth in self-understanding.* In all of our lives, we have been wounded and are in need of wholeness and healing. As we look into ourselves, we come to new awareness of the blocks and wounds that keep us from adoring God and giving ourselves without reservation to one another. We can dare to face the dark places of our lives.

The books *Our Many Selves* (Harper & Row, 1971) and *The Eighth Day of Creation* (Word Books, 1971), both written by Elizabeth O'Connor, provide perspective and suggest specific individual and group exercises in this area.

3. *Growth in community.* Reflection is given to that which facilitates community and that which blocks it. How can caring become a way of life? How can institutions that care be built?

B. The *Outward Journey*

The outward journey is only possible as facilitated and directed by the inward journey. If we move outward without our roots sunk deep in the wells of God's strength and wisdom, our outward movements often turn on themselves and destroy us.

Preparation for the mission-group way of life comes through experiences in the "School of Christian Living."

Classes are offered regularly in all aspects of ministry. A basic curriculum is required before persons may become an intern member of a mission group.

For further information see *The Handbook for Mission Groups,* by Gordon Cosby, Church of the Saviour, 1982 ($3.95). A section on "intern members" includes sample covenants, sponsor's guide, a sample spiritual autobiography, a section on members (their covenants/commitment), samples of spiritual journals, and sample letters of accountability.

For information/books/newsletter of the Church of the Saviour, write: Bookstore, c/o Potter's House, 1658 Columbia Road NW, Washington, DC 20009.

See also Appendix B.

Church Renewal

Cursillo

(A Spanish word meaning "little course"—pronounced "kur-seé-yo.")

Cursillo is an intensive three-day course in love, new life, renewal, joy, listening, discussion, learning, changing, and commitment. First begun in Majorca, Spain, in the 1940s, Cursillo was first held in the United States in Texas in 1961.

While the movement has primarily involved Episcopal parishes and dioceses, several other denominations have used the basic format for the weekend. In its inception the course was aimed at attracting men to a renewed and vital faith in Christ. As women saw and heard of the dramatic changes in their husbands, they, too, wanted to participate in such experiences.

The time is filled with input from spiritual directors, discussion, prayer, singing, sharing, and reflecting on God's grace and direction for our lives.

For information on who to contact in your local area, write the National Episcopal Cursillo, P.O. Box 113, Cedar Falls, IA 50613.

Fuller Seminary Christian Formation and Discipleship

A number of seminaries are sponsoring "faith renewal experiences." Some happen on campus; others, like "Faith Renewal," are taken to the local congregations for a weekend experience led by a team of folk from the school.

Fuller also has a relatively new department of "Christian Formation and Discipleship" (CFD), headed by Dr. Roberta Hestenes. A variety of resources, including books, tapes, and Bible studies have been created to complement formal course work. Write: CFD, Roberta Hestenes, Fuller Seminary, Box 256, Pasadena, CA 91101.

Institute for Church Renewal (IFCR)

P.O. Box 172, Tucker, GA 30084.

The Institute provides basic resources for all aspects of church renewal and growth. Samples from several resources include:

1. *Basic Training for Disciples*—A series of four 8-week, small-group, intensive training programs designed to produce more fully committed and capable disciples, including:

   a. training for devotional life

   b. training for relationships

   c. training for service

   d. training for witness

2. *Life-Style Stewardship*—A holistic approach to the Christian life and resources.

3. *Daring Discipline*—Training of a core group to reach out to those who are marginal/inactive.

4. *Lay-Witness Mission*—A weekend renewal experience for the entire congregation.

Life-Style and Discipleship

Is there any discernible difference between the values of our lives and those of the world? The Christians in America need to ask themselves this question. The clearest answer to this question is revealed in *how we spend our time and resources*.

Two key areas present themselves for reflection:

1. The impact of the media, especially TV, upon our lives and values and

2. Our consumerism mentality.

TV and Life-Style

A network study of TV viewing habits indicated that the TV is on in the average American home *over 6 hours each day*. Each person watches, on the average, more than 5 hours of TV a day. For perspective, in the United States the average person spends 2,000 hours a year in front of the TV (equivalent to a 40-hour work week for the year!), 200 hours reading the newspaper, 200 hours reading magazines, and 10 hours a year reading books.

If only half of the persons in our local congregations are average, think how much time is potentially available for ministry if people carefully reflect on how they spend their time! One person who chooses to cut his or her TV viewing time in half, from forty hours a week to twenty, could invest that twenty hours in ministry. That is the equivalent of a half-time salaried employee!

We need to help people reflect on how they invest the energy of their lives.

A. Television Awareness Training (TAT)

TAT is a workshop plan developed to enable individuals and families to assess the positive and negative ways in which TV affects their lives. Twelve different areas of the TV experiences have been developed into workshops:

1. TV—an overview	7. news
2. TV and violence	8. strategies for change
3. TV and stereotyping	9. sports
4. TV and advertising values	10. minorities
5. children	11. theology
6. human sexuality	12. soaps/game shows

A core of workshop leaders has been trained to lead local sessions. An excellent participants' manual, *TAT: The Viewer's Guide,* is available for $13, plus $1 postage. It contains 280 8½-by-11-inch pages of workshop resources/background/articles basic to those concerned. For names of leaders in your area and for book orders contact:

Television Awareness Training Marc (Media Action Research Center), 475 Riverside Dr., Suite 1370, New York, NY 10115. Tel.: (212) 663-8900.

B. Growing with Television (GWT). Specifically developed for use within the life of local congregations, GWT helps us examine our TV viewing habits from the perspective of the Christian faith. Each person is encouraged to take a deeper look into his or her beliefs and values and examine the impact of TV on them.

Growing with TV is not an antitelevision crusade. Its emphasis is on critical awareness of the positive and negative roles TV plays in one's life and the life of one's family, and it leads the participants to reflect, in light of the Scriptures, on specific changes they may want to make in their lives.

Within each age-graded course there are four units of study:

1. World views—compares commercial TV with biblical teaching to identify what is real and what is unreal in life; a study of fact and fantasy.

2. Life-styles—examines the impact of TV commercials and their promises on our lives.

3. Relationships—examines whether people are really like the stereotypes on TV; a look at images—sex and sexuality, isolation and community.

4. Concept of self—What am I? How does God evaluate my worth? How should I behave? How do I react toward other people?

Can be ordered/purchased through most religious bookstores.

Consumerism

We are continually bombarded with messages that would convince us that we are not fully human unless we purchase certain products.

One family in the Midwest who had a good yearly income but unsteady month-to-month income spent over $800 one Christmas. When work was short in the summer, they were worried about foreclosure on their house. "Well, we *had* to have a good Christmas, and besides, there was graduation for our daughter; we *had* to buy her something."

This buy-now-pay-later, "dollar down and a dollar a week" mentality has led to an average personal family debt in excess of $6,000 (1981), over and above automobile and home financing.

We have a four-trillion-dollar corporate debt in the U.S.A. and a national debt of one trillion dollars. These figures do not include the personal debt figures already mentioned.

Why should these figures bother us? This planet is God's

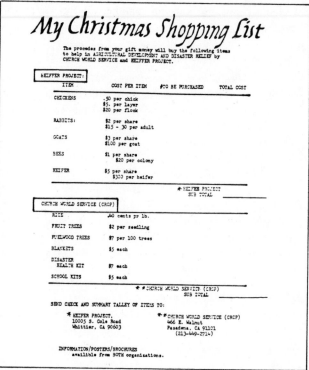

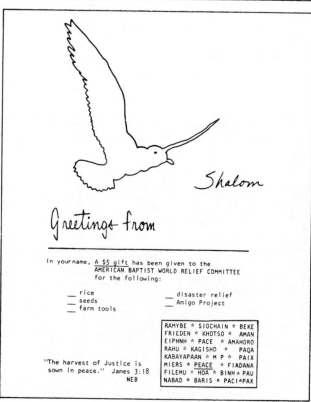

garden, and we are called to be good stewards. We need, as God's people, to help one another disengage from the consumer society and redirect God's resources into creative use.

Reflection upon our life-styles as Christians is imperative. Opportunities present themselves at every turn as we look for alternatives.

Alternatives

Alternatives, an alternative life-style newsletter, 1124 Main St., Forrest Park, GA 30050. Tel.: (404) 361-5823.

''Working for simpler life-styles through alternate celebrations'' is the theme that underlies all of the work of Alternatives, an organization to help persons who voluntarily choose simplicity so as to take charge of their lives.

Alternatives, a quarterly newsletter, includes background articles, book and resource reviews, program plans, specific celebration ideas, personal stories, and information on workshops held around the country. It costs $6 per year.

Also available are their *Alternative Celebrations Catalog,* 1982 edition ($8.95 plus postage) and a great variety of books and packets.

Alternative Games

The Cooperative Sports and Games Book, Challenge Without Competition, by Terry Orlick, Pantheon Books/ Random House, 1978 ($5.95).

This is a fantastic collection of cooperative and challenging games for all ages—arranged by age group. Samples for ages 3-7 include:

Cooperative Musical Hugs
Cooperative Musical Hoops
This Is My Friend (an introduction game)
Big Turtle (children under a ''turtle shell'' make it move)
Caterpillar (constructing a mountain by fours).

This is a delightful book with games that are equally fun and exciting for youth and adults.

Covenant Group for Life-Style Assessment

For those interested in exploring life-style issues in a small group context, this series of plans for twelve 2½-hour sessions is one of the most useful and comprehensive tools available.

The group covenant includes four parts:

1. to participate in each session;
2. to do preparatory study and share leadership;
3. to express oneself honestly and to listen carefully;
4. to be faithful in keeping promises to make specific changes.

These areas of life-style change are considered:

1. consuming
2. conserving
3. sharing
4. playing
5. advocating
6. giving

Sessions are designed to include an exciting variety: Bible study, discussion, activities, reports on readings, participation in Bread for the World and IMPACT networks, and consideration of and commitment to specific changes. Three

of the sessions are open to the member's entire family and include a shared meal and other enjoyable family activities.

The Covenant Group for Life-Style Assessment *Participants Manual* was written by William E. Gibson in 1978, revised in 1981, and published by the United Presbyterian Program Agency as an outgrowth of the interest of several denominations.

It is available from *Alternatives* for $4 plus shipping.

Simple Living

1. *Freedom of Simplicity,* by Richard J. Foster, Harper & Row, 1981 ($9.95). Foster skillfully moves from the paradox of simplicity as both a grace and a discipline into the nitty-gritty of the practice of simplicity in the modern technological society.

2. *Living More with Less,* by Doris Longacre, Herald Press, 1980 ($6.95).

''More with less is not a slogan—it is a glimmer of hope for disciples of Jesus in an unjust world,'' says Wilbur Heisey of Elizabethtown, Pa.

This is a book for people who know something is wrong with the way North Americans live and who are ready to talk about change. Over 350 people submitted "working ideas" from their lives with respect to their struggles to deal with a materialistic society in a world of hunger. These personal testimonies provide practical and workable models. They are not theoretical remarks from the "ivory tower." They come from ordinary people who have begun a pilgrimage toward simplicity.

While the book *Freedom of Simplicity* focuses on spiritual discipline, *Living More with Less* offers blueprints for family and community development towards simplicity. Categories include: money, clothes, homes, homekeeping, transportation, travel, celebrations, recreation, meetinghouses, dating, and strengthening one another. A companion volume is the *More-with-Less Cookbook.*

3. "Kingdom in the Streets," a record album by Ken Medema, Word Records, Waco, Texas, 1980 ($8.95). Male vocalist challenging our life-style assumptions with rare creativity.

Inflation

People Power: What Communities Are Doing to Counter Inflation, by Esther Peterson, Director, Consumer Information Division, United States Office of Consumer Affairs, Washington, DC 20201.

Limited copies are available from the Office of Consumer Affairs and also in the reference section of your local public library. This manual is organized in general categories and contains information on what local communities are doing to work together to "beat inflation." While the majority of the people involved are not motivated by their faith in God, the ideas can be utilized by anyone.

The manual's categories include health, energy, housing, and food—four hundred pages full of ideas and resources.

This manual is well worth finding at your library. It will stimulate lots of thoughts and lead you to many other folk who are experimenting in these areas.

Trading Skills—Alternatives to Money

G-Plan, by Pat Phillips, 14586 Dogbat Road, Grass Valley, CA 95945. Free flyer available (enclose SASE).

Instead of exchanging money for services rendered, the members exchange "G's" or "G-certificates," each of which is the equivalent of one hour of labor valued at approximately $5 per hour. Members accumulate the G's by performing special services or providing goods for other members. The G's can be traded for services or goods which are needed. The group's motto is "Give as much as you get," from which the name "G-Group" emerged.

Work done is inclusive—everything from house sitting, cleaning, milking, fence building, plumbing, electrical work, cooking, to child care.

Members meet once a month for an informal potluck to get acquainted with new members and to let one another know of interests and needs. A directory is published to facilitate contacts. Annual dues of $3 cover the costs of printing and other expenses.

Trading—"Circulation Day"

First Christian Church (38 Teloma, Ventura, CA 93003), under the direction of Rev. Austin Coe and Steve Lacey, has a day each year when people bring items from home which they are no longer using. People from the church and community are invited to come and take items that they can use—*for free.* It is a real time of meeting one another's needs in the Lord.

Sharing Equipment

Why not have a sharing system for specialized tools and equipment needed in home/auto repairs? A covenant could be worked out for those interested in using them. Another idea would be a free tool-lending shop—on the idea of a rental shop but with no fees, using a deposit system to guarantee return of the tools and a testing system to guarantee trustworthiness.

Housing, Foster Care, and Adoption

How many families in your congregation have large homes with rooms standing empty? A child has already left the nest, or all the children have become independent?

Have you considered challenging your congregation to find two families willing to become *foster parents* this next year? And what about two more families the year after that? The nationwide need for healthy, constructive family environments in which to place children from troubled homes continues to grow.

Adoption is another way to share our love and resources.

There are thousands of children worldwide who are homeless and need parenting and the basic elements of human survival. Have you considered seeking two couples a year in your congregation who are open to adopt a foreign-born child?

While the costs of adoption continue to soar (over $3,000 per child in 1983), many families have the resources to adopt (it costs about the same for natural birth). Some churches have even gone together on the actual costs of adoption for families willing to care for the children.

We have two Korean children: June-Young, 12, and Kim-Diane, 8, as well as Kent, our natural-born, 8, and Kristi—living in heaven. The children have added greatly to our enjoyment of life and have given us far more than we feel we have given them.

Another possibility for using extra space would be to *share a room* (for a reasonable rent) with a needy single person or couple this year. Housing is an issue we can do something about if we begin to learn to share what we have. (See pages 81-83.)

Evalgelism

"Follow me" (Mark 2:14). These simple yet profound words, used by Jesus in calling his disciples, call us and all individuals in the world to a new way of living, to become bearers of the Good News. Evangels—*all* of God's people are to be bearers of the Good News.

The "Little Bo-Peep" Theory

Remember Little Bo-Peep? She was the one who lost her sheep. Remember the advice she was given about how to get them back? "Leave them alone and they'll come home, wagging their tails behind them."

Many churches practice the "Little-Bo-Peep Theory of Evangelism"—just "leave them alone and they'll come home." Parents say this of their teenage children. Pastors and deacons say it about inactive members. We say it about families in which there has been a crisis. We say it about older members who can't get out any more. We say it about young married couples just starting their families. The end result is passivity.

This same attitude is often held toward those who have been estranged from the church, maybe over seemingly insignificant things. Avoidance of pain and conflict often leads to no contact, and we miss the opportunity to clarify true feelings and to encourage reconciliation.

Matthew tells a story about another shepherd who had lost a sheep. He left the fold and went in search of that one sheep and brought it back.

Which shepherd will we follow?

This idea is from Ted W. Land, Montgomery Presbyterian Church, P.O. Box 69, Montgomery, WV 25136.

Evangelism in recent years has taken on a limited definition in some circles and is used in a confined way to describe only the specific process of calling a person to commitment to Christ.

To use a garden metaphor, evangelism would be limited to the process of picking tomatoes. It is one thing to send a person into the garden to pick tomatoes, with the instructions on how to do it. It is another thing to train persons in the *process of gardening*. True, there are some "tomatoes" ripe and waiting for the picking—those who are ready to enter the kingdom. But many others are in no way ready for harvest. The ground is still to be turned, the seeds of love planted and nourished, and the plants tended and pruned before the harvest can come.

Those who attempt to pick the tomatoes before they are ready do great harm; it is better to approach with a gentle squeeze—or careful observation—testing to see the state of ripeness. Those who would sit and watch the fruit and do nothing are equally guilty of unfaithfulness to God's call to "go into the fields for harvest."

There are those who would sit and reminisce about the gardens of their past and endlessly discuss books on gardening techniques. In short, they are no longer in the practice of gardening but have formed a gardening club to celebrate the history of gardening and to study current techniques—without ever picking up a shovel or spreading the odoriferous fertilizer necessary for growth.

Evangelism involves the entire process of preparation and the picking. That's because evangelism reaches the whole person.

All too often, a Christian has been defined as one who has certain beliefs about Jesus. We believe that God is calling us, through Jesus, not only to acknowledge Jesus as God intellectually and verbally but also to demonstrate many new attitudes and behaviors as we become followers of Jesus.

A Christian is a person who—

EXPERIENCES:
I have experienced God at work in my life—God's love, justice, mercy, forgiveness, presence, filling of the Holy Spirit (Ephesians 2:1-10; 1 John 1:9; Romans 6:23).

COMMITS:

I am committed to be a follower of Jesus and I have asked Christ into my heart (John 1:12, 8:31, and 12:44-50; Acts 16:31; Mark 1:15).

BELIEVES:

What do I believe about God? Jesus? people? sin? salvation? the Bible? the church? the Holy Spirit?

BELONGS:

I am committed to a group of Christians (local church) who are part of the body of Christ (Acts 2:42-47; Matthew 18 [especially v. 20]; Galatians 3:27-29 and 6:1-10; 1 Corinthians 12).

SERVES (''Does Ministries''):

I will serve God within/among the body of Christ, and in the world (John 13:1-16 and 14:12; Matthew 10:1-10; James 2:14-26; Luke 4:16-18; Isaiah 58:3-12; Micah 6:8).

SHARES:

I will share faith experiences and resources of life (Matthew 10:37-42 and 25:31-46; James 1:27; 1 John 3:17-19).

LIVES ATTITUDES:

I will live in a way that can be seen as different (Colossians 3:5-17; James 2:1-9; Galatians 5:13-26).

LOVES:

I will learn to love myself, my neighbors, and my enemies (Matthew 5:38-48 and 22:34-40; John 13:34-35; 1 Corinthians 13).

Evangelism, then, reaches the whole person.

To "give witness," in its original use in the New Testament, meant to answer questions. When a person was a "witness in the city square or in the court," he or she gave information when asked. Too often witnessing or evangelizing is now perceived to mean "giving information" whether or not the other person has any interest in receiving it.

Any area of a person's life can be a stimulus for questioning purpose and meaning. Any crisis can provide a potential entry point for love and caring, for the message of hope, and for God's comforting presence in the midst of pain.

When there is a need in a person's life, reaching out to help meet that need can be a means for establishing a *relationship of integrity* with that person. In the midst of the relationship will come the questions about *why* we are doing these caring things. Questions regarding our source of hope/faith then open up an opportunity to share our faith and source of hope.

This approach in no way suggests that we should be passive in opening the doors of spiritual issues or concerns. It does suggest that we should respect the other person's life and not proceed without permission or interest from him or her.

Jesus certainly was sensitive and imaginative in his approach to each one he called. In the following pages you will find a variety of tools for evangelism. These tools are not ends in themselves but are to be used as you are guided by the Holy Spirit.

An excellent book that is helpful in understanding the definition of ''Christian'' is *I'm Saved, You're Saved . . . Maybe,* by Jack R. Pressau, John Knox Press, 1977 ($7.50).

This volume uses Kohlberg's states of moral development for looking at the nature of commitment and faith from a variety of theological perspectives. It is an excellent book for building bridges between individuals and communions with different definitional assumptions and understandings.

It is too easy to conclude that ''others'' are ''weird,'' a decision that cuts off dialogue and blocks our fulfilling the law of Christ to love others as we love ourselves.

Creative Public Outreach

A Cup of Cold Water at the State Fair

At the hot and dusty DuQuoin State Fair in Illinois, the only group giving out cups of water was from the Baptist Churches of the Great Rivers, a group working together in sponsoring an evangelism booth at the fair. Each year ten to twelve thousand cups of water, along with appropriate literature and personal conversation and concern, are distributed in Jesus' name.

Dr. Madison Bittner, Regional Evangelism Coordinator, 425 E. Second St., Centralia, IL 62801.

Bread Day—Free Fresh Bread

University students passing the religious center in Goleta, California, on Fridays are surprised with the offer of free fresh bread, still warm from the oven. Each week, students meet to bake the bread and then serve it themselves to passersby with words of greetings, comfort, encouragement, and support.

Because offering something free, especially to a stranger, is cause for mistrust in our culture, these young people use no "hard sell" in the sharing process. They have just chosen to demonstrate God's love and concern in this quiet, effective way.

UCSB University Religious Association, 777 Camino Pescadero, Goleta, CA 93017.

Public Entertainment

In Lockport, New York, members of the First Baptist Church provide concerts, recreation, storytime, and other attractions to bring in youth and adults from the community. Visitors to these events are eventually contacted personally to share an invitation to Christ and to the church.

The laity also lead a weekly mission program to the Tuscarora Indians on a reservation near town, which includes varied activities for children, youth, and adults. The response has been tremendous.

First Baptist Church, Pine at Genesee St., Lockport, NY 14094.

Softball Evangelism

As associate pastor I had resisted requests to organize a softball team, questioning its value in ministry. "There are more important and serious things to do."

However, some laymen of Hatboro Baptist in Pennsylvania took it upon themselves to get things moving and formed a team. After two years, three top-notch couples had been recruited from the softball enthusiasts as sponsors for ministry with youth, and a number of families and youth had made commitments to Christ and become active. I was forced to change my mind!

At the First Baptist Church of Oak View, in Ventura, California, a slow-pitch team also became a tool for ministry and, over a two-year period, was used by God to bring three new families and six young people into the life of the congregation.

Cul-de-sac Puppet Show

For three years the Hanapepe (Hawaii) Corps of the Salvation Army has been involved in a "cul-de-sac puppet show" ministry. A van is used to transport equipment to a neighborhood, including a portable puppet stage made of a plastic-pipe frame with a curtain covering. The van serves as "backstage."

The stage is set up in front of the van's side door, and the children sit on mats right on the street, in the cul-de-sac. The program includes songs, Bible teachings, and puppet plays with a message; it concludes with an invitation to follow Jesus. Then refreshments are served.

The *content* of the program is not unusual, but the *setting* is. The project works for two powerful reasons: (1) the cost is minimal, and (2) since few parks are available in the area, the cul-de-sac provides a safe (dead-end) street that is close and accessible for gathering the children.

Jack Allemang, Lieutenant, Hanapepe Corps, P.O. Box 1, Hanapepe, HI 96716.

Evangelism with Seniors

Given a small congregation with a predominance of senior members and ample building space, how could the available resources be used to meet their needs?

A small group of five people met to pray and begin planning. What were the specific needs of these seniors? How could the building be used? What funds would be needed? How would leadership be organized?

This discussion led to the formation of the Neighborhood Seniors Council (NSC), made up of representatives of five organizations in the community, including First Baptist of Oak View, which had been the catalyst to get things moving.

The project began simply with a weekly potluck meal at noon. From this evolved a "hot-lunch" meal program in cooperation with the Senior Nutrition Program of Ventura County, which now provides a part-time coordinator for the program.

The NSC continues to provide overall supervision of the Golden Age Activities Center, and it plans special programs, bazaars, bake sales, and projects/trips. The center's program now includes bimonthly blood pressure checks, tax and homeowners' counseling, legal counseling, two different exercise groups, a food-sharing process for surplus day-old bread and produce, weekly tournaments and bingo games, and seasonal parties.

Because a portion of the funds to renovate the building came from federal sources, sectarian religious programming is not possible. This has in no way been a hindrance to evangelism! Several seniors come to a weekly "Prayer and Praise" service in the adjoining building; many people who have been befriended by Christians have been attending worship, and several have made commitments to Christ and joined the congregation. Personal relationships are what count, and those cannot be regulated.

Needs Evangelism: The Voice of Calvary

A vital ministry demonstrating the absolute necessity of translating personal faith into social concern is the Voice of Calvary Ministries, led by John Perkins.

Evangelism, as defined and practiced by the Voice of Calvary, might best be summarized: "Find the Need and Meet it in Jesus' Name." *Needs evangelism* is based on the principle that the best way to people's hearts (their deep spiritual needs) is *through* their physical needs, at least the needs that those persons can identify for themselves. Jesus often called and ministered to people in this way.

The cycle of God's will and action as experienced in Voice of Calvary's history and development is instructive for all of us. Listen then to the story of God's call to John Perkins.

A Quiet Revolution, by John Perkins, Word Books, 1976 ($5.95).

John Perkins grew up in the black community in Mendenhall, Mississippi. His family was involved in bootlegging moonshine. John was successful in "making it" out of Mendenhall and eventually settled into a good career in California.

God had other plans. John's son began attending a small Church of Christ Holiness Mission church school and came home absolutely filled with love and joy. His son continually invited John to come with him, and finally he went to see what was happening that had so changed his son.

John got excited about studying the Bible in the adult Sunday school class. He eventually made a personal commitment to Christ and gave his life to Him. For the first time he experienced a deep sense of peace, even though there were still problems in his life. He was discipled through one-on-one Bible study and prayer for over a year by brothers in Christ.

God called John and his family to go *back* to Mendenhall, the thought farthest from their minds since they made their escape from that southern town.

Back they went. John and his family began a whole series of personal outreach evangelism ministries in Mendenhall: child-evangelism Good News clubs for children, similar programs within the public schools, and occasional tent meetings. They began a Bible institute to train people in the faith and eventually formed the Voice of Calvary Ministries (VOC).

Evangelism was continued through establishment of a day care center, a nutritious meals program, tutoring, recreation for children, housing, and health care.

Employment and economics soon emerged as an issue. People were still poverty-stricken after becoming Christians. Sin had clearly become institutionalized in the form of assumptions and laws which kept blacks in a state of educational, economic, and social inferiority. John and his church set out to be people

of "Good News and justice" in their world of hatred and hopelessness.

Jobs were created in the Bible institute and at the Headstart and child-care programs. Farming and housing cooperatives, thrift stores, and health-care systems were initiated—all moving toward the vision of economic justice.

Injustice occurs when power creates victims. When the leaders of Voice of Calvary Ministries began to address economic issues, they were hauled into court and jailed many times on spurious charges. Living for justice has had high costs. Many people have judged them to be extremists and labeled them "communists" or "nigger lovers." Only with God's heart of love and the support of the Body of Christ near and far can they face the violence they encounter on a daily basis.

As we can see in the story of the Voice of Calvary Ministries, there is a natural progression from personal faith to needs evangelism.

1. *God's call* to us to come live in him.
2. *Evangelism*—with living people and sharing the Good News of Christ with them. This may entail *relocating* ourselves and *reconciling* ourselves across racial or cultural barriers.
3. *Social action*—identifying needs and meeting them in Christ's name, bringing "flesh" to the words of love.
4. *Economic development* and equality—the logical steps as people become free from their dependence on an oppressive system.
5. *Justice* becomes essential as the forces of evil attempt to maintain the status quo of the old order and keep God's kingdom from breaking in. We must open ourselves to *redistribution* of our resources and wealth, of which we are temporary stewards.
6. *The church* is the living organism of the kingdom and supports its members as they suffer in the cause of justice.

The dynamic interchange of all these areas of ministry is shown in the following diagram (adapted from *A Quiet Revolution,* pp. 14, 199, with permission of John Perkins © 1976).

Perkins calls the Christian church to a genuine evangelism.

There are two places where we as the evangelical church can get involved but still lose our witness. . . . The first is *cheap evangelism.* If we create a style of evangelism that

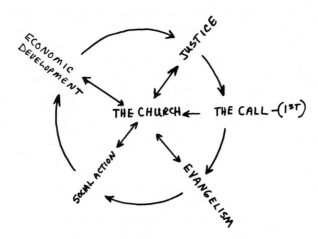

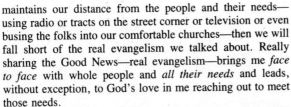

maintains our distance from the people and their needs—using radio or tracts on the street corner or television or even busing the folks into our comfortable churches—then we will fall short of the real evangelism we talked about. Really sharing the Good News—real evangelism—brings me *face to face* with whole people and *all their needs* and leads, without exception, to God's love in me reaching out to meet those needs.

If we make our evangelism real, we can still fall short of a real witness by participating in *cheap involvement*. Cheap involvement is *charity*, meeting some random symptoms a person has without getting down to the real needs, without asking those difficult questions about why those needs are there, what causes them, and how we get down to the root of the problems (*A Quiet Revolution*, p. 100, author's emphasis. Quoted with permission of Word Publishers © 1976).

As Perkins envisions the potential magnitude of this revolution if genuine evangelism is put into practice by God's people, he quotes a number of statistics from a speech by Senator Mark Hatfield. "If each church in America were to take responsibility for caring for 10 persons over 65 who are living below the poverty level, there would no longer be a need for the welfare system for the aged. If each congregation cared for only 18 families (72 adults and children) who are eligible for welfare, there would be no need for the existing federal or state welfare programs."

Figures from the prison system are equally challenging. If each congregation in America took responsibility for two prisoners, there would not be enough prisoners to go around (based on 1983 figures of 500,000 persons in prison). It is pertinent to note here that it costs taxpayers approximately $28,000 per prisoner per year to keep them in prison.

Write VOC for an annual report of their programs; their newsletter, *A Quiet Revolution*; information on their Jubilee conference; and book resources.

VOC Ministries, 1655 St. Charles Street, Jackson, MS 39209.

Evangelism Programs

Neighborhood Bible Studies

Effective outreach and evangelism can be accomplished by establishing neighborhood/community Bible study sessions.

Two simple questions are asked from door to door: (1) "Would you be willing to have a Bible study in your home for people in this neighborhood interested in learning more about the Bible?" and (2) if the answer is no, "Would you be interested in attending such a Bible study?"

Of course, the conversation in which these two questions are asked would include more general subjects. Identify who you are and which congregation you represent; state your purpose, and then inquire about the person's interest in hosting or attending Bible study.

While you are listening for the answer to the first question, other sharing questions will present themselves. For example, "Do you have a church home?" is a good one to help you discover a person's involvements and commitments without "attacking." The answers you receive can lead you to affirm the person's involvement and encourage reinvolvement: "We are glad that you have a church home and trust that you will continue to explore your faith actively. . . . We are not trying to steal people away. . . . we just want to reach out."

After some conversation and depending on the content and feelings expressed, question #2 may be asked.

A basic four-session Bible study can be developed around God's purpose for the Bible, God's message in the life and ministry of Christ, Jesus' call to all of us, and our response. Following this basic series, appropriate follow-up with individuals will reveal feelings, decisions, and interest in further Bible study, inquirer's groups, or service.

Variations of this simple process have been used in the development of new congregations, as well as in the outreach of existing ones.

Adult Inquirer Groups

For over thirteen years, Pastor Joseph Baker has been using four-session Adult Inquirer Groups (AIG) as the principal evangelistic tool with congregations he has served. Over 150 groups have been held, and Faith Baptist has received more than 1,380 persons into the life of the church, 98 percent of whom have come through these groups.

AIG attenders are secured by the pastor and laity through calls on new arrivals and Sunday visitors or through referrals by members and friends. Generally, specific enlistment is done on the second call in the home, and people are asked to attend a session that begins a month or two in the future.

In 1981 Pastor Baker began training lay-leader couples to facilitate the groups. He now attends only the first session and follows up personally with each person/family after the final session.

The first session provides time for getting acquainted; participants share their answers to certain questions and the pastor shares his or her four primary goals of ministry (to tell people the truth about Jesus Christ; to urge the uncommitted to come to Jesus Christ; to help the committed grow in grace and knowledge of Jesus Christ; and encourage the committed to witness and serve Jesus Christ).

The second session includes an audiovisual slide presentation of the history and ministry of the congregation and a "quest for answers" regarding the American Baptists, showing the similarities and differences among Baptists.

The third session is focused on Christian symbols and the church setting: the cross, baptistry, pulpit, Bible, Communion table, flowers, offering plates, candlesticks, and the Christian and American flags.

The final session includes church expectations of its members, a review of constitution and bylaws of the congregation, and a discussion of Christian stewardship of the congregation.

A complete set of resource materials, including a leader's guide and four 90-minute tapes of actual AIG sessions, is available for $12.

Rev. Joseph Baker, Faith Baptist, 6600 Trier Rd., Fort Wayne, IN 46815. Tel.: (219) 485-1646.

Episcopal Renewal

The Episcopal churches in the New York City area have had a pilot project in evangelism and renewal in nine congregations, according to Rev. Wayne Schwab of the Evangelism and Renewal Office.

The first three years of the process include: specific "growth partners training," which includes the rectors and representatives from each congregation. Workshops include Bible study and specific planning and goal setting for evangelism and outreach. Follow-up meetings are held regularly to continue the sharing by parish teams.

Some sample strategies, developed by parishes and based on their needs, include: introductory pamphlets about the church for real estate agencies, name tags for all church members and visitors, newcomer luncheons, "tracking systems" for visitors, calls on visitors by clergy and laity, newcomer activities, and training for church membership. Following decisions for Christ and church membership, some new congregants are assigned to fellowship groups/committees/tasks or participate in defining their gifts for ministry in the church and the world.

Rev. A. Wayne Schwab, ER Office, the Episcopal Church Center, 815 Second Ave., New York, NY 10017.

Operation Timothy 2:22

Operation Timothy 2:22 is a ten-week course in relational evangelism developed by Rev. Russel Jones prior to his becoming Director of Evangelism for the ABC Pacific Southwest.

The foci of the ten sessions with laity include: (1) the basis for evangelism—making the most of your contacts; (2) the use of your personal testimony; (3) gospel presentation in outline; (4) handling objections; (5) how to deal with the backslider; (6) different types of unsaved persons; (7–10) how to deal with particular kinds of persons—the "concerned," the self-righteous, the indifferent, and those with intellectual objections to faith.

The course is being used by a number of congregations in the Pacific Southwest with exciting results. One of these is Calvary Baptist Church of San Bernardino, Rev. Larry Dobson, pastor (3701 N. Sierra Way, San Bernardino, CA 92405).

Evangelism with Youth in the City

The Reverend Bill Konicki, associate pastor of St. Joan of Arc Roman Catholic Church, 570 Lincoln St., Worcester, MA 01605, has trained an exciting team of adults and youth in outreach into the parish and community.

Sixty-eight percent of this 1,200-family parish are one-parent families. The parish also has a high percentage of low-income families and a large population of seniors. Personal interviews with individual youth revealed deep needs for friendship, love, and support. In 1978, Pastor Konicki began with a core of three married couples; in 1983, more than twenty-four adults take responsibilities in different areas of leadership with a team of youth. In all, over 200 young people are active.

The ministry teams are divided into work-focus areas:

1. meeting planning—weekly one-hour meetings, with speakers/serious input/Bible study/games
2. ministries—worship, special seasonal parties and picnics for seniors in the congregation, baby-sitting, yardwork, and snow removal
3. athletics—several teams/banquets/awards
4. newspaper publication—monthly, September–June
5. social activities
6. public relations and publicity
7. servants' team—planning for spiritual life of the group, prayer focus; informing group about sick persons, deaths in families, and families in crisis

The 1982 theme of "Reach Out and Touch" resulted in sixty-seven youth committing themselves to a biweekly visit with an elderly person for fellowship, reading, walks, errands, and prayer. Partners were "hooked-up" at the annual youth-sponsored parish picnic.

Youth also regularly visit other youth and train still others for the three stages involved in visitation:

1. a *telephone call* (to a potential member or a former member)—"May we come and visit with you? Why? We care and want to share information with you. It's easier to talk face-to-face."
2. a *visit* (with former member)—sharing how the group has grown, exploring feelings of difficulty the person may have with group or individuals in it, inviting them to a "drop-in" meeting (which is easier to attend than a formal meeting), offering to pick up him or her.
3. a *letter*—a personal, handwritten note, reinforcing feelings of care and love for the person, affirming the desire for his or her involvement, and expressing thanks for the visit.

These three stages may be repeated, depending upon the response, feelings shared, problems discovered, and appropriateness.

A personal call to commitment to Christ is shared in person, using the pamphlets created through the public relations group. The story of "Sam and Samantha" provides the context. Sam and Samantha are "with it" teens who are sophisticated and bored with life; they feel rejected by adults and are hostile toward the world.

There is good news! There is a time to embrace. No, we're not talking about dating or making out or anything like that. We are talking about opening our arms and hearts to other people, who fear being hurt. These next few pages are more than a description of programs; they are about a miracle: parishioners, parents, and friends all working together to get

rid of the Sam/Samantha syndrome. There is room for you. In a silly way, we left out the most important person as we were writing—Jesus—because we didn't want to turn you off. You see, he's the one performing the miracle. He's the one inviting you to come to himself and to become part of the "St. Joan of Arc Youth Ministry."

The Reverend Bill Konicki, Associate Pastor, St. Joan of Arc Church, 570 Lincoln St., Worcester, MA 01605.

Evangelism in the Asian Community

In the United States among Baptists alone, over fifty Asian congregations have been formed since 1970. Included are separate missions to Laotians, Hmong, Thai, Vietnamese, Koreans, Filipinos, Chinese, Japanese, Taiwanese, and Cambodians. About half of the worship services are conducted in a language other than English; one-third are bilingual or trilingual.

Evangelism happens through small group Bible studies in homes, revivals, friendships made in language classes, use of the Bible in language training, and, most significantly, through invitation by family and friends to come to fellowship and to Christ.

The culture of the Hmong people is organized in tribal units; if the leader is converted, the whole tribe joins. This concept is surprisingly similar to the biblical concept of the "household"; when the master became a Christian, the whole household was often won to Christ.

Calvary Baptist Church of Providence, R.I., has more than eighty Hmong people in its fellowship. In Southern California, the fields are "ripe for harvest" with an estimated 100,000 Hmong, not counting other Asian groups.

Katie Choy, Director of Asian Ministries, American Baptist Churches, P.O. Box 851, Valley Forge, PA 19482-0851.

Institute for American Church Growth (IACG)

The IACG has done extensive research on the bases for church growth within the local congregation. Training courses and ongoing support groups help a congregation look at its own history with respect to growth, do a "growth check-up" and analysis of its current situation, assess needs within the church and community, devise specific programs of outreach into the community, and focus on discipling and retaining visitors and new members rather than watching them go out the "back door."

Congregations and judicatories can participate in a three-year, in-depth program of assessment, planning, and growth. The American Baptist Churches of the Pacific Southwest has over thirty congregations participating in this kind of training of pastors and lay leaders.

Excellent book, film, and training resources have been

developed, along with study guides. Write for a list of resources and the "Church Growth Resource News," a free quarterly publication. A monthly magazine, *Church Growth: America,* is available for $14 a year. Institute of American Church Growth, 150 S. Los Robles, Suite 600, Pasadena, CA 91101. Tel.: (800) 243-4844 (toll free).

The Master's Plan

The Master's Plan is an excellent resource kit for use by a local congregation in helping to open its members' eyes to their personal opportunities to invite their households to Christ.

First Baptist Church of Ventura, California, under the direction of Rev. David Gallager, is using this resource effectively. *The Master's Plan* is available through the Institute for American Church Growth.

Why and how do people come to Christ? How do they choose a church? The Institute for American Church Growth asked more than 14,000 lay people the question "What or who was responsible for your coming to Christ and to your church?"

The results were startling and humbling (that is, for pastors). Here are the results shared in *The Master's Plan for Making Disciples,* page 43:

special need	1-2 percent
walk-in	2-3 percent
pastor	5-6 percent
visitation	1-2 percent
Sunday school	4-5 percent
evangelistic crusade	½ of 1 percent
church program	2-3 percent
friend/relative	75-90 percent

In New Testament times, the church, led by God's Spirit, spread like a brush fire. That growth was felt as people were committed to Christ and then went home to share with their households.

A household then included an average of four generations, several families—brothers and sisters, servants and helpers. Today's household ("oikos"—our sphere of influence) includes: (1) common kinship—larger family; (2) common friendship—friends, work relationships, and recreation acquaintances. These webs still provide the primary paths for most people in following Christ today.

MARC

The Missions Advanced Research and Communications Center (MARC) is the working arm of the strategy group of the Lausanne Committee for World Evangelization. MARC provides materials, seminars, and resources for all aspects of planning for ministry, and it also helps in implementing plans within local churches and the church worldwide. An incredible data bank of information on worldwide missions and ministry is maintained by MARC.

MARC was founded "to undergird the task of Christ's church by providing strategy information on the work of the church worldwide by applying a management systems approach to the task of missions at home and abroad, and by doing cooperative research in evangelism and church growth."

The MARC Newsletter is a bimonthly publication on the work of MARC, including the needs and news of mission research and essays on strategic planning in missions. Free.

An excellent handbook on planning and the goal-setting process using "PERT—Program Evaluation Review Technique" is *God's Purpose and Man's Plans* by Edward R. Dayton, MARC, 1976 ($2.50).

Write for newsletter and list of publications to MARC, 919 W. Huntington Drive, Monrovia, CA 91016. (MARC is a ministry of World Vision.)

Macedonia Ministries (MM)

MM is a lay-witness and renewal program designed to enable people to discover their calling in Jesus Christ, grow in their faith, and support one another in applying their faith in life situations.

Biblically based on the call to all persons to follow Jesus' command to love one another, MM takes its name from the book of Acts, which describes how Paul heard the call for help from Macedonia. In the work of Macedonia Ministries, committed laity hear the call from others to "come over and help" in the process of renewal. MM involves three approaches:

Renewal—A team of lay persons directs an intensive weekend process for individual and congregational renewal through worship, study, prayer, shared meals, visitation, and celebration.

Group-Life Development—A small group is trained and equipped to establish support groups for ongoing spiritual growth.

Life-Ministry Support—Members of MM help congregations to provide a support-group focus within the "dailyness" of their lives—home, neighborhood, school, community, or job.

MM is not an end in itself; it is a means whereby the total life and ministry of a congregation can be strengthened. It is a powerful process for renewal and commitment.

Macedonia Ministries, National Ministries, American Baptist Churches, P.O. Box 851, Valley Forge, PA 19482-0851.

Resources: MM Packet, for use in training team members, $3; descriptive leaflet #408-1-2224, free.

Evangelism-Communication (EV-COM)

EV-COM is a training process developed by ten denominations to help train trainers who then train members of local congregations in evangelism and communication skills, using the common media tools available in most communities.

Local congregations are helped to decide upon their own unique and specific biblical/theological definitions of evangelism and their own practical foundations for active evangelism. They are also taught some communication theory and techniques.

Specific focus is then given to the development of strategies for using the following tools: church newsletters and bulletins, direct mail, advertising, audiovisuals, radio, commercial and cable television, telephones, and newspapers.

For information of national training events or for the names of trainers in your area, contact:

EV-COM, Rev. Eugene Schneider, Director, 105 Madison Ave., Suite 909, New York, NY 10016.

Evangelism Explosion International (EEI)

EEI is committed to the development of lay leaders trained in one-on-one visitation and evangelism. Dr. James Kennedy, founder, trains pastors and key lay leaders in workshops held throughout the nation. These folk then become the leadership core for training and mobilizing their congregations.

The core of the method is a framework of reflective questions providing a flexible structure for discussion of a person's commitment to Christ, surety of salvation, and role in ministry in the church.

EEI, Dr. James Kennedy, P.O. Box 23820, Ft. Lauderdale, FL 33307. Tel.: (305) 781-7710.

Example:

Rev. Howard Stewart has taken the basic framework of EEI and rewritten it for his congregation, correcting what he sees to be the Calvinistic biases of the theological assumptions. He particularly appreciates the adaptability of the framework for those using it, in contrast to the inflexibility of tools that are preprinted and fixed in format, regardless of where the users may be in their personal spiritual awareness or faith journeys.

Rev. Howard Stewart, Ocean View Baptist, 1900 S. Western Ave., San Pedro, CA 90732.

Campus Crusade for Christ (CCC)

CCC offers a variety of evangelism materials and programs, including resources on how to use the *Four Spiritual Laws* booklet with integrity, manuals for training, and follow-up discipleship series.

The Transferable-Concepts Study Series includes ten focus areas: How to Be Sure You Are a Christian; Experiencing God's Love and Forgiveness; Being Filled with the Spirit; Walking in the Spirit; Witnessing; Introducing Others to Christ; and Prayer—to name some.

Ten Basic Steps Toward Christian Maturity is another basic Bible study series including these topics among others: The Christian Adventure, Abundant Life, Holy Spirit, Prayer, The Bible, Obedience, Old Testament, New Testament, and Witnessing.

CCC, Arrowhead Springs, San Bernardino, CA 92414.

Department of Evangelism, National Ministries, American Baptist Churches, U.S.A.

The Department of Evangelism (DE) (P.O. Box 851, Valley Forge, PA 19482-0851) has developed, through creative local pastors and leaders, an incredible set of resource materials for congregational use in the study and implementation of evangelistic outreach ministries.

Featured extensively in the discipleship section of this book (p. 39) are excerpts from *Growing as a Caring Community,* by Bill Cline, focusing on a process for opening up communications with and reclaiming inactive members.

Carl Gittings has written an easy-to-use diagnostic tool for local congregations around an acrostic of the word

"GROWING." The title is *How Are We Doing? A Congregational Life-Style Assessment* ($1).

These and five other excellent booklets are described in a catalog: "Out of Death, Life Resources for Evangelism," available free from the DE.

Discipleship and Mission in Today's Cultures

These materials are distributed by Partnership in Mission, 1564 Edge Hill Rd., Abington, PA 19001 ($19.95).

John Stott has said, "'Gospel and Culture' is not a topic of purely academic interest. On the contrary, it is the burning practical concern of every missionary, every preacher, every Christian witness, for it is literally impossible to evangelize in a vacuum."

These tapes and study materials grew out of the "Consultation on Gospel and Culture" sponsored by the Lausanne Committee for World Evangelism. Seven study modules include these titles, among others: Looking at Culture; Jesus in Culture; Incarnation: God Speaking in Culture; Interpreting the Bible in Culture; and the Church in Culture.

An excellent study tool and resource for a local committee planning for evangelism either locally or in another country.

Finding the Way Forward

The United Methodist Churches have created a study series titled *Finding the Way Forward,* written for the evangelism committee of the local church. The book and a film by the same title feature several case studies of local congregations as stimuli for theological study, reflection, and planning.

Additional material from local congregational ministry is published in a periodical called *FORWARD,* available from Dr. Charles Kinder, Director of Foundation for Evangelism, 1910 Adelicia Street, Suite 206, Nashville, TN 37212.

Growing Churches for a New Age

By Owen W. Owens, Judson Press, 1981 ($7.95). This concise book documents the growth in ten local congregations, varying from small to large, in rural, suburban, and metropolitan communities. This cross-denominational study (United Church of Christ, Baptist, Presbyterian, Independent) focuses on churches as evangelistic communities, looking at five specific qualities. The churches described are *"visionary* in their teaching and preaching. . . . *incarnational,* acting on and embodying the Good News of Christ in distinctive ways. . . . *witnessing,* bringing persons to a knowledge of Christ and joining them to the Body of Christ. . . . *relational* in their inner life and decision making, expressing the teachings and life-style of Christ. . . . *activist,* influencing the values and structures of their community."

The American Bible Society

The American Bible Society has done a magnificent job of creating attractive reprints of salient selections of Scripture for use in a host of different contexts: seniors' centers, laundromats, doctors' offices, beauty parlors, barber shops, train and bus stations, and hospitals. Prices are rock-bottom.

Write for a complete catalog of materials: American Bible Society, Box 5656, Grand Central Station, New York, NY 10163.

Concern for People

> "I believe in person to person; every person is Christ for me, and since there is only one Jesus, that person is the only one person in the world for me at that time."
>
> (Mother Teresa, quoted in the *New York Times Magazine*, December 9, 1979)

Children's Groups Other Than Church School

Children Together, Vols. 1 and 2

Vol. 1, by Louise Spiker (Judson Press, 1980) and Vol. 2, edited by Elizabeth W. Gale (Judson Press, 1982). These resource books are designed to be used with groups of children in grades 3-6 whenever children gather other than in Sunday church school. Throughout there is an emphasis on the group as a Christian community. Each session has a multitude of things to do. There are no printed learner's materials or packets to buy.

Children's Worship Bulletins

For ages 3-12. Crossword puzzles, dot-to-dot games, word games, matching games, pictures to color, places to draw—all using biblical resources.

Concordia Publishing House, 3558 S. Jefferson Avenue, St. Louis, MO 63118.

The Gathering Place

This activity is conducted every afternoon from 1:30 to 5, five days a week in the summer for young people in grades 3–7. A sampling of their activities includes:

weaving in the biblical fabric center;

swimming in the "Dead Sea" or the "River Jordan";

working in the carpenter's shop;

molding, firing, and glazing clay in the "Potters' House";

listening to stories told in the "Old Nomad's Tent";

singing right next to the "Wailing Wall";

preparing and eating food just as Jesus and his disciples did.

A special Friday-night festival was also planned for friends and family as an outreach into the community and an opportunity to share the exciting "products" of the week's learnings and the spirit that was evident throughout the week.

The program was operated by a staff of twenty persons of various ages.

Bobbie Roland, Coordinator, First Presbyterian Church of Oxnard, 850 Ivywood, Oxnard, CA 93030.

Youth Ministries

Youth-Club Program, Inc.

700 Dewberry Road, Monroeville, PA 15146. Tel.: (412) 372-1341.

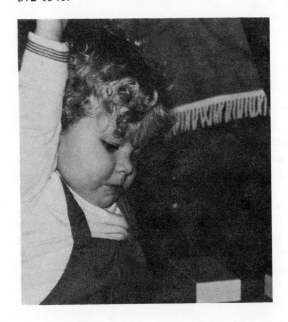

Over 3,000 churches in the United States are using the basic concept and format created by the Youth-Club folk for an effective midweek after-school activity and training time for children and youth. Each year Youth Club offers workshops for those who would like orientation and training in the establishment and administration of youth clubs.

The Youth Club is organized around four activities: recreation, Bible study, training in worship, and a shared meal. The club involves pastors, parents, and adults with the youth in the church; it helps *do* "Christian education." It is not a fad or gimmick but a reasonable program involving the whole family in the Christian education process.

Trinity Baptist in Santa Monica, California, has enthusiastically operated a Youth Club for a number of years. Hatboro Baptist Church in Pennsylvania is just beginning a club.

Have you considered this exciting tool in your congregation?

Funtastics: Handicapped Youth

Funtastics is a once-a-week youth club providing crafts, music, activities, dances, games, and trips for young adults with developmental disabilities in the southeastern Indianapolis area.

While the club is clearly seen as a ministry of the church "to go into the highways and byways and bring them in," the program is open to all and is not "preachy." Of the more than thirty youth who participate, only two have parents who are members of Judson Church, the sponsoring organization.

Here is a clear example of finding a need and meeting it, in Jesus' name.

Rev. Larry Wills or Rev. Estel Haywood, Judson Baptist Church, 6950 E. Raymond Street, Indianapolis, IN 46239. Tel.: (317) 353-2079.

Runaway/Alienated Youth

Vallejo First Baptist Church has formed Respite, a nonprofit corporation for outreach ministry to runaway and alienated children and young people whose needs are not being addressed by any existing agency, public or private, in their community.

Respite was begun in January, 1983, with an initial commitment of nine families willing to provide temporary housing for no more than five days for youth with emergency needs, and twenty-three persons willing to staff a telephone hot line. This ministry includes personal counseling, efforts to establish contact and reconciliation with parents, help with planning and making decisions for vocational/job futures, and good old-fashioned TLC—tender loving care.

For information write to Dr. Ralph Lightbody, Pastor, Vallejo First Baptist Church, 538 Carolina St., Vallejo, CA 94590.

Youth for Christ

Youth for Christ reaches out to teenagers and their families through five basic ministries: campus-life clubs, youth guidance, family concern, literature, and media. Clubs are organized in local high schools through the work of a local campus-life board and a staff member. The youth-guidance ministry is directed to delinquent, predelinquent, and disadvantaged youth. The family concern ministry is a seminar, and the literature ministry is aimed at families of youth.

A number of creative resources have been evolved for leadership, including two living-unit group manuals, volume 1 and volume 2, prepared for use in the small group setting. Volume 1 includes a topical approach to Scripture: dating, friendship, family, etc.; a book-by-book approach to Scripture: 1 John, Romans, Proverbs; and studies on the *Chronicles of Narnia*, by C. S. Lewis. Each session includes specific "how-to" helps for use with the group.

Both volumes are available from YFC Teen Sales, Box 419, Wheaton, IL 60187. Ask for a complete literature list.

Youth Magazines

1. *Campus Life:* Quality reading in contemporary format for today's high school student. With companion *Leader's Guide*. Christianity Today, 465 E. Gunderson, Carol Stream, IL 60187.

2. *Venture:* A lively, pertinent magazine for young men 12 to 18 years of age. Published by Christian Service Brigade, Box 150, Wheaton, IL 60189.

3. *HIS:* Inter-Varsity Christian Fellowship magazine, aimed primarily at Christian college students on secular campuses. Inter-Varsity Christian Fellowship, 5206 Main St., Downers Grove, IL 60515.

4. *Group:* Published eight times a year ($13.00). Complete edition for leaders is available. Use the magazine as a basis for Bible study and reflection on the meaning and practice of Christian faith. T. Schulz Publications, Box 481, Loveland, CO 80537.

Group magazine offers books and resources for youth ministry, including books such as *"More . . . Try This One"* ($5.95). Hundreds of ideas for use in local groups.

A yearly national conference for youth and youth leaders is sponsored, usually in Colorado.

5. *Youth Magazine:* United Church Press, 132 West 31st St., New York, NY 10001. Published quarterly ($11.60 for a single subscription); reduction for group subscriptions. Write for information. Contains articles by and about youth,

written on topics of interest to youth relating to life issues and personal spiritual growth.

C-4 Resources (Christ, Covenant, Community, Change)

210 W. Church St., Champaign, IL 61820. Tel.: (217) 356-9078. Publishes *Youth Ministry Update,* a free-of-charge newsletter, and a variety of printed resources including *The Youth Worker's Handbook,* materials on teenage sexuality, Bible-study resources and retreat guides, and the C-4 devotional journal for use by individuals during weekend retreats (poems, prayers, short stories, and Bible study suggestions for thirty days of devotions). *Repairing Christian Lifestyles,* developed in cooperation with the Alternatives organization and nineteen different denominations, focuses on the process of making life-style changes to improve the quality of our own lives and to help us to be better stewards of the world's resources.

Study is biblically based and includes a variety of instructional methods: simulation games, journal writing, values clarification, service projects, etc.

Resources for Creative Ministry with Youth

Recycle Community

A number of groups are creating their own ideas and sharing the creativity of others in the area of ministry with youth. See creative networks and Dennis Benson, *Recycle I* and *Recycle II,* described on page 25.

Youth Specialities

1. Publishers of the "fantabulous" *Resource Directory for Youth Workers,* published (and updated) annually. While

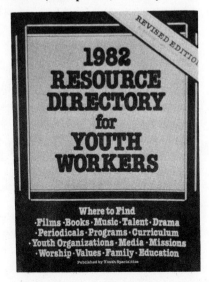

focused primarily on youth ministry, it includes resources applicable to all ages. The Table of Contents reads like a library of ministry:

- Books of youth ministry—high school, junior high school, programming, recreation
- Camping ministries—organizations, publications, camps, and people providing resources
- Curriculum publishers—nondenominational, denominational, Catholic, elective
- Denominational youth ministries
- Drama—professional groups, play script sources, publications, puppet and clown ministries
- Family ministry—organizations, periodicals, program and curriculum resources, books
- Films and video—producers/distributors; cassettes
- Mission and relief agencies—service projects, publications, leadership training, music/songbooks, periodicals, newsletters for leaders and youth
- Simulation games and role plays
- Singles' ministries
- Talent, values, and moral development
- Worship resources

Odds and ends—college/career planning; counseling, sexuality; tapes/television; substance abuse

This publication has over 140 pages and is well worth the $7.95 purchase price.

2. Compilers and publishers of *Ideas—Library,* a 28-volume library of ideas created and used by local leaders with youth. Organized by category, it includes crowd-breakers, games, creative communications, special events, camping, skits, publicity, and service projects.

3. Sponsors of the National Youth Workers' Seminar each year. Dozens of workshops are led by top leaders from local congregations and creative ministries throughout the world.

4. Publishers of the *Wittenburg Door* magazine—a "Christian *Mad Magazine*"—aimed at humorously helping stimulate creative reflection on our work and ministry (see p. 33).

Youth Specialities, now handled by Abingdon Press, 201 Eighth Ave., S., Nashville, TN 37202.

Basic Encyclopedia for Youth Ministry

By Dennis C. Benson and Bill Wolfe, T. Schultz Publications Group Publishers, 1982, 352 pp., hardcover. Write to Dennis Benson, Box 12811, Pittsburgh, PA 15241 ($15.95 plus $1.50 for mailing and handling).

This encyclopedia contains 240 articles on every aspect of youth ministry. It was written to assist youth advisors at the local level in all aspects of their work: understanding roles, programming, building leadership, interfacing with the congregation and community, and many others.

Each topic entry from A to Z is cleverly identified and catalogued; each defines a problem or a concern and then includes a story of how someone else has dealt with the problem in his or her situation.

Larry Richards, author of *Youth Ministry*, a foundation book of theological/practical considerations, has this to say about the *Basic Encyclopedia for Youth Ministry:* "A practical and theologically sound guide that is rich in insights—for *everyone* involved in youth ministry. . . . a simple resource which will encourage your workers as well as point the way to flexible, effective youth ministry."

The Complete Youth Ministries Handbook

Volumes I and II, edited by J. David Stone, Abingdon Press, 1980 ($12.95). Background articles and curriculum ideas focus on real needs of youth, using insights from John Westerhoff and others.

Consists of three tracks, each having four components and together making a complete rainbow:

Educational:
1. Telling your story—finding common ground.
2. Belonging—risking trust.
3. Planning life together.
4. Establishing a Christian support family.

Leadership:
1. I do it.
2. You and I do it.
3. You do it; I'll support.
4. You do it; I'll move on to something else.

Theological:
1. Experience.
2. Affiliate.
3. Search.
4. Feel ownership.

Songbook for Youth Groups

Songs that speak of life, love, faith, truth, and feelings.

- Gospel
- Folk
- Oldies
- Hymns
- Country
- Popular
- Jesus Rock
- Timeless
- Classics

Songs songbook, used by more than 500,000 folks weekly, helps individuals to participate rather than watch. Using materials and leadership philosophies that reflect "participation dynamics," groups can increase their singing involvement by 70%. The anthology of over five hundred songs, reflecting classic and folk hymns, psalms, and popular selections, is uniquely compiled to mix all kinds of songs and expressions. Fixed categories are avoided to give a feel of "life in its wholeness."

By Songs and Creations, Box 559, San Anselmo, CA 94960. Tel.: (415) 457-6610. Write for catalog.

Retreats—Planning and Program Ideas

Retreat Handbook, by Virgil and Lynn Nelson, Judson Press, 1976 ($5.95). (See page 31.)

Respond and Explore Program Resource Books

Respond, Volumes 1-6, contains programs and program resources for senior highs, plus articles for leaders; published by Judson Press. *Explore,* Volumes 1-4, contains programs and guidance for leaders of junior highs; also published by Judson Press.

Mission and Study Opportunities for Students

Each year *Eternity* magazine publishes a directory of seminaries and missions opportunities called *Doors ['84].* Included are descriptions of schools, their program areas and strengths, and missions organizations that can use the energies of Christian students. This publication is primarily focused on more traditionally conservative schools and organizations.

Information and copies available by writing: *Doors,* Inquiry Service, P.O. Box 13040, Philadelphia, PA 19101.

Ministry with Singles

The Lutheran Church in America has held a number of consultations on "Ministry to and with Singles in Cities." The consultations, held in Atlanta, Los Angeles, New York, Minneapolis, and Washington D.C., included persons ranging in age from nineteen to sixty-seven. Single participants included those who had never married and those who were divorced, widowed, or separated.

A variety of interesting comments and recommendations were made, according to Harvey Peters of the Lutheran Church in America Division for Mission in North America:

1. The word "singles" means *many different* kinds of people with a *diversity of needs*.

2. Many churches unconsciously gear most of their programs to "the family," which they assume to be a traditional nuclear family but which statistically is less present than ever in our society.

3. Most participants rejected the idea of "specialized singles ministries" that isolate the unmarried. Ministry, while it may be specialized at times, needs to be consciously inclusive.

For information write to the Lutheran Church in America, Division for Mission, 231 Madison Ave., New York, NY 10016.

Solo: **The Magazine for Positive Singles**

8740 E. 11th Street, Suite Q, Tulsa, OK 74112 ($12 per year).

This is a magazine that helps the single person take a realistic look at life as an individual, work out his or her own feelings about that life, and then move ahead positively.

A great gift by a congregation to its single members.

Further Resources

For further resources see the *Resource Directory for Youth Workers,* Youth Specialities, p. 63.

Ministry with International Students

Thousands of international students attend colleges and universities in our country. We have a unique opportunity to minister to them while they are here, and we hope that they will return to their native lands as indigenous leaders in the Christian faith—with no added mission dollars being necessary.

Hundreds of international students attend Colorado State University. In 1972, American Baptist Church of Fort Collins (600 S. Shields, Fort Collins, CO 80521) organized a sewing class when one of the student wives expressed concern over the high cost of clothing in this country. Twelve sewing machines were purchased and nursery care was arranged. Attendance soon reached a capacity of forty per week.

Women from fifty-four nations have since participated in this class, many having made lasting commitments to Christ. A natural outgrowth of the sewing class was instruction in English as a second language. These classes are filled with women who want to learn while their husbands are studying.

Is your congregation near a college with international students? Have folk in your community considered having an exchange student from another country come and stay for a year? It is worth thinking about.

Ministry with the Handicapped

Historically, persons with physical and mental handicaps have been treated as subhuman. It took the vision of an English Christian, John of Beverly, for example, to see that deaf people were, in fact, intelligent and could know God's Good News of hope.

Ministry with the Deaf

Rev. Daniel Pokorny, who holds the "John of Beverly Chair" at Concordia Seminary (801 Demun Ave., St. Louis, MO 63105), is one of the key "movers and shakers" in the encouragement and training of persons and congregations for ministry with the deaf. He suggests the following as some beginning resources for a congregation feeling called to minister in this area:

1. Church school curriculum for children: contact the Mill-Neck Foundation, Box 100, Mill-Neck, NY 11765. Materials are free, and sample copies are available. The Foundation also has training videotapes on how to use the materials.

2. Background books and materials on understanding the nature of deafness:

   a. *Be Opened!* by William Yount, Broadman, 1976, 240 pp. ($8.95).

   b. *Ministering to the Silent Minority,* by Edgar D. Lawrence, Gospel Publishers, Springfield, Mo., 1978 ($1.50).

   c. *Creating the Caring Congregation, Guidelines for Ministering with the Handicapped,* by Harold Wilke, Abingdon, 1980 ($4.95).

   d. General awareness materials for churches—bulletin inserts, articles, bibliography. Contact Donald Zuln, Lutheran Churches Missouri Synod, secretary to Ministry of Deaf, 1333 South Kirkwood Rd., St. Louis, MO 63122.

Several Lutheran churches around the country are made up of deaf members. Names and addresses of two such churches are: Holy Cross Lutheran Church for the Deaf, Pastors Moody and Radke, 101 N. Beaumont St., St. Louis, MO 63103. Pilgrim Lutheran Church for the Deaf, Rev. A. Auptman, 1233 S. Vermont, Los Angeles, CA 90006.

For those ready to begin to learn specific communication skills with the deaf, Dana Farley, of Santa Barbara, shares basic resources from his years of training people for deaf ministries:

1. *A Basic Course in American Sign Language,* by Tom Humphries and Carol Padden; Terrence J. O'Rourke, publisher: 517 Silver Spring Ave., Silver Spring, MD 20910 ($10 paper, $15 hardback).

2. *Conversational Sign Language II: An Intermediate-Advanced Manual,* by Willard J. Madsen, publishers: Gallaudet College, Washington, DC 20002, 1972 ($15).

3. *A Dictionary of Idioms for the Deaf,* by Maxine Boetner and John E. Gates, edited by Adam Makkai, rev. ed. 1983, Barrons Educational Series, Inc. ($8.95).

4. For help in understanding children and the experience of deafness, *They Grow in Silence; The Deaf Child and His*

Family, by Eugene D. Mindel and McCay Vernon, National Association of the Deaf, 1971 ($7.50).

Dana has created a list of resources and has written a variety of curricula for use with youth and adult groups in church schools and camps. Dana Farley, 259 Vereda Leyenda, Goleta, CA 93117 (SASE).

Ministry with the Developmentally Disabled

Resources for working with the handicapped and developmentally disabled are not easy to find. Folk in Santa Barbara who have ventured ahead in the creation of their own materials are Joyce Walters, Mary Slater, and Dorle Obitts. They are leading a Wednesday evening program for fifteen to twenty persons varying in chronological age from early teens to mid-twenties. They have used basic Pioneer Club curriculum books and have adapted the suggestions to meet the unique needs of their groups.

Calvary Baptist Church, 736 W. Islay, Santa Barbara, CA 93101, is planning to have, each October, a Handicapped Awareness Sunday to help the congregation be more sensitive to the special gifts, talents, and needs of the developmentally disabled person.

Mary Slater would be happy to share with those interested in similar ministries. Write to her, c/o the church, enclosing a SASE.

Busing of Handicapped

The American Baptist Church of Ft. Collins, Colorado, buses twenty to thirty adults with special handicaps to church each Sunday and offers other regular programs of worship, study, and fellowship (600 S. Shields St., Fort Collins, CO 80521).

Ministry with the Blind

Recording for the Blind, 215 E. 58th St., New York, NY 10022, is a library of the spoken word, which includes over 50,000 texts and adds 4,500 new titles each year.

Thousand Pines Conference Center established a "trail walk" for blind campers during one of its summer sessions for persons with visual handicaps.

The American Bible Society has scriptural resources for the blind, including the Bible in Braille, as well as Scriptures in several translations recorded on tapes. American Bible Society, Box 5656, Grand Central Station, New York, NY 10163.

Ministry with Seniors

Hello Today (Care and Call Program)

Lucille Driggers, Hello Today Administrator, University Baptist Church, 2515 Church Avenue, Bakersfield CA 93306. Tel.: (805) 871-0840.

The "Hello Today" program is a ministry between persons who live alone. Its purpose is to encourage a *daily telephone call* just as a matter of prudence. This ministry is open to any in the church or community, whether or not they are members of the church or seniors' program. A simple instruction sheet is shared with members.

A specific time is decided upon for each day's call. The partners take turns, one being the caller for a week, the other the recipient. Conversation is kept to less than a minute. (If people want to chat, they are encouraged to agree on a call-back time.) This is *critical* to the success of the program; when people get into talking or feeling obligated to talk, rather than just calling, there is an increased likelihood of their not making the thirty-second–one-minute call and the effectiveness of the program is lost.

If there is no answer, callers are instructed to try again in thirty minutes. If there is no answer, they are to call a relative of the person; if later there is still no answer, they are to call the church, the pastor, or program administrator. One of them will go in person to visit. If none of these people can be reached, participants are to call the police.

XYZ Club

First Baptist Church, 1130 San Vincente Avenue, Salinas, CA 93901, has a number of exciting ministries, including XYZ Club for seniors—"Xtra Years of Zest"! This group, led primarily by lay seniors, plans spiritual and fun activities year-round for seniors.

The congregation, under the direction of Pastor Fred Fels, is also involved in many other creative ministries, such as ministry with the deaf, ministry with men and boys in correctional institutions, weekend camping outings called "Wagon's Ho," youth development with evangelism and discipleship in view, ministry with singles, and the variety offered by three morning services led by two different preaching pastors.

More of this exciting work is documented in the book *Growing Churches for a New Age,* by Owen D. Owens, Judson Press, 1982 (page 60).

Ombudsmen: A Patient's Best Friend

In a day when nursing homes and convalescent hospitals may be operated by impersonal corporations concerned primarily with the bottom line of profits, there is an intense need for concerned people to keep watch on behalf of individual patients and all of the residents.

In Ventura County, the local chapter of the National Council of Jewish Women has contracted with the area agency on aging to train volunteers and administer a county-wide ombudsmen program in nursing and convalescent homes.

The basic goal is to be an advocate for the patient. People in rest homes are vulnerable and often alone, with nobody in the outside world looking out for them. Ombudsmen are like good surrogate relatives, relatives who listen and get results.

The project has trained more than sixty people since its first graduating class in 1981.

For information on the program and its operation write: Shirley Radding, Director, Ombudsmen Program, 7620 Foothill Rd., Ventura, CA 93004; or Ombudsmen Training Manuals, California Department of Aging, c/o Bill Benson, 1020 19th St., Sacramento, CA 95814.

Visitation in Convalescent Hospitals, Home-Delivered Meals

Over 150 volunteers from thirty-six congregations in the Santa Monica area work together to visit in convalescent hospitals and to deliver meals to homebound seniors. The Westside Ecumenical Conference is the coordinating vehicle for these activities.

Helen Wallace, Executive Secretary, Westside Ecumenical Conference, P.O. Box 1402, Santa Monica, CA 90406.

Day Care for Seniors

Elderhaus is a day-care center for the elderly, which allows them to remain living in their homes longer by providing professional care during the day. Participants may involve themselves in individual growth programs and receive counseling and occupational therapy. In addition, a registered nurse is on duty at all times, helping to provide generous doses of tender loving care, along with other staff. Elderhaus is a ministry of the American Baptist Church of Fort Collins, Colorado, under the leadership of Dr. Don Lambert and Betty Mosely (for address, see p. 66).

Family Ministries

The institution of marriage/family is undergoing radical change in our culture. We see it moving from being an assumed societal form to being an intentional relationship based on companionship. It is becoming less grounded in its structural-functional aspects and more in intimacy. Both men and women have far higher expectations of marriage and family relationships than ever before.

Only 17% of the nation's families currently fit the model of the traditional family: father–breadwinner, mother–homemaker, children–doing chores around the house.

The family configurations that are increasing include:

1. The *single parent family*—an adult living with a child or children. The largest number are divorced persons; second largest, and growing, are those never married who have children.

2. *Remarried persons*—75% of divorced women and 83% of divorced men remarry within three years, and 44% divorce a second time, with 50% of those remarrying for a third time. This means an *increasing number of children* who have multiple parent figures and *adults* who are parenting children that are not biologically theirs. It also means children living with other children to whom they are not biologically related.

3. *Unmarried people living together*—a dramatically increasing number of people do not bother with marriage or remarriage.

(This data is based on 1982 studies of 1981 statistical reports by Rev. Larry Dobson, American Baptist Churches of the Pacific Southwest, Family-Life Task Force, 970 Village Oaks Dr., Covina, CA 91724.)

Often our congregations' unconscious definitions of family assume the traditional model. Look through your regular program and ministries and reflect upon which of them consciously take into account the needs/dynamics of the above data. Our planning for ministry needs to reflect the diversity of needs within our congregations as well as our communities.

Two basic questions emerge: (1) How do we deal with these changes from a biblical/theological perspective? and

(2) In what ways can we minister most effectively to persons in these varieties of family structure?

Some implications suggested by the task force include:
—The family in our culture is a major mission field.
—The metaphor of the church as the "family of God" is a powerful one today.
—The church can be extended family, providing loving care and acceptance lacking elsewhere.
—The family can be challenged and enabled to fulfill its

God-given role in the life of individuals and society.
—Ministry with families in many forms can be an effective evangelism and church growth tool because it potentially touches the felt needs of many people.

Comprehensive Family-Support and Care Systems

An overall system of family support and care has been developed by the Church of Jesus Christ of Latter-Day Saints (LDS), in which a family that is in a crisis is helped financially and spiritually as the need presents itself.

In each stake (area), the entire membership fasts one meal each week, and the money is set aside in a special fund for emergencies in the lives of families. The money is used to help with bills, rent, or other crises. It provides for payment to people to do specific work for the church or for other families in need in the church.

There is specific counseling with the family in crisis, and one person takes charge of coordinating the work of the fellowship with that family. Focus will be on whatever is needed: budgeting, job skills development, job search process, or locating housing.

Clothing, furniture, and other physical needs are met through a regional network of clothing sharing and distribution warehouses. Food warehouses provide sources of canned foods, salvaged foods, and other items secured and stored for emergency use. These centers are usually regional and dispense supplies to local stakes through the appropriate coordinating persons.

Jobs are created in these regional centers, and the funds for them come through the offerings and small donations made by other church members for items acquired.

This whole system of ministry is well documented in a film called *Welfare: Another Perspective*. This film is usually owned by each local stake, and would probably be available for viewing if you contacted the local leaders. It is also available through Brigham Young University Film Library, BYU, Provo, Utah 84602.

Family Devotions Created and Shared by Families in the Church

Morris F. Anderson, Pastor, First Baptist Church, 2421 W. Point Rd., Green Bay, WI 54303.

To encourage families to participate in establishing and practicing family devotions together, lay members of the church created seven family devotions for use by other families in the church during the month of May.

The home focus identified Christianity as a "homemade" religion. Jesus grew up in a home even as we do, and Jesus' symbolism continually referred to family images: God as "Father" or "my Father."

Each devotion had background information and activities appropriate for different age groups within the family. Even some simple role-plays about values were included. After meeting twice a week for the month, families were encouraged to create their own "Eighth-Day" devotional activity and then share it with the church family for later use.

Family Home Evenings

The Church of Jesus Christ of Latter-Day Saints has most consistently emphasized and practiced the disciplines of the Family Home Evening. No church functions are scheduled on that evening (often Monday), and all the families are encouraged to spend the evening together in a variety of activities, including singing, games, Bible study, and sharing projects. Extensive materials are prepared each semester for the family to use in planning for and leading this process.

Specific samples of materials and information about this program may best be obtained by contacting the local stake of the LDS church ward in your community or by writing LDS, Church Distribution, 50 E. North Temple, Salt Lake City, UT 84150.

Our Family Night In: Workbook of Covenant Living

By Lois Seiffert, Upper Room, 1981 ($4.95). This stimulating volume is organized around the theme "Covenant": covenants of new beginnings in Christ, of the Christian church, of Christian love, and of Christian prayer. Each of these four areas is divided into six outlines for use in planning a "family night in." In reality, these twenty-four session plans can easily expand.

Gatherings are arranged simply: preparation, beginning, sharing suggestions (appropriate ones are given for each age group/stages), closing, and things to do during the next week.

Families Sharing God: Devotions and Activities at Home and Away

By Barbara O. Webb, Judson Press, 1981 ($3.50). Thirty-five anytime, anyplace devotions for use at home, on a trip, visiting with friends, indoors or outdoors. Each devotion includes a Bible verse, an interpretative story, plus a creative project to attract and hold children's attention.

Barbara has written several other excellent devotional books for families: *Devotions for Families: Fruit of the Family, Devotions for Families: Building Blocks of Christian Life, Prayers for Families,* all of which are published by Judson Press.

Family Nights Throughout the Year

By Terry Reilly and Mimi Reilly, Abbey Press, 1980 ($2.95). (Series II). Activities for each session include: opening prayer, thought questions, activity ideas (divided with separate suggestions for young families, middle-years families, adult families), snack time, entertainment, sharing, and closing prayer.

Celebrate the Feasts: Of the Old Testament in Your Own Home or Church

By Martha Zimmerman, Bethany House, 1981 ($4.95). Excellent documentation of the significance of seven major

Jewish feasts, the materials needed for their observance, and full details on how to celebrate them as Christians. Powerful ways to experience biblical principles as families in the reenactment of these great religious feasts.

Activities for Families and Church Groups

Roland and Doris Larson have created a fantastic volume entitled *Values and Faith: Value Clarifying Exercises for Family and Church Groups*, Winston Press, 1976 ($5.95). This volume of faith/values clarifying and sharing exercises is a basic tool for those designing programs in educational or family ministries.

Within each section there are eight basic tools used: voting, ranking, continuum, "either/or," listening, dilemma, interviewing, and goal setting. Blank work forms are included, with permission granted to duplicate for group and family use. Themes include: valuing, my faith, my family, myself and my gifts, others, the old, and the new.

This book is a virtual encyclopedia of great ideas and tools adaptable for use in numerous contexts within the life of the church and family.

Mothers' Morning Out

A popular ministry for mothers of young children has been initiated by many congregations to give mothers a morning out. In some instances, there is merely provision for child care, and the mothers are free to shop, do errands, read or whatever they choose.

Community Presbyterian Church (115 Lincoln Drive, Ventura, CA 93003) has chosen to organize the morning for the mothers as well, including time for small-group sharing, prayer, input from presenters, and refreshments. There is creative child care during the time the mothers are in session.

Program input is from a Christian perspective and deals with subjects of interest for mothers of young children. The focus is outreach to new families; there is no hard-sell, merely an opportunity for friendship, relationships, reflection, and sharing. Speakers state their convictions clearly; there is no apology made for the gospel. As a result, many women have made commitments to be followers of Jesus and have drawn their families to God as well.

BURP—Bringing Up Real People

Oxnard Presbyterian Church (850 Ivywood Dr., Oxnard, CA 93030) once had a class with the exciting name "Mothers of Young Children." One year the planning committee decided to change the name; their first session was a howling success (no pun intended!). Now called BURP (Bringing Up Real People), the group meets the second Thursday of each month from 9:30-11:30 A.M.

Marriage Encounter

Two major movements offer resources to couples and to congregations in the strengthening of the marriage ties between wives and husbands.

Marriage Encounter began originally within the Roman Catholic community as a weekend renewal experience and has spread to many other denominations and organizations; Presbyterians, Episcopalians, Southern Baptists, and American Baptists also have marriage encounter.

Marriage encounter can be misunderstood by those who still associate the word "encounter" with the encounter movement of the 1960s, with its often stereotyped accounts of knock-down, drag-out confrontations between persons.

Marriage encounter does not take the place of therapy; it works from a positive base of assumed mutual trust and encouragement in an effort to help good marriages become better. This is done throughout the weekend retreat and in follow-up "spiral groups," in which couples are encouraged to participate to help keep their commitments to communication growing.

For information, inquire among leaders in your association or denomination, or write: Marriage Encounter, 560 Paterson, Wichita, KS 67212. Tel.: (316) 722-3644.

Christian Marriage Enrichment (CME)

This is another organization, organized independently to support the church's desire to build Christian marriages and strengthen families.

It regularly offers workshops and seminars throughout the country for couples, and others for pastors and leaders who are working with families in the church. CME also has created a wide range of resources for use by pastors, marriage counselors, lay "shepherds" working with families, or counselors working with troubled persons in the local congregations.

Resources have also been developed for ministry with single persons, including *Single Vision,* a periodical directed to singles and those working with them.

Highlights of some other resources:

Seasons of a Marriage, by H. Norman Wright, Regal, 1982. Norman Wright has been a key mover in the growth of the CME movement. In this book he shares a variety of "seasons" including: initial expectations, early years, mid-life transitions, the empty nest, affairs and unfaithfulness, the healing process, parent-child reversal, and a time to die.

Excellent for use in premarital counseling and discussion and also with couples groups.

Before You Say I Do: Study Manual, by H. Norman Wright and Wes Roberts (Harvest House, 1978), *After You've Said I Do,* by Dwight H. Small (Jove, 1976), are two separate workbooks designed for joint couple study and sharing. They include Bible study, worksheets on goals/expectations, expressing appreciation, personal needs analysis, dreams for the relationship, and many other planning-sharing tools. The latter volume includes many exercises that are similar to the first and probably should not be used with the same couple.

Marriage and Family Enrichment Resource Manual, by H. Norman Wright, 1979 ($12). This 8½-by-11-inch manual has 135 pages of background information and exercises for use with couples and small groups in the life of the church. It contains reflective tools, work charts, sharing instruments, planning guides, and lesson plans. Excellent.

CME offers training workshops for pastors and counselors in the use of the Taylor-Johnson Temperament Analysis, an excellent personality inventory for use with an individual or couple seeking perspective and feedback for growth.

Write to CME for a complete catalog of resources and training opportunities: CME, 1913 E. 17th St., Suite 118, Santa Ana, CA 92701. Tel.: (714) 542-3506.

Tool for Counseling with Couples and for Assessing Strengths of Church Leaders

Rev. Jack Bailey, First Baptist Church, Santa Paula, California, has found the "Firo-B" inventory to be a good tool for use in premarital counseling, in his work with couples, and in leadership within the church. It is less cumbersome than the Taylor-Johnson Temperament Analysis and, while less specific, can still give quick feedback regarding potential areas of concern.

The "Firo-B" gives information in three broad categories: inclusion, control, and affirmation. It rates a person's desire to give and receive each.

"Firo-B" and interpretive material for use by counselor/leader in scoring the instrument are available from: Consulting Psychologists Press, Inc., 577 College Ave., Palo Alto, CA 94306. (Write for catalog.)

The Secret of Staying in Love

The "daily bread" of dialogue is the answer, and the process is aptly described by John Powell in his book *The Secret of Staying in Love,* Argus, 1974. Although words are easy to say, the daily practice of communication beyond the routine is not natural for many, if not most, couples.

This book is ideal for shared reading and interaction by wives and husbands, engaged couples preparing for marriage, and couples' groups within a congregation. The first sections deal with (1) the human condition—needs, options, addictions; (2) human needs and the experience of love; (3) love and communication; and (4) emotions.

The last sections introduce a specific discipline of dialogue, using a format called "10 and 10"—ten minutes spent in writing a love letter and then ten minutes of sharing feelings regarding the letters, which have been exchanged and read. The closing chapter includes a host of specific suggestions for the focus of the daily "10 and 10" and instructions on how to think up your own questions for reflection and sharing of feelings.

This process is very similar to that used in marriage encounter, described earlier.

I Need to Have You Know Me

This volume by Roland and Doris Larson (Winston Press, 1980, $6.95) is filled with fifty exercises to help couples define what is important to them, clarify their goals as individuals and as a couple, and crystalize plans for putting their hopes and values into action. Excellent for use with individual couples or groups of couples.

Topics cover all aspects of marriage: money and finance, health, time, work, humor, relatives, rest, talents, fears, and forgiveness, to name a few. Couples are encouraged to keep a journal of learnings and reactions, feelings, and unfinished business, in conjunction with their use of the exercises.

Homosexuality

An area in which strong feelings prevail is likely one in which we need the spirit of openness and the gifts of God's spirit (Galatians 5:22)—patience, gentleness, kindness, and the like. An excellent book for those wishing to explore the theological dimensions of this arena is *Now That You Know: What Every Parent Should Know About Homosexuality,* Betty Fairchild and Nancy Hayward; Harcourt, Brace, Jovanovich, 1981 ($8.95).

Men's and Women's Roles

In the 1970s a number of national conferences on men and masculinity were held across the United States to explore the effects of the feminist movement on men. With the help of the National Organization for Women, *Ms.* magazine, and the legislative move to pass an Equal Rights Amendment, women were raising many issues that affected the roles of men, such as birth control, domestic violence, equal relationships, coparenting, women clergy, gay and lesbian relationships, androdgyny, as well as patriarchy, the ideological base for the dominance of men over women.

Economically, however, women were still treated as second-class citizens in the work force by being paid 57 cents for doing the same work that men were receiving $1 for doing. Because the gender roles were stereotyped and reinforced by families, churches, schools, businesses, and government, a profeminist men's movement was created. Emerging now in the 1980s are a National Organization for Changing Men, *M.* magazine, and mutual support for legislative action.

Several books and periodicals worth noting are:

1. *Woman and Nature: The Roaring Inside Her,* by Susan Griffin, Harper & Row, 1979 ($4.95).

2. *Our Bodies, Ourselves,* by the Boston Women's Health Book Collective, 2nd rev. ed., Simon and Schuster, 1976 ($8.95).

3. *For Men Against Sexism: A Book of Readings,* ed. John Snodgrass, Crossing Press, 1980, 240 pp. ($6).

4. *Women, Men, and the Bible,* by Virginia Ramey Mollenkott, Abingdon, 1977 ($4.95). A classic work describing the relationship between men and women from a biblical perspective. Organized for use by study groups; cassettes and leader's guides available.

5. *Man as Male and Female,* by Paul K. Jewett, Eerdmans, 1975 ($3.95). Theological and exegetical work examining the relationship between men and women; valuable

reading for those considering this question from an evangelical perspective.

6. *Changing Male Roles in Today's World,* by Richard P. Olson, Judson Press, 1982.

7. *Quest: A Feminist Quarterly,* $2.75 per issue.

8. *M., Gentle Men for Gender Justice,* 306 N. Brooks, Madison, WI 53715. $2.50 per issue.

For a complete bibliography write to Food for Thought Books, 67 N. Pleasant St., Amherst, MA 01002.

For the material in this section we are indebted to Rev. Timm Peterson, 283 E. Vince St., Ventura, CA 93001.

Marriage and Parenthood Study Series

This study series was created to accompany full-length books on different aspects of marriage and family. Each book and accompanying discussion and study guide is suitable for 12 or 13 one-hour sessions for church school classes or complete groups. Guides also include suggestions for adapting to 6 two-hour sessions.

1. *Family Problems and Predicaments,* by Paul Welter, Tyndale, 1977. Welter explores how Christians can respond to anxiety, hurt, anger, and the struggle for independence ($4.95). Guide: LS15-331 ($2.95).

2. *Friends, Partners, and Lovers.* A personal and practical view of marriage by Warren L. Molton, Judson, 1979 ($5.95). Guide: LS15-335 ($2.95).

3. *You Can Have a Family Where Everybody Wins,* by Earl H. Gaulke, Concordia, 1975. A biblical perspective using the tools and skills of Parent Effectiveness Training ($2.50). Guide LS15-333 ($2.95).

Other book titles (with accompanying guides) include: *Expecting,* by Elizabeth A. Hambrick-Stowe, Judson, 1979; *Parents and the Experts,* by Diane Cooksey Kessler, Judson, 1974; and *Love and Negotiate: Creative Conflict in Marriage,* by John Scanzone, Word Books, 1979.

Discussion and study guides were created by leaders recruited for their special skills by the Department of Adult Ministries, Educational Ministries, American Baptist Churches in the U.S.A. Write to them at P.O. Box 851, Valley Forge, PA 19482-0851 and request pamphlet LS15-313, "Sources and Resources for Family Ministry, 1982," or order any of the above books and study guides from Judson Book Store, at the same address. Tel.: (215) 768-2097.

Planning for Family Ministry

Joe H. Leonard has written an excellent volume entitled *Planning for Family Ministry: A Guide for a Teaching Church,* Judson Press, 1982. Included are step-by-step planning helps, procedures/outlines for gathering information about family needs, and a list of family ministry program ideas. Appropriate for churches of any size, the book also includes background on the changes taking place in families today, the biblical foundation of family ministry, the nature of family ministry, and content and skill areas of family ministry.

Christian Education in Family Clusters

By Mel Williams and Mary Ann Brittain, Judson Press, 1982 ($6.95). Each of the thirty-eight sessions include group builders, table talk, Scripture, blessings, learning experiences, songs, and closing activities. Theme clusters include beginnings, faith, friendship, conflict, Advent, Lent, values, and marriage.

Training in Parenting Skills

The Parent's Handbook: Systematic Training for Effective Parenting (STEP), by Don Dinkmeyer and Gary McKay, American Guidance Service, Circle Pines, MN 55014. (Write for current catalog and prices.)

STEP is a practical, day-to-day approach to parent/child relationships. It provides a systematic approach to examining the motives for behavior/misbehavior, the intended results of this behavior, alternative actions for parents based on our understandings of the dynamics involved.

Additional sessions focus on self-understanding, learning how to encourage children and build feelings of self-worth, communication/listening skills, learning to explore alternatives, examining and allowing for natural and logical consequences of behavior, and a session on regular family meetings.

The course is designed for 8 or 9 two-hour sessions and comes complete with a leader's guide, cassette tape resources, table and wall charts, and flyers.

Rev. Larry Dobson of Calvary Baptist Church (3701 N. Sierra Way, San Bernardino, CA 92405) has used this course and feels that it can easily be complemented with appropriate Scripture for use in the church. He has taught the course to Christian couples in the congregation and has used it as an effective outreach in the community. Parents who have learned the tools have told others, and now even the PTA is requesting a course through the school. In the whole process, many valuable contacts have been made with families, some of whom have found Christ and have become active in the congregation.

Training in Family Stewardship and Personal Finance

How many families in your congregation would you guess actually know where their money goes? How many could indicate with some accuracy how much was spent last month

for food? for utilities? for transportation? for clothing? for entertainment? for God?

Most families manage from the bottom line of the bankbook or from the projected income of the next paycheck set against the current pile of bills on the desk.

This fact, coupled with our culture's "buy now, pay later . . . . a dollar down and a dollar a week" mentality, has led to a personal debt for the average family of *over $6,000*, not including home mortgages or auto loans!

Personal Financial Management Seminars

Pomona First Baptist Church has decided to do something about the problem of family financial planning by offering its members a ten-hour seminar in stewardship and personal financial management. Led by Christian CPAs and business educators, the seminar tries to teach members how to get their finances together so that they can function in favor of God and themselves. It is not a "wills and bequests" seminar or a subtle fund-raising gimmick.

Sessions include biblical study of stewardship, clarification and establishment of family goals, analysis of a family's current financial situation, help with the setting of objectives, suggestions for dealing with inflation, establishment and maintenance of a family budget and record-keeping system, and the formulation of individual action plans for each family.

For information/brochure write: Storehouse Ministries, First Baptist Church, 586 N. Main St., Pomona, CA 91768.

Are you in a small community with several churches? Why not go together and offer such a course to members of several congregations at once? Leadership could also be shared across denominational lines.

Family Clusters

In 1970 Dr. Margaret Sawin began a program of intergenerational education called "family clusters." The aim of this style of church education is to overcome the loneliness and impersonality of modern, especially suburban, life.

A family cluster is made up of four or five family units who covenant to meet together over an eight-to-twelve-week period of time. Meetings are usually held weekly, and at the end of each period, a decision is made by the cluster whether or not to continue.

Some of the objectives Dr. Sawin outlines for family-cluster education include:

1. to provide an intergenerational educational experience in which families share their values, insights, and faith, and grow together through mutual support and encouragement;

2. to provide an opportunity for families to discuss serious subjects;

3. to provide an opportunity for families to model aspects of their family systems for one another;

4. to provide an opportunity for parents to understand their own children more fully through contact with other children and for children to understand their parents more fully through contact with other parents.

Resources:

Family Enrichment with Family Clusters, by Margaret M. Sawin, Judson Press, 1979. Packet of descriptive materials from Family Clustering, Inc., P.O. Box 18074, Rochester, NY 14618. Also, "Approaches to Intergenerational Education" pamphlet, ALS 15-316, available from Judson Book Store, P.O. Box 851, Valley Forge, PA 19482-0851 (50 cents).

Many churches and denominations have taken basic resources from family clustering and adapted them for their own special use. The First Baptist Church of Redlands, California, with Rev. Bob Wallace and Rev. Hugh Huntley, developed a Bible-study format for use in their clustering program.

Intergenerational Education

St. Paul's United Methodist Church in Ithaca, New York, has developed an intergenerational Sunday church school, which meets for an hour at the usual church school time. A typical class of around twenty-five persons might include five sets of parents, a single adult, two third graders, one fourth grader, several sixth-to-eighth graders, and a few high school students. Attempts are made to match children in each group so that no child is the only one of a given age.

Everyone is responsible for helping with goal establishment, choosing curriculum resources, and providing leadership. Each group has a convener instead of a teacher. The church staff support the conveners and provide planning and resource assistance.

Some learnings from the experiences of St. Paul's Church:

1. The families involved have had a higher degree of commitment to the church school program, primarily because of their functions in leading/participating in the group.

2. Families are spending time together rather than in age-level groups and are interacting with single adults and others.

3. Adults have learned that learning to be a Christian can happen through means other than lecture and discussion. Many adults needed encouragement to get into the activities and find meaning in them rather than sit back and observe.

4. Creating curriculum from scratch takes a lot of church and leadership time and energy.

Further discussion on this experiment and a listing of resources can be had by sending for the pamphlet "Approaches to Intergenerational Education," prepared by the Division of Family Life Education of the American Baptist Churches. (To order, see information under "Resources" on this page.)

For information about the program at St. Paul's Church, write to the church, 402 N. Aurora, Ithaca, NY 14850.

Creative Resources for Teachers

1. National Teacher Education Program, 7214 E. Granada Rd., Scottsdale, AZ 85257. Tel.: (800) 528-2805. Regular information regarding workshops, training opportunities. Fantastic classroom teaching resources and learning-center kits. Has specialized in the development of learning centers for use in the Christian education classroom.

To receive the *NTEP Informer* free, write to get on the mailing list.

NTEP publishes *Church Teachers' Magazine*—a magazine with one purpose: to help Sunday school teachers—and *Family Devotional Guides* for use during the Advent and Easter seasons. Special learning-center resources are developed around the church year.

2. *Christian Education Catalog,* edited by Ruth Gordon Cheney, Seabury Press, 1981. Contains descriptive information, summaries, and reviews of books and resources. Helpful to those who work with children, youth, and families; and to curriculum publishers, both denominational and independent. Also has wider application for special ministries: singles, divorced, aging; for the church: theology, mission, education, worship, spiritual growth; and for human awareness: sexuality, justice, world hunger, the arts and drama.

3. Brethren House Ministries, 6301 56th Avenue, North, St. Petersburg, FL 33709. Tel.: (813) 544-2911.

Training and resources for use within the local congregation in all kinds of worship and education settings. Worship and church school resources include a wide range of items: "doing" psalm/hymn activities and world mission activities, Bible teaching resources, world hunger resources, and media materials.

These creative folk also publish the *Brethren House Times,* a newsletter published five times a year for only $4. They also tour the country taking their learning laboratory on the road to help local congregations to be more effective in leadership training in the church school and in young adult ministries. Special resources are developed around the seasons of the church year.

Death Education

Anticipating and Planning for Our Own Death

Estimates show that seven out of ten Americans do not have a written will. As a result, millions of dollars pile up every day, waiting for the courts to determine appropriate distribution.

Christians, especially, as stewards of God's resources and as those whose God has conquered death, need to plan seriously for those who survive them.

In California, if both parents are killed at the same time and if there is no written will stating who the parents want to raise the children, the state determines who will raise them, according to its assumptions about family relationships.

A local congregation can take charge and offer specific sessions on making wills and planning estates from a Christian perspective. Sometimes denominations have resource persons available for this kind of education. Or a congregation can find a Christian lawyer and work with her/him in planning.

Most wills can be drawn up at a cost of $50 to $100, depending upon their complexity.

Schedule this kind of opportunity for *your congregation* next year!

Wills also provide a unique opportunity for you to give continuing support to ministries that you appreciate. Remembering them will continue to advance God's cause long after you are gone.

Memorial Societies

Rev. David Stone, of Trumbull Neighborhood Ministries, 75 Jackson Dr., Campbell, OH 44405 (tel.: [216] 755-8696), has organized a memorial society for members of the community. For a low-cost membership fee of $10, lifetime members are kept informed of low-cost burial plans available through the society's standing contracts with funeral parlors. This kind of a group contract provides for fixed price, low-cost services at the time of death.

Members become involved in the process of planning ahead by making out a sheet detailing their wishes regarding memorial service, cremation, open/closed casket, burial location, and the like. Planning for living memorials well in advance of death is also encouraged by the society in order to increase our stewardship of God's resources—some of which are saved in the low-cost preplanned burial arrangements.

A number of other societies have sprung up in response to the high cost of dying. For information on a memorial society in your area write to: The Continental Association of Funeral and Memorial Societies (CAFMS), 1828 L Street NW, Washington, DC 20036, or Memorial Association of Canada, Box 96, Station A, Weston, Ontario, Canada M9N-3M6.

Preparation for Death and Burial

A basic reference and study tool for use in preparation for death and burial is *A Manual of Death Education and Simple Burial,* by Ernest Morgan, 9th ed., Alternatives, 1980, 64 pp. ($2,50), available from CAFMS.

This manual provides clear theological and philosophical bases for the practice of simplicity in funeral arrangements, along with advice on procedures at time of death, suggestions for memorial services, directories of memorial societies, societies of cooperative mortuaries, and addresses of medical schools, eye-banks, and so forth, should a person want to leave his or her body to be used for medical research or organ transplants.

Putting My House in Order is a two-page planning form, a convenient tool for pastors and churches to use in helping each person and family consciously plan for and face death.

Included is a list of information needed when a person dies, ranging from burial wishes to insurance policies and location of personal and legal papers. Using this form is a good way to save hassles for those we love.

Single copies, 40 cents; $1 for three; available from CAFMS (address given above).

Two basic books documenting and analyzing the costs and customs of American funerals are also available from CAFMS: (1) *The High Cost of Dying,* by Ruth M. Harmer, CAFMS, n.d. ($1); and (2) *The American Way of Death,* by Jessica Mitford, Fawcett, 1979 ($2).

The Living Will—A Directive to Physicians

If it is your desire not to be kept alive by artificial means at tremendous costs to your survivors, then you can sign a directive to your physician, in advance of your being in that situation, indicating your wishes.

Copies of sample statements can be obtained by sending a SASE to The Society for the Right to Die, 250 West 57th St., New York, NY 10019. After you receive your information, you will want to talk to your doctor and a local lawyer to be sure that the form is acceptable in your area. For example, California law has required exact wording at several points. A portion of the California wording is as follows:

. . . I, _____, being of sound mind, willfully and voluntarily making known my desire that my life shall not be artificially prolonged under the circumstances set forth below, do hereby declare:

1. If at any time I should have an incurable injury, disease, or illness certified to be a terminal condition by two physicians, where the application of life-sustaining procedures would serve only to artificially prolong the moment of my death, and where my physician determines that my death is imminent whether or not life-sustaining procedures are utilized, I direct that such procedures *be withheld* or withdrawn, and that I be permitted to die naturally. . . .

Some states provide that this form must be re-signed every five years in order to force people to be clear about their intentions.

As congregations, we need to encourage our fellow members to consider these issues in advance of facing them firsthand. Doing so will reduce the pain of indecision and the likelihood of the family being trapped in an untenable economic situation.

Resources for the Bereaved

Many of the scholarly books dealing with death and grief are written from a secular point of view, and yet they provide an excellent resource for pastors, counselors, and others working with those who have experienced death in their families.

One such is *A Time to Grieve: Loss as a Universal Human Experience,* by Bertha G. Simos, Family Service Association, 1979. This volume deals with all aspects of mental health associated with death and other losses; for example, psychological security, occupation, financial status, appreciation, etc.

Those who may be faced with the prospect of caring for a terminally ill person will find Evelyn M. Baulch's book *Home Care,* A Practical Alternative to Hospitalization, Celestial Arts, 1980, a very practical how-to-do-it manual. Mrs. Baulch is the widow of a pastor who died following years of invalidism.

How to Recover from Grief, by Richard Lewis Detrich and Nicola J. Steele, Judson Press, 1983, is written primarily for the person who has lost a spouse. Based on their extensive experience in counseling with such persons, the authors discuss the way in which a person can deal with the grief and begin to reconstruct his or her life. Suggestions are also included for helping a friend who is grieving.

One final volume, *The Hospice Way of Death,* by Paul DuBois, Human Science Press, 1980, 223 pp. ($24.95), traces the development of understanding and treatment of terminally ill persons in Europe and the United States and the subsequent development of the hospice movement. The book contains a thorough analysis of the psychological and sociological benefits of the hospice and documentation of several specific programs.

Compassionate Friends

For families who have experienced the death of a child from any cause—disease, suicide, violence, or accident—there is a nationwide network of small self-help groups called Compassionate Friends. Begun by Rev. Simon Stephens in 1969 in Coventry, England, the organization quickly spread to America, and by 1972 the first chapter was formed in Miami, Florida.

Local groups set their own meeting patterns, usually monthly, and support one another in the positive resolution of the grief experienced after the death of their child. Focus is on helping people care for their own physical, emotional, and spiritual health and that of the rest of their family.

Chapter members watch local papers and initiate calls to families whose children die—offering a compassionate listening ear and the opportunity for a safe place to come and share. As parents whose two-year-old daughter was killed in an automobile accident, we can attest to God's use of the people in this group.

To secure information on chapters near you or on how to form a chapter, write: Compassionate Friends, P.O. Box 1347, Oak Brook, IL 60521. Tel.: (312) 323-5010.

Concern for Community

The *New York Times* estimated that in 1982 as many as 4 million Americans joined the ranks of those officially classified as poor—that is, those with an annual income of less than $9,287 for a family of four.

In a time of increasing poverty, the church is called to question our national priorities, our life-style, our morals, our stewardship of resources—with the hope of redeeming the people and bringing into reality our Lord's prayer that the kingdom would come here on earth as it is in heaven.

Food

The amount of food wasted in America is beyond comprehension.

1. A grower in Oxnard, California, indicated that over 50% of what is grown never makes it to market. Those in Food-Share (p. 78) found out that his estimates have been fairly accurate.

2. Former Secretary of Agriculture Bob Bergland said that nearly 20% of all food produced in the United States is lost each year, a total of over 140 million tons, enough to feed forty-nine million people for one year!

3. A study by the University of Arizona of the garbage in Tucson, Arizona, indicated that in 1970, $9 million worth of edible food was thrown away by families. This represented just over 10% of all food purchased in that community that year.

While people "shall not live by bread alone," people do need a minimum protein and calorie intake daily to survive. What are the churches in America doing in the name of Christ to help those in their communities who need food for the body as well as the soul?

Emergency Food Pantries

Many congregations have organized an emergency food closet/pantry to help in times of crisis. Some limit access to "members" only; others see this as a form of outreach to the community.

Focus on Food, in Ventura, California, is a shared effort by more than twenty churches and organizations. Food and funds are collected during special holiday seasons, and many groups have one Sunday a month of ingathering, collecting a single item from a needs list. For example, this month may be "Peanut Butter Month"; each person brings a jar of peanut butter. One item is much easier to remember at the store than a whole list, which is easily left at home.

Referrals of people in need are made from pastors, church secretaries, or counselors after they have checked a central coordinator to see if these folk have already been helped.

Sixteen volunteers provide the core of the operation, staffing the pantry three afternoons a week. Recipients are given enough food for three days, based on a standard list, with the quantity depending on family size. Cash budget for this program for an average year is around $6,000, plus donated food; over 600 families are served, comprising over 1,900 individuals.

Write: Focus on Food, Barbara Born, P.O. Box AE, Ventura, California 93002, for a pamphlet and list of staple items. Enclose a SASE.

Food Salvage and Distribution

St. Mary's Food Bank in Phoenix, Arizona, is credited with being one of the first major food banks, operating in

conjunction with Second Harvest, a gleaning operation. Supermarkets, bakeries, food processors, and wholesalers all discard large quantities of usable foods, which can be collected for a food bank.

Second Harvest is now working to coordinate a nationwide network of food banks, contacting major companies (General Mills, Kellogg, and the like) regarding donations to the system from the manufacturers and processors.

For information on the national system of food banks contact: Second Harvest, 1001 N. Central, Suite 303, Phoenix, AZ 85004.

Food Gleaning and Salvage

Two early food-gleaning groups, based on the spirit of Leviticus 19:9-10, are Senior Gleaners and Food-Share in California. Senior Gleaners, founded by Homer Fahrner in Northern California, is made up of groups of seniors who go into the fields after the last commercial harvest and pick for distribution to nonprofit organizations, seniors, and food banks.

Food-Share (FS) in Ventura County, in Southern Cali-

fornia, is similar, except that its more than four hundred members are not limited by age as long as they are over eighteen and sign a covenant to respect every farmer's property and handle the food carefully.

FS was begun in 1978 by a group of eighteen people. Growth has been slow and steady, both in numbers of persons and in produce secured/distributed. In 1979, 40 tons were handled; in 1981, 346 tons; and in 1982, over 600 tons, with more than 75 nonprofit organizations distributing to families, individuals, and seniors.

For an information packet send $1 and a SASE to: Food-Share, P.O. Box 4596, Ventura, CA 93004. Packet includes: covenant, list of officers, crop totals, IRS regulations, copy of letter to donors, and miscellaneous information.

Surplus Food Commodities—U.S. Department of Agriculture

Most food banks have been distribution vehicles for handling USDA excess food commodities, primarily including cheese and powdered milk. Many other products are potentially available. These items were purchased to guarantee prices for a given item, and are being stored at tremendous cost—for example, in 1982, the cost of storing cheese alone was over $1 million a day.

Local nonprofit organizations can organize for distribution of commodities by forming a food bank. Contact Second Harvest or Food-Share for general information; also contact the regional office of the USDA nearest to you.

Brown Bag Programs

Food banks have often established "brown bag" distribution systems to specific individual seniors who have low incomes. Once a week each member receives a brown bag of food items; on occasion, depending upon supply, the distribution may be more frequent.

The Brown Bag program of the Santa Clara Food Bank in San Jose, California, was one of the first in the nation to develop this system of distribution. Individual low-income seniors join, after determination of their eligibility, and are requested to donate $2 a year to help with transportation costs.

Write for a manual of operation: Brown Bag Program, 312 Brokow Rd., Santa Clara, CA 95050.

A distribution system need not be large! Do you know *five* seniors who could use some additional food? You can get started! Begin with your church. Find another who shares your vision; then begin contacting other groups, or just start contacting market managers for past-dated bread/products, dented cans, etc.

Soup Kitchens

Hospitality for the homeless is offered in Clifton Presbyterian Church. A house of hospitality now provides shelter to thirty men and women per night, morning showers, a clothes closet, and a soup kitchen for all who come in at specific times. Other churches are being encouraged to provide more space for the homeless, the majority of whom are older, disabled people who have no income.

Over 1,200 meals are served each week, and more than 150 persons were sheltered in nine months during 1982.

Write to Rob Johnson, Open Door Community, 910 Ponce de Leon Avenue, NE, Atlanta, GA 30306. Tel.: (404) 874-9652.

The Catholic Worker movement (CW) has been instrumental in the establishment of hospitality houses and soup kitchens in most of the major cities in the U.S. They are staffed by volunteers who commit themselves to live and work with the poor and destitute of society.

The Los Angeles kitchen provides lunch to over nine hundred people daily, primarily on food that has been salvaged from the city's produce market. A health clinic has been opened, the only facility treating people absolutely free in the City of Los Angeles. A tot-lot play area has been established next to the kitchen, and Nuestra Tienda (Our Store), an "at cost," membership grocery store, has been opened.

The Los Angeles CW community publishes *The Catholic Agitator* each month, providing background articles on the causes of poverty, descriptions of its victims, and spiritual resources for meeting the persons in need and challenging the systems of oppression in our culture. Fantastic articles by a wide variety of authors including, for example, "Prayer and Peacemaking," by Henry J. M. Nouwen, December 1982 issue.

Write: LACW, *Agitator,* $1 per year. 632 N. Brittania, Los Angeles, CA 90033. Tel.: (213) 267-8789. For information on hospitality houses or soup kitchens in your area, contact the Los Angeles House, or NYCW, St. Joseph's House, 36 E. First St., New York, NY 10003.

Food—Cooperative Purchasing

The possibility of extending resources by purchasing large quantities (bulk or case lots) of certain items is one tool that is being used by groups within many congregations.

The Bible Fellowship Church, Ralston St., Ventura, California 93003, began a bulk-food co-op—"Basic Food Co-op"—with an initial group of about thirty persons. Each family contributed a refundable $25 to a common pot as a working capital fund.

A simple division of labor includes one coordinator, one person taking orders and collecting money, one handling the receipt and distribution of food, and another handling the treasury. Individuals covenant to share four hours a month in receiving food and repackaging it for orders as they come in. The group has limited itself to one large bulk order every 4-6 weeks.

Individuals are encouraged to calculate the amount they save by this process and contribute all or a portion of the savings to a special missions project of their choice.

Food wholesalers—see the Yellow Pages of a metropolitan area near you—are usually willing to sell to co-ops, as long as their minimum quantities are met for a given item/order. (Sometimes a local supermarket manager will cooperate on case lots and give a good price.)

Food—Family Preparedness

The preparation of families for potential economic or natural disaster has long been a practice of the Church of Jesus Christ of Latter-Day Saints (LDS). Each family is encouraged to keep a constant supply of all basic staples and water, adequate for an entire year.

With this preparedness comes the examination of basic issues, such as eating habits and life-style, since the stock of wheat, grain, and other items need to be in continual rotation to prevent waste. This means a move away from preprocessed and packaged foods, back to basic preparation from scratch. While this move may mean that we must take more time in preparing food, it is a clear step toward the preservation of the resources of the earth and is a powerful move toward simplification of life-style in terms of energy use.

Family preparedness is accomplished through the process of bulk-buying at prices well below those in the supermarket.

For information on bulk purchasing in your area, contact the LDS stake nearest you. A simple 29-page pamphlet, *Essentials for Home Production and Storage,* can be had for $1 from the LDS Church Distribution Center, 500 E. North Temple, Salt Lake City, UT 84150.

Center-City Food Cooperative

The community served is a fifteen-block section in the inner city of Indianapolis. It is a low-income area, declining in population, with 85% black population, 24% female heads of households, and substandard housing. More than half the senior citizens do not drive, and over ⅓ of the adult population does not have a driver's license. No major grocery store is located in the area so there is a real need for a local source of food.

The staff and volunteers of the Edna Martin Christian Center (EMCC) started a food-buying club in 1981, which expanded into a mini-store-front operation in June of 1981. Seed money was received in the amount of $9,000 for the purchase of equipment and supplies.

The co-op aims to be self-sufficient, not profit making, by a standard 20% markup on all merchandise. Even at this, prices are well below nearby convenience stores.

Members may work two hours a month to get a 10% discount on all food purchases. Their jobs include ordering, pricing, wrapping, bagging, cleaning, bookkeeping—all under the direction of a social worker who spends eight hours a week training/supervising the work of the members in the co-op.

EMCC, Food Corp., 1979 Carolina Ave., P.O. Box 18129, Indianapolis, IN 46218.

Resources on Starting a Cooperative

1. "Co-op How-To," *Food Monitor* (magazine), #13, Nov./Dec. 1979 ($2). P.O. Box 1975, Garden City, NY 11530.

2. Food Co-op Directory Association, P.O. Box 4218, Albuquerque, NM 87196 ($5).

After cooperatives grow in their volume of sales, there are a number of co-op distributors who will distribute to them. For example, the Intra-Community Cooperative, 1335 Gilson St., Madison, WI 53715, distributes over $5.5 million dollars worth of cheese and other items to food cooperatives around the nation per year.

Community Gardens

Those who lived through World War II are familiar with the concept of "victory gardens." Today we need a revival of this concept in "survival gardens."

First Baptist Church, Santa Paula, California, had five families who cooperated in the planting and cultivation of a 50-by-100-foot garden. It grew enough food for all of the families, with plenty left over to share with the congregation.

Care-and-Share Table

Individuals who have gardens or fruit trees can be encouraged to bring their excess to the church on Sunday and place it on a table in the entry area. Those who have surplus produce bring it; those who need items take what they can use. There need be no extensive organization—short of someone who will be sure that the area is kept cleaned and straightened after each use.

Often people are encouraged in this process to make a small donation for local or world hunger ministries—although this is clearly a "donations accepted, but not expected" situation.

Community Gardens in Cities

Some communities have organized community gardens using small parcels of vacant land among buildings or in transition/park areas.

Organizing and operating principles differ from community to community. In some, small portions are given to each participant and choice of crops is strictly up to the individual gardener. Some request a small donation to cover the cost of water, etc. Some are organized so that one person grows an entire crop, and then the harvest is shared with the others, who are growing different crops, and with the broader community.

It takes only *one* person to be the catalyst to get something going. How about you?

Gardening is really "growing" in the Washington, D.C., area. For information contact: Community Gardens of Hope, c/o Rev. Rodney Young, Council of Churches of Greater Washington, 1401 Massachusetts Ave., NW, Room 213, Washington, DC 20005. Tel.: (702) 332-2080.

Farmers' Markets

Local congregations and groups working together through the Interfaith Hunger Coalition (IHC) of Los Angeles have effectively organized several true farmers' markets in the parking lots of churches in several communities.

Farmers are certified, following personal contacts with them regarding their interest in marketing directly to the public. The farmer gets far more profit than usual, and needy families get good fresh produce at far less than market prices.

Write IHC, 1010 S. Flower St., Room 404, Los Angeles, CA 90015.

Solar Greenhouses—Urban Gardening

Christian Action Ministry, a local church coalition, 5130 W. Jackson, Chicago, IL 60644, was instrumental in the establishment of a model, 880-square-foot greenhouse for gardening year round.

The success of this venture led to the formation of the Center for Neighborhood Technology (CNT), a nonprofit corporation aimed at educating others around the country in the establishment of similar programs. CNT's solar project has grown to include four greenhouses with a total of 12,000 square feet of growing space, providing tons of produce to people in need in Chicago.

The process of building the greenhouses has provided employment for neighborhood folk through the CETA (Comprehensive Employment and Training Act) and the Action VISTA (Volunteers in Service to America) programs.

Some rural communities have constructed greenhouses as well. For example, Laramie County, Wyoming, has several projects organized through the Community Action Agency.

Community Canning

In days past, people gathered to share in the canning process, meeting in homes and working together to make the load lighter. The same thing can be done today, even if there are only four or five families cooperating together. Why do it? Canning frees funds for other ministry in the name of Christ; it is also a move away from the energy-intensive food systems we have created in our nation in which sixteen calories of energy are spent for every calorie of food that reaches our table.

Some cities/areas have established community canning projects in which individuals can their own food. One such group is Community Self Reliance (CSR), 16 Armory St., Northampton, MA 01060. The cannery conducts ongoing food preservation classes and helps low-income families can their own tomatoes, applesauce, and tomato juice. Over 100 families canned over 4,000 containers of food. Overall, the cannery canned 20,000 pints of produce in one year. Community residents are allowed to purchase fresh produce using food stamps as well as cash.

The Church of Jesus Christ of Latter-Day Saints has an effective nationwide system of canneries for use by its members. In California alone, six canneries are operated by members of the church structure—sharing produce with their churches around the nation.

G-Plan of Trading Energies

This sharing system can effectively be applied to food (see page 48).

Housing

While Jesus was committed to a life of total simplicity and had neither his own home nor possessions, we must make some provision for our physical needs, such as adequate shelter, food, and water. Jesus did have the home of his parents and those of his friends and disciples to which he could go.

In our own nation there is a critical housing shortage which, coupled with high unemployment, has forced thousands of families to live in "tent cities," public parks, recreational vehicles, and campers. Two families in Oak View, California, lived for nearly two years in a motel, paying $300 a month for a 10-by-11-foot room and a bathroom; both families had two children under four years of age. Even when one has a job, to move into an apartment means having enough cash for the first and last months' rent, plus a cleaning deposit, all of which usually adds up to over $1,000.

People moving into communities to look for work are often desperate to find some temporary housing for a couple of weeks in order to check things out.

The Bible is filled with the Old Testament call to "hospitality," taking in the "wayfarer and the stranger" for food and lodging. We need to be open to creative ways in which we can provide the same ministry in our culture and time.

Ideas for Thought and Stimulation

—find unused RV's and travel trailers that are in storage and establish certain areas where they may be used on a temporary basis.

—change zoning laws to allow dormitory-style living.

—change zoning to allow increased density in single-family areas, allowing for the changing of two-car garages into small apartments for seniors/families.

—divide large homes into two living units; divide empty warehouse space and old school buildings into living units.

—use portions of church facilities for housing.

—establish households of faith where one or two nuclear families are joined by a number of single persons, perhaps of differing ages (see page 28, *Living Together in a World Falling Apart*).

Seniors' Housing

1. *House Sharing*—a special program matching seniors and others with seniors who are willing to share homes. The city of Ventura has initiated such a program: Ms. Gloria Nelson, Director, 461 E. Main St., Suite C, Ventura, CA 93001.

2. *Boarding Homes*—several self-sufficient aging persons sharing one home, with house parents responsible for some support services. Trinity Lutheran Church of Ventura is exploring this idea, hoping to purchase a home or two from its own members as a beginning. Write Rev. Stan Gjervick, Trinity Lutheran Church, 196 N. Ashwood, Ventura, CA 93003.

Transitional Housing

The American Baptist Church of Fort Collins (600 S. Shields, Fort Collins, CO 80521) uses a church-owned house to provide transitional housing for refugee families until they can get jobs and become self-sufficient. Another space is available for a maximum of two weeks for local families who are in transition.

Jubilee Housing (Cooperatives)

Housing cooperatives can be organized in a variety of ways, depending upon the creativity of the group designing them.

Jubilee Housing was begun as an outreach into the poverty community in Washington, DC. As a nonprofit organization, Jubilee Housing purchases and rehabilitates old apartment buildings for ultimate transfer of ownership/management to the tenants. This training and rehab process moves slowly, but it is a light of hope to hundreds of families living on less than $5,000 a year.

Jubilee Housing, 1750 Columbia Rd., NW, Washington, DC 20009. Tel.: (209) 332-4020.

Habitat for Humanity

One of the most radical departures from normal assumptions about housing construction is that of Habitat for Humanity (HFH) in which homes are built and sold to poverty families with *no profit* and *no interest*.

Based upon the biblical injunctions in Leviticus 25:35-38, Clarence Jordan began this variation of the old-fashioned "barn-raising" as a way to make possible decent homes for people with limited financial means.

In 1982, a 3-bedroom home was finished in San Antonio, Texas, and sold for $18,000, the actual cost of the land/materials. The purchasing family is paying $190 a month interest-free for a new home.

The purpose of Habitat is not "to provide homes for those who have access to regular means of financing and just cannot locate a home." Instead, it is a clear commitment to work with impoverished families who have demonstrated their stability of character and the discipline to meet regular monthly obligations.

Love in the Mortar Joints: The Story of Habitat for Humanity, by Millard Fuller and Diane Scott, New Century, 1980 ($4.95) and the *Habitat: How-to Manual* ($10) both document this exciting ministry. Both are available from HFH, 419 W. Church St., Americus, GA 31709. Tel.: (912) 924-6935.

Kentucky Mountain Housing (KMH)

Dwayne Yost, a Church of the Brethren minister, has been a key visionary and mover behind the KMH Development Corporation (Box 431, Manchester, KY 40962), which has built new homes for purchase by more than 200 families with annual incomes under $5,000. Another 500 families have had their homes restored through this ministry.

Lots of volunteer help, CETA workers, one paid foreman, and lots of donated materials help keep the costs down, with houses costing around $18,000, less than half the cost of comparable housing in the area. Purchasers get financing through USDA's Low-to-Moderate-Income Housing loans (Section 502) program. Renovation funds come through the Farmer's Home Administration's Very Low Income Housing Repair Loans and Grants (Section 504) program. Loan information: Farmer's Home Administration, USDA, 14th St. and Independence Ave., SW, Washington, DC 20250.

Credit Unions and House Mortgages for Urban Poor

What can one person do about housing and credit needs in the inner city? A lot, if that person is involved in real estate and/or credit union operation, and if that person is seeking to live by "kingdom values."

Robert Lavelle, Christian owner/director of Lavelle Real Estate and Dwelling House Savings and Loan (DHSL), has centered his work in the Hill District ghetto of Pittsburgh. Where other financial institutions illegally practice "redlining" (a practice of drawing red lines around areas where they will not finance home mortgages because of changing/deteriorating neighborhoods), Robert Lavelle is aggressively providing home mortgage loans to low-income minority families.

He has had few foreclosures in his twenty years of work because of the personal involvement he and his staff have with their clients. Currently there is 40% home ownership in the Hill District; Lavelle's goal is 90%. Lavelle sees home ownership as a key to many of the problems of the inner city. When there is access to ownership, people build equity, which helps to change the economic base of the neighborhood from prostitution, dope, and numbers to home ownership. Increased home ownership leads to demands for and implementation of better city services, such as trash collection, and to more service from private businesses.

Carrying on ministry in economics, Lavelle receives investments in his credit union from around the country. He pays 5½% and does not apologize for the noncompetitive rate.

Robert Lavelle, DHSL, 501 Herron Ave., Pittsburgh, PA 15241.

Local Congregational Credit Unions?

Yes, some larger congregations in the low-income community have established their own credit unions for their members and community, lending at less than half the going commercial rates. Mt. Zion Baptist Church in Los Angeles is one such.

Even a small congregation, rather than *giving* money in times of need, might consider making loans, so that when times improve, the money can come back to be passed on to others.

Denominational groups have come together to organize credit unions for leaders of local congregations. One of these is the American Baptist Credit Union, 101 S. Barranca Ave., Covina, CA 91722. It has thousands of members and assets over $7 million, lending only to member Baptists and employees. Your denomination could do a similar service for its leaders.

Keeping Down the High Cost of Buying/Selling

Why not have a Christian real estate brokerage house, which persons would join when they were ready to purchase a house? All the title searches and fees would be somewhat normal. When the time of sale came, all of the preliminary work would have been done. There would be no need to do it again, and therefore the sale could be completed at less cost to seller/buyer, possibly without points, and all other duplication of fees. How would the sales persons live? A fixed price for joining could be established, regardless of the sale price of the house, as opposed to having the member pay a percentage of the sale price.

Sharing Home and Apartment Leads

Why not a central apartment/housing referral system operated out of a church for the benefit of a community? Commercial variations charge $30–$40 to join; such a system could be operated on a token $10 joining fee, and listings could be solicited from Christian landlords and home owners.

Use of Federal and State Funds for Housing

Many congregations have chosen to organize nonprofit housing corporations to take advantage of federal and state funds for meeting housing needs. A number of examples are included in this chapter.

Mountain T.O.P. (Tennessee Outreach Program) (MTOP)

A Christian summer mission program designed to help youth groups grow spiritually and increase their social awareness of poverty, MTOP also aids in meeting the home improvement needs of others.

The week-long experience includes renewal group activity, work-team experience, worship, study, recreation, and music. Open to youth from all denominations, MTOP asks groups to bring their own tools; materials are furnished by the home owners. MTOP staff provide leadership through the week and assign the work teams to various two-day projects.

Applications must be received from interested groups by February 1: MTOP, Box 23536, Nashville, TN 37202.

Renew, Inc.—Inner-City Housing Renovation

1016 W. Washington St., South Bend, IN 46625.

A local parish priest, Father Ken Maley, began Renew when several people came to him in desperation looking for housing. A number of deteriorating homes stood empty, and Father Maley was able to raise $1,000 to make the down payment on one house. Funds were borrowed to renovate it, and it was sold when finished. Since that humble beginning in 1972, more than sixty families have purchased homes from Renew. The average annual income of purchasers has been $8,000.

Potential purchasers are screened and then enrolled in classes in which they learn basic home maintenance and repair, budgeting, taxes, loans, and other survival subjects.

Self-Help Home Repairs

Brothers Redevelopment was formed by Rev. Richard Magnus, Don Schierling, and Joe Giron in response to the housing crisis in Denver. This self-help group has evolved from a single church volunteer with building skills interested in helping people do home repairs. Over 80% of those who are helped go on to help others in some way, even if only preparing food for the work crews. Since 1973, Brothers Redevelopment has completed eight hundred repair/renovation projects.

From small beginnings, tiny mustard seeds planted in faith, grow tremendous plants when watered by God's spirit of love and concern.

Brothers Redevelopment, 2519 11th Ave., Denver, CO 80204.

Neighborhood Improvement Project

The Milwaukee Christian Center Neighborhood Improvement Project (NIP) is a nonprofit program providing free home repairs for elderly, disabled, and low-income families on the south side of Milwaukee. The majority of work is done by high-school-age youth under the supervision of young adults.

In 1982, forty-five youth were employed with the NIP, and approximately 120 houses were improved, using a budget of $495,000 of state and federal funds.

Repairs are made by painting; installing rain gutters; repairing windows and screens; doing light carpentry in repairing porches, steps, fences, roofs, sheds, and garages. No structural repairs are done or major roofing/foundation work.

An incredible "ripple effect" has been felt in the neighborhood as trained youth return home to fix their own homes and those of neighbors. As neighbors see improvements, they are inspired and motivated to improve their homes.

Employment and training in the skilled trades for both the supervisors and the workers is an immeasurable contribution to the lives of the youth and to the community.

NIP, 1223 South 23rd St., Milwaukee, WI 53204, Ken Smith, Director.

Prisoners—Building Houses?

Operation Fresh Start (OFS), 2322 Atwood Ave., Madison, WI 53704, is helping youthful offenders learn valuable job skills while renovating homes for low-income residents. Law Enforcement Assistance Administration funds, along with local monies, provide for supervisory salaries, and $19,500 was borrowed for the purchase of the first old house and its rehabilitation. Write Jack Osteraas, the spark plug behind this project, for information. Why not start a similar project in your community?

Public Education

Historically, the church provided the impetus in America for the establishment of a system of public education. In many parts of the country, major social crises are being faced, and for some in the religious community, the solution has been to "flee" the issues and establish private schools.

An excellent discussion series entitled *Critical Issues in Elementary and Secondary Education* has been created to engage church people in discussion of the underlying goals and issues critical to education at the elementary and secondary level, and to clarify the church's role as an advocate of public education.

Complete teaching packet, including wall charts and discussion guide, is $8.50. Discussion guide only, $2.50; 5 or more, $2 apiece. From Education in Society, Room 710, National Council of Churches of Christ in the U.S.A., 475 Riverside Dr., New York, NY 10115-0099.

The Public School

The Public School (TPS) is a series published by Pilgrim Press. Each book covers a different perspective on public education.

TPS and Public Policy, by M. Stanley, $1.95.

TPS and Education of Whole Persons, by M. C. Richards, $2.95.

TPS and the Family, by H. J. Leichter, $1.95.

TPS and Moral Education, by H. C. Johnson, $5.95.

TPS and Challenge of Ethnic Pluralism, by C. A. Grant, et al., $2.95.

TPS and Finances, by M. R. Williams, $3.95.

The Education of the Public, by M. L. Warford, $2.95.

The Anti-Muffins, by Madeleine L'Engle, $7.95.

Write to Pilgrim Press for prices on the entire set and various combinations, as well as discussion guide information. The Pilgrim Press, 132 West 31st St., New York, NY 10001.

Tutoring Project

The American Baptist Church (600 S. Shields, Fort Collins, CO 80521) began a pilot tutoring program in one junior high after discovering that 70% of minority youth drop out of school by then. After the youth had had one semester of one-on-one tutoring, the lives of thirty-six of them were reversed motivationally. Subsequently, the school district assumed the program and installed it in all four junior high schools.

Unemployment

Unemployment in this time of rapidly changing technology seems to be a constant factor with which people have to deal. The potential for ministry by the local congregation in this area of need is incredible! We do not have to solve the job situation directly to be of help. We can provide a supportive, caring community to help people plan, cope with stress, and keep their integrity as persons while they search for meaningful employment.

Support Groups for the Unemployed

First Baptist in Evanston, Illinois, is an old, established, downtown church in the midst of a modern community. New in the community has been the impact of unemployment on the lives of the middle class. Between January 1 and March 31 of 1982, over 33,000 people were laid off in Illinois, in addition to those already out of work.

The congregation of First Baptist maintains a traditional program of Sunday morning worship, some Sunday evening activities, a ministry with Hispanics and Koreans, weekday events for neighborhood children, and a small but growing Christian education program.

Upon learning of more and more members of the congregation who were unemployed, Robert Thompson, the minister, felt that the least the church could do was to provide a support group for those facing this crisis in their lives.

The support group began with only five people (three from the church), but in four months more than fifty were participating in the Tuesday, two-hour, brown-bag luncheons. There is never lack of things to talk about. Discussions center on *feelings:* hopelessness, rejection, powerlessness, anger and frustration—all of which can be paralyzing if ignored. The group also talks about writing resumés, does role plays, practices job interviews, and shares leads on jobs.

While the group has not seen its function as that of a job service agency, a number of job opportunities have been generated; more than twelve members of the group found employment in the first four months.

Bob summarizes the meaning of this ministry in his own words: "I share the pain of my life with you, and you share the pain of your life with me, and out of that transaction we become whole," based on the concepts presented by Henri J. Nouwen in his book *The Wounded Healer*, Doubleday, 1972.

Rev. Robert V. Thompson, First Baptist Church of Evanston, 607 Lake St., Evanston, IL 60201.

Unemployed Management

One congregation creatively involved in ministry with unemployed persons is Park Baptist Church (10 E. Park Place, NE, Grand Rapids, MI 49503). Rev. Ken Whitwer has been the initiator and director of this ministry, which consists of a series of biweekly seminars aimed primarily at unemployed management personnel.

The first session is inspirational, and spouses are invited to attend. Other sessions, in order of focus, include: preparation of resumés, interviewing techniques and role playing, stress and how to deal with it, job prospects in the '80s, handling personal finances while unemployed, and a summary-sendoff led by an industrial psychologist.

The results have been encouraging, both in terms of the development of a support group and in the number of folk who have found jobs. The members of the group have become a referral source for one another in job availability and potential openings.

Neighborhood Action Program

In a New England city of just over 100,000, what does one do when major manufacturers close down, plants move south or out of the country, and there is no "high-tech revival" to create new jobs?

Waterbury, Connecticut, is such a community. The flight of its professional and skilled workers has left behind the elderly, the poor, and the unskilled. Old First Baptist Church now finds itself in an area that is decaying and filled with an ever-increasing percentage of low-income families living in buildings owned by absentee landlords.

Rather than move, its members, under the direction of Rev. Paul Hanneman, have joined in a special neighborhood action program aimed at ministering to the community. A soup kitchen provides meals each day, and on Sunday morning about twenty children eat breakfast in the church. A temporary shelter for the homeless has been developed, as well as a community food cooperative.

These outreach ministries have demonstrated in *action* the members' commitment to caring. Many people have heard and responded to the Good News shared in both word and deed.

Rev. Paul Hanneman, First Baptist Church, 205 Grove St., Waterbury, CT 06710.

Employment Training Ideas

Twenty-five years ago, in New Jersey, several utilities created summer jobs for high school young people in a very creative way. One student was assigned to each utility truck and crew as a "go-for" and general assistant to the crew. The goal was to help the student workers get an overview of the work and then begin to learn the specific skills necessary to become a functioning member of the crew.

The apprentices served without pay—sustained by their interest and desire to learn the job. Other students were placed in laboratories and substations to function in a similar way. This program provided training, and at the same time increased the productivity of existing workers.

The same program could be initiated in any business in which committed Christians are willing to help their brothers and sisters gain a skill and trade. Even though apprentices began without pay, this was better than sitting around feeling depressed and bored, waiting for something to come up. Logical variations, of course, could include minimal salary either at the start or after a certain period of training, and the same program could be extended to include adults.

Contributed by Tony Lamb, Director, Senior Survival Services, 3161 Loma Vista, Ventura County, CA 93003.

Youth Training and Employment

The Morningside United Church of Christ has established Morningside Arts in Inglewood, California. This nonprofit program is designed to educate and enrich young people from all backgrounds. Classes in art, creative writing, dance, acting, music, theatrical costuming, and humanities are taught by professional artists in a series of eight-week, after-school sessions from 3:45–5:45 P.M., and on Saturdays from 9 A.M.–1 P.M.

Instructors and other professionals work with individuals in career exploration through field trips and informal workshops with other established artists.

Morningside Arts, 8722 Crenshaw Blvd., Inglewood, CA 90305; Richard Chrisman, Director; Jennifer Smith-Ashely, Art Director. Tel.: (213) 750-8688.

Church-Placed "Job Wanted" Ads—For Members

Central Baptist Church of Joy, Spokane, Washington, has taken out a display ad in the local paper announcing "We have a few good persons who need employment, and we at Central Baptist Church of Joy recommend them.''

The ad then includes thumbnail sketches of each unemployed person's skills along with his or her phone number. ''If you now have or soon will have an opening, give these people consideration. . . . They are most worthy, faithful, honest, and hardworking. . . .''

Does it work? Yes, not for all, but members are consistently placed through this process.

Rev. Art Jacobson, 19 West Shannon, Spokane, WA 99205.

Why not distribute a church-sponsored paper to local employers listing people from the Christian community who are available for work? This could be a shared ministry of several congregations.

Why not have each church ask employers in its midst to share openings and future openings through a similar paper—''jobs available'' or ''coming jobs available''?

Drawing for Free Labor

Mike Eggleston, First Baptist Church of Oak View (Box 338, Oak View, CA 93022) came up with an idea that is helping members of the church and the community as well as unemployed folk. Individuals donate one dollar per ticket for a drawing for *two free hours of labor*. When fifty dollars are collected, four tickets are drawn and four persons each receive two free hours of labor. They can direct the laborers to do whatever needs to be done.

Laborers are those in the congregation who are unemployed. They are assigned on the basis of skill and interest, and they receive a gift of five dollars per hour for their work. Total funds collected for each drawing—$50; total funds given to laborers for work—$40; funds remaining for advertising, equipment expenses, etc.—$10.

This process generates the money to help with family survival and helps people who need to have work done.

Job-Training Program

A shared ministry of the United Christian Centers in Sacramento is a six-month job-training program in general clerical, data key entry, office technician/secretary, and basic math/English skills. Each student works at her or his own rate of speed, based on entry testing of abilities and placement.

Vernon Freeman, director, believes that motivation and help with job placement are as important as curriculum. During one year, 85 people were trained, and more than 80% of these were placed in jobs. Follow-up is also included, with contact at 30-, 90-, and 150-day intervals.

While the program was initially funded with CETA (Comprehensive Employment and Training Act) funds, the goal has been to move continually toward self-sufficiency since all federal funds are uncertain.

United Christian Centers of Sacramento, Lincoln Center Training Program, 2620 21st St., Sacramento, CA 95818.

Helping People Get Off Welfare

National Women's Employment and Education, Inc. (NWEE), Lupe Anguiano, Director, Box 959, San Antonio, TX 78294. Tel.: (512) 226-6933.

This program is aimed at helping women become independent of the welfare system. In interviews with hundreds of welfare mothers, Ms. Anguiano found that over 90% of them wanted to get off welfare and become self-sufficient.

What were the blocks that prevented this from happening? (1) Most did not have marketable skills and needed specific training; (2) most did not know how to go about finding a job—creating resumés, interviewing, following up, etc.; (3) most did not have adequate transportation; (4) most did not have any possible arrangements for child care.

In one year, more than five hundred women were helped to become self-sufficient and interdependent in new and exciting ways. The creation and implementation of this program involved many in the religious community in San Antonio.

Job Creation—Indianapolis

Quality used clothing is direly needed, since this inner-city community is isolated from major shopping districts both by geography and economics.

The Edna Martin Christian Center has created a thrift store which is open twenty hours a week, selling used clothing, toys, shoes, and household goods at an average price of 50 cents per item.

Coordination of volunteers and staff is accomplished by one staff person, who works eight hours a week doing paper work, training, and communications. Merchandise is all donated by churches in the community. Individual Baptist churches commit themselves to help staff the store one day per month.

Projected income for 1982 was $5,000. All of the balance, beyond expenses, is used in program ministries.

Write to Edna Martin Christian Center, %Rev. Richard Patrick, 1970 Caroline Ave., P.O. Box 18129, Indianapolis, IN 46218.

Volunteerism—A Road to Employment

Churches creating programs for those seeking employment would do well to encourage applicants to follow the advice of Ms. K. K. Wallace, director of Operations Improvement, Inc., an industrial consultant in Chicago, and author of *You're the Boss*.

She advises those looking for work to find a volunteer organization and jump in with both feet. Through volunteer work you will be able to show people what you can do—it is like a free trial offer. In addition, the mental benefits are tremendous.

Just creating and mailing resumés and going for interviews won't work. A person needs to gain visibility and demonstrate persistence.

Congregations and community ministries should look to the unemployed for sharing of their skills—and at the same time devise ways of publicizing information on those who are helping.

Health and Healing—Creative Ministry with the Ill

The number one health hazard in America is the addictive personality, according to a study done by the State of New York. Astounding are the figures they compiled of the numbers of people who are addicted nationwide:

heroin	50,000
prescription drugs	1,000,000
compulsive gamblers	9,000,000
alcohol	**13,000,000**
nicotine	1 of every 3 adults
overeating, overwork	unknown

In addition to those addicted to alcohol, there are many problem drinkers. Conservatively, one in ten Americans is in some way affected by problems related to the use of alcohol. In a church of 150 members, approximately 15 people would be expected to have this struggle. Do you know those persons in your congregation with problems in this area? How does your congregation support/deal with them? What resources are there for spouses/family members who live with them?

Many congregations make space available to Alcoholics Anonymous groups. This is a major step. AA needs to be complemented with other alternatives.

Agape Groups

As a Methodist pastor for many years prior to working with Ventura County in alcohol treatment programs, Rev. Doyle ("Des") Shields became intimately involved with individuals/families wrestling with addictions.

The results of his creative wrestling with this problem have included the Agape process and the formation of Agape groups aimed at learning how truly to love one another. (The process is very useful whether or not there are identified

alcoholics in a given group.)

The Agape process works toward the fulfillment of four basic human longings: (1) to feel good, (2) to improve one's life, (3) to have hope for the future, and (4) to feel worthwhile.

The basics of the Agape process are now in book form: *How to Love Yourself and Everybody Else*, by Doyle and Ann Shields, 1982; available from the Agape Center, P.O. Box 6325, Ventura, CA 93006 ($4). "Des" has a number of other pamphlets and items useful to those open to developing ministries in this area. (Send SASE, with sufficient postage for 2 ounces.)

Substance Abuse (Tobacco/Food)

Other substance abuse is more subtle and pervasive in our culture because it is more acceptable. Most notably this involves tobacco and food.

The Seventh Day Adventists (SDA) have been very creative in helping people deal with these addictions; they see this effort as part of their outreach ministry in the community. "Stop Smoking" clinics are offered regularly in areas where there is a Seventh Day Adventist presence; their books and printed resources are among the best in the field.

For information on contacting Seventh Day Adventists in your area, write: Department of Health and Temperance, General Conference SDA, 6840 Eastern Ave., NW, Washington, DC 20012.

For a catalog of books/resources, write: Pacific Press (SDA), 1350 Villa St., Mountain View, CA 94042.

Healing Order of St. Luke

There are many Christian doctors, pastors, priests, and laity who are committed to the ministry of healing through the International Order of St. Luke the Physician.

The objectives are: "To bring about among the Christian denominations . . . an increasing understanding of *spiritual healing and wholeness* as an essential part of the teaching and practice of Jesus Christ" (author's emphasis). The order was begun in 1932 by the late John G. Banks, S.T.D., priest of the Episcopal Church. Membership includes clergy and laity of Roman Catholic, Orthodox, Anglican, and Protestant churches, as well as laity in virtually every other profession.

The order believes that there is a critical need for Christian healing, including physical healing—doctors and medicine—and spiritual healing—prayer, love, faith, and the laying on of hands. In local congregations, regular healing services are held, usually weekly.

The emblem of the order is usually printed in blue (the symbolic color of healing). The motto translates, "O Jesus, be to me my Saviour (Healer), my Leader, my Light, my King, and my Law."

Information: International Order of St. Luke the Physician, 1212 Wilmer Ave., Richmond, VA 23227, and/or contact your local Episcopal church.

Sharing the Crisis—Coping with Life

When in worship do people really have a chance to share how they perceive God to be at work in their lives? Rev. David Woodworth (First Baptist Church, 5737 Fallbrook Ave., Woodland Hills, CA 91364), takes time in the morning worship to interview one person (for 5-7 minutes) who has gone through a crisis. The tone is casual and gentle.

These "moments that matter" provide an opportunity for the sharing of the depths of faith, as well as a chance for people with similar concerns to find and support one another.

Juggling for the Complete Klutz

Juggling is a great way to relax and is a tremendous source of hilarious laughter as you watch/hear the juggling bags hit the floor. I would never have thought something could be so much *fun*! (Doing it reduces tension, between the shoulder blades and in the neck area.) While watching and laughing at my feeble attempts, the kids wanted to try. Soon they were doubled up laughing at themselves and each other.

Juggling for the Complete Klutz, by John Cassidy and B. C. Rimbeaux, 1977. Klutz Press, Box 2992, Stanford, CA 94305 ($9.50). Includes shipping and three juggling bags. Write for complete catalog.

Healing

Experiencing Inner Healing, by Ruth C. Stapleton, Word Books, 1979 ($2.25). An in-depth study of the healing power of love, faith, service, forgiveness, confession, self-acceptance, release, prayer listening, adversity, and authentic self-identity. Tape series also available for use in small group context, complete with workbook.

Stress—Awareness and Management

The best resources this author has found for clergy and lay leaders in the congregation who are concerned about caring for themselves are *Clergy Burnout* and *Clergy Stress*, both by Roy Oswald of the Alban Institute, published by Minister's Life Resources, 3100 W. Lake St., Minneapolis, MN 55416. (Both for $25, including shipping, prepaid only. Individually, $15. Each volume includes two cassette tapes.)

These "survival kits" for church professionals are readily transferable for use by any person active in the life of a congregation or religious organization. Ideal also for small group use.

They include overview data on stress/burnout; theological perspective: "the theology of self-care"; work sheets for self-reflection (17 in all), such as the Clergy Life Changes Rating Scale that follows; and, most important, specific strategies for dealing with stress in all aspects of life.

Clergy Life Changes Rating Scale (readily usable by laity!)
The significance of your total Life Change Score depends on your stress threshold. The following scoring will give

Clergy Life Changes Rating Scale[1]

Event	Average Value	Your Score
Death of spouse	100	_____
Divorce	73	_____
Marital separation	65	_____
Death of close family member	63	_____
Personal injury or illness	53	_____
Marriage	50	_____
Serious decline in church attendance	49	_____
Geographical relocation	49	_____
Private meetings by segment of congregation to discuss your resignation	47	_____
Beginning of heavy drinking by immediate family member	46	_____
Marital reconciliation	45	_____
Retirement	45	_____
Change in health of family member	44	_____
Problem with children	42	_____
Pregnancy	40	_____
Sex difficulties	39	_____
Alienation from one's board/council/session/vestry	39	_____
Gain of new family member	39	_____
New job in new line of work	38	_____
Change in financial state	38	_____
Death of close friend	37	_____
Increased arguing with spouse	35	_____
Merger of two or more congregations	35	_____
Serious parish financial difficulty	32	_____
Mortgage over $50,000 (home)	31	_____
Difficulty with member of church staff (associates, organist, choir director, secretary, janitor)	31	_____
Foreclosure of mortgage or loan	30	_____
Destruction of church by fire	30	_____
New job in same line of work	30	_____
Son or daughter leaving home	29	_____
Trouble with in-laws	29	_____
Anger of influential church member over pastor action	29	_____
Slow, steady decline in church attendance	29	_____
Outstanding personal achievement	28	_____
Introduction of new hymnal to worship service	28	_____
Failure of church to make payroll	27	_____
Remodeling or building program	27	_____
Start or stop of spouse's employment	26	_____
Holiday away	26	_____
Start or finish of school	26	_____
Death of peer	26	_____
Offer of call to another parish	26	_____
Change in living conditions	25	_____
Revision of personal habits	24	_____
Negative parish activity by former pastor	24	_____
Difficulty with confirmation class	22	_____
Change in residence	20	_____
Change in schools	20	_____
Change in recreation	19	_____
Change in social activities	18	_____
Death/moving away of good church leader	18	_____
Mortgage or loan less than $50,000 (home)	17	_____
Change in sleeping habits	16	_____
Change in eating habits	15	_____
Stressful continuing education experience	15	_____
Major program change	15	_____
Vacation at home	13	_____
Christmas	12	_____
Lent	12	_____
Easter	12	_____
Minor violation of the law	11	_____
Your total Life Change Score:		_____

[1] Adapted by Roy Oswald from the Holmes/Rahe Life Changes Rating Scale.

you a sense of your score in relation to other clergy:

50 or less—unusually low
150 or less—stress manageable
200 or less—borderline mild concern
250 or less—serious concern
300 or less—more serious concern
350 or less—take seriously
above 350—take very seriously

Remember, you may have a very high stress threshold and be able to manage at a score of 350 or more.

Clues to your personal stress threshold are: feeling tired/exhausted, feeling anxious or overwhelmed, or having a lingering cold or illness. (The Strain-Response Survey will be of help in determining where you are in relationship to your threshold level.)

The Life Changes Rating Scale, developed by Holmes and Rahe as a predictor of illness (*The Social Readjustment Rating Scale*, J. Psychosomatic Res. II, 1967, pp. 213-218), proved a highly effective instrument. They hypothesized that the more changes in life to which we must adapt, the more likely we are to be sick.

This data is condensed from pages 15–17, *Clergy Stress: A Survival Kit for Church Professionals*, by Roy Oswald.

As each individual's tolerance for stress varies, the total Life Change Score should be taken as only a rough guide. For each of the events below that you consider yourself to have experienced during the past twelve months, transfer the "Average Value" to the line in the "Your Score" column. Then add these for your total Life Change Score. The Clergy Life Changes Rating Scale on page 89 was adapted from the Holmes/Rahe scale and field tested with clergy groups from various denominations.

Prayer—Meditation

For an outline of background materials and "how-to" resources on prayer/meditation write: Virgil Nelson, 283 E. Vince, Ventura, CA 93001 (SASE).

Hospital Ministries

Some hospitals are fortunate to have full-time hospital chaplains. Most do not. The potential ministry of Christian employees in the hospital context is incredible if they will consciously ask themselves, "How can I share my faith with integrity here—with staff and patients?"

Mrs. Ruth Dexter of Fowler, Colorado, is a nurse. Her concern is shown through *listening* to what people say and asking careful questions about what people enjoy reading. In light of their religious preference, if they have any, she will offer them a good paperback from her vast stock, which includes a variety of authors like C. S. Lewis and John Powell. A number of the books are in Spanish. When she leaves a book with someone, she tries to plan for a follow-up discussion with a comment like: "When you've read it, let's discuss it, OK?"

Based on friendships established with patients, she invites some of them to her home for "how to teach your children about God" sessions.

Why couldn't ministerial associations or small groups of Christians within the hospital maintain a good supply of books on disease/illness, healing, wholeness, and grief—making them available in waiting areas in the hospital and giving them to patients? Each book could be stamped "This book is for your use. You may keep it if you find it useful to you. There is no charge. If you would like to donate to help with purchasing books, please send your contribution to. . . ." Such a note might also include a statement offering counseling, such as, "If you would like to talk with someone—a priest, rabbi, clergyperson, or counselor about your feelings, contact ____*(name and phone #)*____."

American Bible Society reprints are excellent for this kind of use.

Hospital Tape Ministry

Why not establish a tape lending library within the hospital context?

Members of First Baptist Church, Oak View, California, often will make a personal tape with messages of greeting and support for members/friends in the hospital. These messages are followed by musical selections (from records) and the reading of Scriptures. The tape and recorder, equipped with an earplug for easy personal listening, are left in the hospital room.

Healing Centers

A number of healing centers have sprung up around the country, attempting to address health and healing from a holistic perspective that includes physical, spiritual, and emotional factors.

One such center is Meadowlark, 26126 Fairview, Hemet, CA 92343. Tel.: (719) 927-1343.

Dr. Evarts Loomis, M.D., director and founder, coordinates two-week programs for twenty-five persons, tailor-made to each person's unique needs. A regular daily regime is established and implemented, including exercise, meditation, education, consultation, and dietary considerations. Specialized diagnosis and treatment is used, along with the traditional medical approaches.

Christian Yoga

By J. M. Dechanet, Harper & Row, 1972. The author, a Catholic priest, explores his own resistance to and initial thirty-day experiment with yoga postures. He has come to

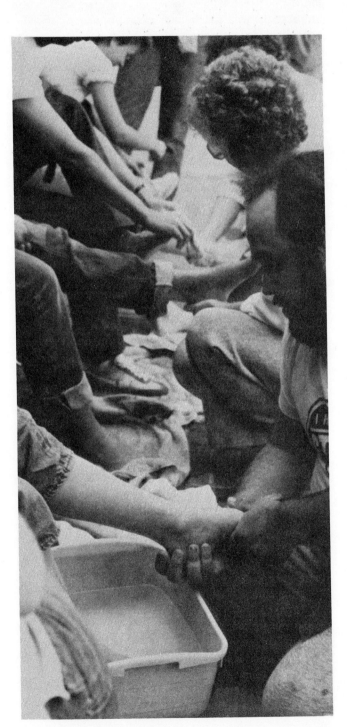

feel that they are a tool and are neutral in and of themselves. When focused on God/Jesus/Holy Spirit, they are a powerful way to deal with the problems of our bodies, spirits, and minds. The second half of the book is divided into sections on getting a beginner started in some simple postures and then leading on to more advanced postures.

Ministries of Touch

Massage

God has made our bodies, and Genesis says that he saw that his creation was good. God, through Jesus Christ, continually used touch as a vehicle for the transmission of healing energy.

One of the most powerful transmissions through touch is in the form of massage. Our culture has "co-opted" the massage, but, unfortunately, prostitution and sex are seen as the primary purposes. Just as a touch or a kiss can be friendly or sexual, so a massage can be caring or erotic.

Christians need to be trained and involved in this ministry of health and healing. Churches could set aside an area for the practice of this service with its members and the community, using professionally trained persons who are Christians and have an overview of the healing process.

Those churches operating counseling centers as part of their current ministries might seriously consider adding massage as another specific tool for use in healing. Counselors and therapists can then work together with an individual. Deep feelings are often released through massage as part of the healing process, and it can effectively accompany counseling as a healing tool. Check with local licensed massage therapists regarding training schools in your area.

We need to experiment with touch as part of the regular life of our congregations.

Foot-Washing Services

It is a tradition in Mennonite churches, and some others, to have regular foot-washing services in the spirit of Jesus, as expressed in John 14. Members know in advance when the service is planned—often accompanying a Communion service—and can dress appropriately.

Logistically, foot washing need not be complicated. Small plastic tubs of warm water can be placed on plastic drop cloths, if it is necessary to protect a rug or floor. Partners can be chosen, or deacons of the congregation can do the foot washing.

A fresh tub of warm water is used for each person. Some soaking time is refreshing; then begins a simple cleansing, possibly using a dash of Epsom Salts rubbed gently into the feet and rinsed off.

The soaking and the cleansing rub can be followed by an "anointing with oil." A few fingers dipped into corn oil is sufficient. Rub the oil deeply into all parts of the foot.

The above process can be done very effectively by washing and massaging hands instead of feet, focusing on the uniqueness and specialness of each person's hands and the gifts God has given each person for love and service.

Racism

There are many ways a congregation can get involved in combatting racism:

1. Bible study
2. Background study
3. Study resources on prejudice, stereotyping, scapegoating, genocide
4. Sharing groups to heighten personal awareness
5. Action to bridge gaps
6. Action to celebrate differences

Racism is both within individuals as personal feelings and within the system of society. It has been institutionalized, being the systematic (conscious or unconscious) exclusion of minority persons from the positions of power in which they could influence the decisions that affect their lives.

Multicultural Fair

St. Paul's Methodist Church in Oxnard, California, each year sponsors a multicultural fair which includes Hispanic, Indian, Filipino, Japanese, Black, Korean, and many other ethnic groups. The day includes cultural displays, crafts, arts, foods, music, and dancing from all of the participating cultural groups. It has become a clear outreach into a community with many walls between groups.

Cross-Cultural Weekend Retreat

Youth from five cultures came together for a weekend of experiencing one another's unique backgrounds—the foods, music and dance, games and play, and Christian worship in their different cultural traditions. Each day was divided into sections with one cultural group planning a "round," which included a meal plus all of these elements or activities.

Rev. Larry Waltz, Philadelphia Baptist Association, 1701 Arch St., Room 417, Philadelphia, PA 19103.

Cultural Understanding and Racial Justice

The San Diego Ecumenical Conference (SDEC) has sponsored a number of events aimed at increasing cultural understanding and cooperation.

1. In response to county racial demonstrations, seminars were sponsored on "Racism in the '80s."

2. Archpriest Vladimir Sorokin from Russia spoke and answered questions about the church and society in his country.

3. A special program on the Byzantine Catholic church was presented.

4. "Folk Faire" in October and "International Smorgasbord" in August celebrated the food, music, and arts of some twenty-two ethnic and cultural groups and provided opportunity for a positive spirit of cooperation among more than 1,000 volunteers.

SDEC, 1875 Second Ave., San Diego, CA 92101.

Ministry in Local Congregation Shared Between Blacks and Whites

Over twenty-five years ago a group of people met in a small frame house to organize the Hillside Presbyterian Church in South Dekalb, Georgia. In the mid-'60s the congregation grew to over six hundred members and was quite proud to have called a second minister. The community around the church was changing. Blacks had begun to move inside the I-285 perimeter. Confrontations occurred in schools, among realtors, and among elected officials. White flight began, and membership in Hillside started declining.

In 1978 the congregation lost its third minister, and the church's dream seemed about to vanish. After considering a wide variety of options, the Presbytery and the congregation decided to call Paul Smith, a Black, as pastor.

Since Paul Smith's arrival, much has happened. Fears of white members leaving did not materialize; approximately 30% of the congregation is not black. Five Blacks serve on the church session; new white members have joined the congregation; and attendance has tripled. A new associate minister (white) has been added as copastor.

The stated goal of the congregation is that "In faithfulness to the Christ who sustains us all, we will be able to transcend race, class, color, and sex barriers. . . . there is, in God, strength sufficient for whatever our needs may be."

Hillside Presbyterian Church, South Dekalb, GA 30034 or the Atlanta Presbytery, Presbyterian Church in the U.S. 341 Ponce de Leon Ave., NE, Atlanta, GA 30365.

Youth—Racism-Minority Relations

Rev. Harry Summers, director of the Interchurch Agency in New Mexico for seventeen years, relates a miracle in which a cluster of churches in Clovis, New Mexico, came together across denominational lines to plan for shared ministry in their community.

Harry believed that the most important need for the community to address was that of relationships between the minority and majority communities: Mexicans, Indians, migrant farmworkers, Anglos, and Blacks. The planning group felt that it was most important for them to deal with youth employment: skills development, job creation, job referral, and work attitudes.

After several years of operation, evaluation of the program and reflection upon its effect in the community shows that it has had a major impact.

● The youth most frequently served have come from the minority communities.

● Churches have had increasing contact with minority persons through these youth.

● Dealing with specific persons and their lives in the job setting has increased the churches' openness to look at the system.

● Looking at the relationship among youth in the community has stimulated reflection on relationships between adults.

It is exciting to see how God can use what we are willing to do as a vehicle for moving us on in the directions in which we need to go.

Rev. Harry Summers, First Presbyterian Church, 20th and Cactus Sts., Silver City, NM 88061.

Racial Cooperation in an Urban Setting

The leadership team of First Baptist Church, Los Angeles, is committed to unity. It is made up of an international, interracial group of Asians, Latins, Blacks, Filipinos, Spanish, Koreans, and Anglos. Over one hundred languages are spoken in the community adjacent to the church, and over 21% of the Los Angeles population is foreign born.

In that mix, the church has developed an incredible ministry with all ages and most stages. Write to Rev. John Townsend, First Baptist Church, 760 S. Westmoreland Ave., Los Angeles, CA 90005, and ask for a copy of the congregation's 1982 or 1983 annual report. The diversity and creativity of ministry will astound you.

Clarence Jordan, a Man with a Dream and a Ministry

The legacy of Clarence Jordan lives on in Georgia and in several nations worldwide. The original 440 acres purchased in 1942 in Sumpter County near Americus, Georgia, continues as *Koinonia*. In the beginning, two families began to work the farm, with a vision for a Christian farming community that could be a resource for the rural poor.

By 1950, fourteen black and white adults and children were living and working there together. Incredible pressures were brought to bear upon them. Preaching a gospel of reconciliation between blacks and whites was not acceptable. More radical still was the sight of blacks and whites living and working together on the same property, sharing the toil, and eating and praying together.

The farm has withstood bombings; an economic boycott by the surrounding community, which made it impossible to buy seed, food, and fuel for years; fences cut down; crops stolen from the fields; garbage dumped on the property; sugar poured in the gas tank of a truck, ruining the engine; three hundred pecan trees chopped down; machine-gun bullets sprayed at night; buildings set on fire; harassment by the Ku Klux Klan and the IRS; and a grand jury investigation accusing Koinonia of maintaining Communist ties and of inflicting the violence on itself for attention and profit.

Despite this deluge of violence, Koinonia has developed the pecan business that has saved the community economically. Significantly for all of us, the violence was transformed by the Holy Spirit into Clarence's *Cotton Patch Version* of parts of the New Testament.

The flavor and depth of Clarence Jordan's commitment to Christ is reflected in his many writings and tapes of his sermons. Write for a complete list of resources: Koinonia Partners, Rt. 2, Americus, GA 31709-9986. (One entire issue of *Sojourners* magazine, June 1979, focused on his ministry. For address see p. 16.)

Resources on Racism

1. *For Whites Only,* by Robert W. Terry, Eerdmans, rev. ed. 1975 ($3.95).

While this volume may be seen as old by some, it is still basic for Christians in the white community who wish to understand and come to grips with their own prejudices and stereotypes and with the racist system of which all white people are a part.

Robert Terry exposes the racism of liberals as well as

conservatives. The alternative is what he calls a "new white consciousness"—the awareness that the racism is not a black problem but a white problem, since the institutions of society that are oppressive are run and controlled by Whites. Strategies and tactics are suggested for the white persons who desire to work to bring about an end to racism and its effects.

Robert Terry was formerly an associate director of the Detroit Industrial Mission and drew heavily on his experiences in Detroit industry for the material included in this book.

2. *Blaming the Victim,* by William Ryan, Random House, Vintage Press, rev. ed. 1976 ($2.45).

This volume explores in depth how and why we, as a society, prefer to put the blame for poverty on its victims rather than on the inequalities and injustices of our society.

Did I choose which family I would be born into? Did I choose the income level of my parents or the community into which I would be born?

A baby born into a poor, uneducated coal-mining community in Appalachia does not have the same chance in life as a child born into a home with financial resources and an attitude of support for education. A child born with black skin did not choose his or her lot.

This is a basic volume for those interested in addressing injustice and racism in our society.

3. *How Black Is the Gospel?* by Tom Skinner, Holman, 1976. Skinner, in this volume, shows how the gospel is relevant to the black person's condition and is basic in liberating and teaching both black and white people to fight against injustice. Jesus, the reconciler, is central to our being able to work together in following his way as the radical who broke through the barriers that separate people.

4. *A Quiet Revolution,* by John Perkins, Word Books, 1977. Perkins clearly demonstrates the vision of God's kingdom here on earth through the ministries of Voice of Calvary and the call to the church to be God's people in a world of brokenness, hatred, and injustice. (See pp. 53-55.)

5. Rev. Milton Owens and Ms. Virginia Sargent have compiled an excellent annotated bibliography of books, program resources, sources of church bulletins, and films/filmstrips on Afro-American history.

For a copy write to Educational Ministries, American Baptist Churches, U.S.A., P.O. Box 851, Valley Forge, PA 19482-0851.

6. The National Conference of Christians and Jews (NCCJ) is a long-standing organization committed to "promote justice, amity, understanding and cooperation among Christians and Jews and to analyze, moderate, and strive to eliminate intergroup prejudices which disfigure and distort religious, business, social, and political relations with a view to maintaining at all times a society in which the religious ideals of brotherhood and justice shall become the standards of human relationships."

The program of NCCJ continues in many areas: anti-Semitism, Christian-Jewish relations as affected by instability in the Middle East, desegregation, quality integrated education, equal job and housing opportunities, women's rights, abortion, police-community relations, and many more. Workshops, community forums, in-service training, education, media piece production—all are part of the "tool kit" used by NCCJ to foster love and justice.

"Brotherhood-Sisterhood Week," the last week of February each year, is sponsored in over 2,000 communities nationwide in conjunction with NCCJ. Resource flyers, posters, and background materials are available.

Write: NCCJ, 43 West 57th St., New York, NY 10019.

Violence—Ku Klux Klan

Southern Poverty Law Center, 1001 S. Hull St., Montgomery, AL 36101.

An excellent resource on racism and the Klan is published by Klanwatch, a program of the Poverty Center, and is called *Special Report: The Ku Klux Klan: A History of Racism and Violence,* 1982.

Contents of the 68-page, 8½-by-11-inch book include articles in several key areas:

History: origins of the KKK, birthplace of an invisible empire, the Black Codes, slave patrols, myths of reconstitution, race riots—complicity and the law

Victims: murdered by the KKK, lynch law

Racism: roots—a brief history of American racism, learning prejudice, genetics and intelligence

Voices: voices against the KKK, when the Klan comes to town, media and the Klan

Christianity: Christianity and the Klan, the Klan terrorizing a young preacher

Today: the Klan today, key figures, reflections on the Klan and poor people, the heart of a former Klansman

The document provides useful background for Bible study and discussion for junior high students and older on racism, brotherhood, relationships with enemies, God's view of the poor, and the ways we relate to our brothers and sisters.

New curriculum regarding the history of racism in America and the resurgence of the Klan is available for schools, churches, and other groups: *Violence, the KKK, and the Struggle for Equality.*

This curriculum resource was developed in conjunction with the National Education Association and the Connecticut Education Association. A 72-page kit contains comprehensive background information and eleven detailed lesson plans with resource materials on such topics as: the birth of the Klan, beginnings of white supremacy, the process of scapegoating, and countering the Klan. Annotated bibliography and glossary are also included.

Price information, catalogs, and discount information are available from the Council on Interracial Books for Children, 1841 Broadway, New York, NY 10023. Tel.: (212) 757-5337.

For other resources on the Klan: National Anti-Klan Network, 348 Covenant Ave., Second Floor, New York, NY 10031.

Farmworker and Migrant Ministries

Migrant workers are just that—workers. They are persons on the move from one area to another, hoping to keep up with the crops; they pick and then move on. Most of the immigrants are economic refugees, having fled their homeland in hope of work in the United States.

1. Fr. Rosendo Urrabazo, priest of Our Lady Queen of Angels Church, 100 W. Sunset, Los Angeles, CA 90012, indicates that their parish had such an influx of migrants that they found it necessary to hire a full-time social worker to help in the management/counseling process for handling the overwhelming need.

In addition to providing counseling, regular access to lawyers skilled in immigration law, clothing, meal coupons for redemption in a nearby restaurant, and overnight/short-stay hospitality with members of the parish, the church also seeks to provide an informal job referral/match process, since work is what everyone is desperately trying to find.

2. Rev. Bill Ruth, pastor of the Ascension Lutheran Church, 14855 Pacific Ave., Baldwin Park, CA 91706, has members of his congregation integrally involved in work with immigrants and Hispanics through a day-care center for children, an interchurch soup kitchen, a bulk-food-purchasing cooperative, a community garden, and ongoing forums/workshops in the church and community on community needs and national priorities.

Rev. Ruth has also been active locally and in Los Angeles, helping the police and the community deal with police abuse of minority persons.

3. Faith Presbyterian Church (pastors: Jaqueline and Richard Thomas, 5 Patricia Ave., Dunedin, FL 33528) has long been involved in immigrant and farmworker ministries, beginning with study programs to document the needs in the community and state and leading to aggressive economic and political action on behalf of farmworker needs. For example, in 1975 the average farmworker worked 5½ months a year for a total of $1,737. Only about 9% of all families received any welfare help. The average family of 5 lived in 1.9 rooms, with 90% of the families having no sink, 95% no toilet; 96% no tub. Infant mortality among migrant families that year was double the national average.

Extensive Bible study in Acts 2:42-45 led to a definition of ministry focused around three aspects of servanthood: *study, share,* and *serve.* As a result of its commitment to this definition of ministry, the congregation pledged to give away a minimum of 51% of all of its income to benevolent causes.

Write to the church (SASE) for a summary of the history of these ministries and for information about an exciting peace ministry that has had impact throughout the Presbyterian Church (U.S.A.).

4. Individual contact with migrant families has been part of the ministry of the Primera Iglesia Bautista Church of Shafter, California, under the direction of Rev. Raul Moreno. During 1982 and 1983, work has expanded from occasional help with clothing and food to ongoing regular worship and programs for children and youth. Adults have been expressing interest in groups for themselves after seeing the youth having such a great time.

Rev. Raul Moreno, Primera Iglesia Bautista, 285 E. Lerdo Hwy., Shafter, CA 93263. Tel.: (805) 746-4862.

Refugees

According to *The Other Side* (see p. 110), there has been a dramatic drop in the number of churches willing to sponsor refugees. Friends at Jubilee Partners indicate, "The major barrier to refugee resettlement today is not the lowered admission quotas, but the lack of churches willing to be sponsors." For the thousands of black Haitians locked up in detention camps, this is an acute problem.

For information on refugee resettlement contact: Church

World Service, 475 Riverside Drive, New York, NY 10115-0099.

Churches of many denominations have answered the scriptural call to care for the widows, orphans, and homeless by opening their hearts and sponsoring families and individuals fleeing their homelands. Ravaged by war and political oppression and facing starvation, these persons come hoping desperately that they can start a new life.

It does not take a large church to minister in this way. It does not take a lot of money. What it takes is commitment and a great deal of time and energy—helping the refugees with learning the language, getting settled, finding adequate/affordable housing, finding a job, dealing with the necessary social agencies, learning how/where to shop, handling currency, banking—in short, helping them to become part of an entirely new society and culture.

The financial burden to the sponsoring church is minimal. An initial amount is granted to help with starting expenses. Federal funds have been made available to help, and many states will provide interim public assistance during the time needed by the refugees to establish job independence.

The Southside Community Church in Sacramento, California, which is only four years old, has developed an ambitious outreach to Indochinese refugees. In 1981 Sacramento County had more than two hundred refugees a month seeking housing, education, and employment in that area. When the pastor, Dr. A. L. Muro, heard of the need, he approached the church board and an outreach project developed. Retired teachers volunteered to teach English, and in one day 185 hopeful students had signed up. Classes are held three nights a week from 6–8 P.M., with fifty students enrolled. Six teachers and several aides help, along with an interpreter. Ruth S. Going, the director of the program, is a retired schoolteacher with training and experience as a reading specialist. She emphasizes a "survival English" approach, which involves learning English words for common objects, parts of the body, clothing, furniture, telling time, asking directions, using the phone, and other essential functions of daily life.

Dr. A. L. Muro, P.O. Box 28635, Sacramento, CA 95808.

First Baptist Church of National City, California, is engaged in an exciting ministry to Laotian refugees living in their area. The ministry was the result of a single pastoral visit in a Laotian home and an invitation to attend the church. The family came, and soon a special class for Laotians was established, with Pastor Charles Molnar teaching and a Laotian serving as interpreter. Families were invited into homes of the congregation for fellowship. Clothing and furniture were collected for new families. Help was given

in the interpretation of legal matters and the forms of society. An English language class was begun. Some Laotians are being helped to find better housing and jobs. Response to these many hands extended in love has been great. In a nine-month period, twenty-two Laotians joined the congregation upon confession of their faith and baptism; eight more are in a new members' class. More than seventy-five Laotians of all ages are involved in aspects of the church's ministry.

The results of this ministry will spread throughout the United States as these families find work and join their relatives in other parts of the country.

Dr. Charles Molnar, 635 E. Seventh St., National City, CA 92050.

Interchurch Cooperation

The First Baptist Churches of Ojai and Oak View, California, cooperated with the Presbyterian Church over a two-year period to help in the resettlement of two Vietnamese families. The Oak View Church has fifty-five members, the Ojai Church around two hundred, and the Presbyterian Church around four hundred.

A joint committee was established, with one person coordinating each aspect of the family's needs: employment, housing, tutoring, health and medical needs, and physical needs such as clothing, furniture, etc. There was a commitment to keep each family off public assistance, so $3,000 was raised for one year's estimated expenses. During the year, budget planning began, and by the end of the year, the family was able to pay its own way. Five retired school teachers developed curriculum materials for tutoring the adults and children and organized the tutoring schedule for each adult each week.

Larger congregations have sponsored a whole series of families. Has your congregation considered this form of outreach ministry?

Undocumented Immigrants

Undocumented persons include those who have entered the country without papers and those who had proper papers but stayed in the country beyond their expiration.

How many people are in the United States as undocumented persons: three million? twelve? sixteen? Nobody is really sure. It is something like asking, "How many lost subway tokens are there in the city of New York?" The very fact that they are lost precludes counting them.

In the Pacific southwest, there is a continual "revolving door" from Mexico into the United States and back. "Coyotes" take advantage of the desire of persons to get into the country, charging $700 or more to help people cross the border; the "migra," or Border Patrol, rounds them up and takes them back over the border.

Thousands have fled to this country from Central and South American countries—El Salvador, Guatemala, Honduras, and many others—fleeing political oppression and poverty.

The scriptural calling is very clear—yet controversial in many congregations. Leviticus 19:33-34 is a call to the people of Israel never to forget their alien or sojourner status in the country of Egypt, and because of that always to be kind to the stranger/sojourner/alien in their midst.

Many myths exist about the "undocumenteds":

1. Jobs are being stolen from Americans; unemployment is being aggravated. Studies have shown that this is not the case. Undocumenteds are working in the fields, in homes and hotels as maids, in restaurant kitchens, and other places, doing menial work most Americans would not consider doing. They are also working at minimum wage or less.

2. Undocumenteds are adding to the welfare rolls and draining the system. A study in San Diego County showed that undocumenteds paid $36 million dollars into the system in taxes in the year studied but received only $3 million in services. (To get on welfare in California, one must have proof of citizenship.)

Few people understand the intense pressure these aliens face. Undocumenteds live in constant fear—fear of exploitation, fear of being caught, fear of violence. They have no recourse when they are robbed or when ten persons are charged $100 a month apiece to live in one small room. To complain is to be discovered.

Potential ministries include direct services such as health, food, employment, survival, and advocacy. Other potential ministries include dealing with the legal structure of the Immigration and Naturalization Service in order to find creative overall solutions to the border problems, and working on the international situation to improve U.S./Mexican relations and reduce the discrepancy in the standards of living.

El Rescate

El Rescate ("the rescue") provides social and immigration services and rescue from forced deportation for refugees from Central America in the Southern California area. It coordinates efforts of local congregations and organizations to provide direct services to individuals and families in crisis.

El Rescate is a project of the National Center for Immigrants' Rights, organized by the Interfaith Task Force on Central America, administered by the Southern California Ecumenical Council. Information on programs, issues, and beginning similar efforts can be had by writing to El Rescate, 1550 W. 8th St., Los Angeles, CA 90017.

A Question of Justice: Undocumented Persons in the U.S. and Lutheran Ministry

By Lutheran Social Services of S. California, 2468 W. Pico Blvd., Los Angeles, CA 90006. Tel.: (213) 385-2191 ($10). This 8½-by-11-inch volume of over one hundred pages is set up to be used in four or more class settings to examine biblical background relating to immigrants, to learn some of the history of migration from Mexico and varying immigration policies over the years, to look at an overview of Christian values and issues, and to focus on public policy and what individuals and churches can do.

Each class outline includes extensive appendix materials taken from unpublished studies and papers, reviews, newspaper articles, and speeches. A bibliography includes other printed materials and media resources, as well as the names of resource persons who are well informed on this issue.

Refugee Camp Simulation

World Concern has created a simulation experience called *Refugee Camp: 24 Hours of Nothing, Nothing, Nothing.* The experience is aimed at helping participants, usually youth, get some feeling for what life is like day after day in refugee camps all around the world.

The experience actually begins several weeks earlier with a "contrast" evening: four hours with everything—a food feast, a rich man's scavenger hunt, exciting video games, bowling, and ice cream treats. The close of the evening is a film: *East Africa: Land of the Dying.*

The point is not to induce guilt but to dramatize contrasts and encourage reflection and the commitment to help raise sufficient funds to support one refugee person for two weeks—estimated cost, 50 cents a day.

Students secure sponsors and pledges, and then comes

the "24 hours of nothing" experience. A leader's manual of specific activities, devotions, Bible studies, and films has been created and provides an excellent structure to use "as is" or modify to fit your particular group. Numerous variations are suggested for activities and time slots, all aimed at giving some experiential glimpses of what living every day in a refugee camp would be like.

For information and materials, write to: World Concern, Refugee Camp, Box 33000, Seattle, WA 98133.

Resources for Ministry with Refugees

1. "Strangers Within the Gate," *Engage/Social Action* Forum 68. Present policy, problems, and theological perspectives. Write United Church of Christ, 110 Maryland Ave., NE, Washington, DC 20002 (75 cents each).

2. *Refugees—Friends Without a Home.* A set of materials for use in the church school classroom with younger students, ages 4-10. Includes a teacher's guide, activities book, filmstrip, map, poster, and record. Write the Mennonite Central Committee: AV Library, 21 South 12th St., Akron, PA 17501.

3. *Borderlands.* This 20-minute filmstrip about the U.S./ Mexico borderlands in Texas was produced by the Methodist Board of Global Ministries. Available for $15 from the United Methodist Service Center, 7820 Reading Rd., Cincinnati, OH 45137.

4. *The Other Side/El Orto Lado.* Produced by the American Friends Service Committee, this 25-minute slide show looks at root causes of migration to the United States and at the impact of U.S. investment in Mexico. Available for rental or purchase in English or Spanish versions, from AFSC, 1501 Cherry St., Philadelphia, PA 19102.

Hispanic Ministries

Formal Study

Mexican-American Program, Perkins School of Theology, Southern Methodist University, Dallas, TX 75275.

Hispanic Ministry—City/Refugee

Rev. "J" (José) Franciscas, Calvary Baptist Church, 747 Broad St., Providence, RI 02981.

The congregation is ministering in a transitory, changing community to resident Hispanics, as well as those who continue to pour in from South and Central American countries. They come without clothes or luggage, without household items, and without jobs.

The congregation has trained each member to be a leader and has effectively discerned the gifts of the Holy Spirit given to each one. Those who are settled in the community give specific and regular assistance to the new arrivals, helping them with locating housing, looking for work, enrolling in English training, and learning to survive.

"J" describes his ministry as informal, going when people need him, knocking on doors, meeting and talking with people on the street. Spiritual nourishment is offered also through programs of the congregation: prayer/Bible study, women's group, an active youth fellowship worship, and a Bible Institute training series.

The congregation has a core of seventy persons from ten countries and continues to grow steadily.

Amigo Project

The American Baptist Churches of the Pacific Southwest has begun a creative project working with its sister Baptist churches south of the border. The project will be a training school in the skilled trades and will be located in Mexico. Seed money has already been secured, land located, and people committed for leadership.

Once operable, the program will provide individual participants with marketable skills for use *within* the Mexican economy. Outgrowths of this, it is hoped, will be the formation of cooperatives and the generation of enough additional seed money to "duplicate" the initial project in several other states in Mexico.

For information, write to Rev. David Luna, Director of Hispanic Ministries, ABC,PSW, 970 Village Oaks Drive, Covina, CA 91724.

Hispanic/White Shared Ministry in an Upper-Middle-Class Community

Hispanic and white pastors ministering in the same upper-middle-class, predominantly white community? Does this sound unbelievable?

It isn't. Exciting ministries are happening in and through the folk at White Plains Baptist Church in New York. The congregation has chosen to hire a full-time Hispanic pastor as a second pastor.

In addition to traditional worship, Bible study, and prayer groups, the church's ministry through its second, Spanish-speaking congregation involves housing, job-hunting, and documentation, supporting those fleeing the violence in Central America.

All of this is done through one church budget and one membership. When Hispanic persons join the congregation, they join First Baptist Church. Both congregations meet together for joint worship once a month and on special occasions. On Communion Sundays, both pastors participate, and the Scripture, prayers, and one hymn are in both languages.

Additional efforts are coordinated in seeking just legislation for immigration, refugee relief, and assistance with documentation.

Rev. José Valencia, the Hispanic minister, was born and raised in El Salvador. For more information, write to First Baptist Church, 456 North Street, White Plains, NY 10605.

Prisoners

Christ calls us (Matthew 25:40ff) to share his love with those in prison. There are over 6,000 correctional facilities in the U.S., according to the American Correctional Association, with between 400,000 and 500,000 prisoners in jail at any given time. (The above figures do not count more than 5,000 local community jail systems.)

The costs of incarceration to us as taxpayers have climbed to over $30,000 per prisoner per year. As citizens and Christians we have the opportunity to influence both individual lives and the entire prison system. We can also respond to the fact that over 40% of local jail systems have no religious services for their inmates.

Our work need not be confined "within the walls"; in fact, opportunities for working with families, assisting those on parole/probation and those on work furlough, or setting up halfway houses are available for those who are willing.

Services Within the Prison Walls

—traditional worship services
—small groups: Bible study groups; problem focus groups for those with problems related to alcoholism, child/spouse abuse, etc., and for sex-related offenders (see the "Yokefellow" model, pages 40–41).
—one-on-one prisoner sponsorship for friendship/support
—tutoring: basic educational and trade skills
—work-furlough programs: trade school/training in community

Service Outside the Institution

—ministry with family/friends of inmates: for every person in jail, six others are affected; ministry can quickly expand to include this group.
—support for the family: both emotional and physical, such as getting to/from prison for visits, child care, stamps and stationery for writing, friendship and meaningful activities.
—upon prisoner's release: there is a desperate need for halfway houses—semi-independent living situations away from the old neighborhood/friends and influences. Homes with small numbers of people and with houseparents constitute one variation which can have a real impact.

—after prisoner's release: offering friendship/inclusion in the life of the church, helping with housing, job search, and the nitty-gritties of life.

Small Group Ministry

Awareness of the needs of prisoners in the nearby state prison led the members of the Royersford (Pa.) Baptist church to form a prison committee.

One member of the congregation had a concern for prisoners. Contact with the chaplain and prison officials confirmed what was most needed—personal, regular, and practical one-to-one contact with inmates.

A set of purposes was formulated in cooperation with the chaplain at the prison and some inmates:

1. to help inmates experience redemptive changes that would help them to cope more successfully with life in and out of prison;

2. to help visitors from churches ("outmates") experience redemptive changes that would give them concern for the imprisoned and motivate them to involve others from the church and community;

3. to show inmates that Christians are concerned about their needs and are willing to act;

4. to help all persons in the group establish new personal contacts in which Christ could be shared in an atmosphere of love and acceptance enabled by the Holy Spirit.

Needs for prison ministry were shared with the congregation through sermons, Bible study groups, and classes. A prison committee was formed to work out particulars. The model was begun with a group of six volunteer "outmates" and six inmates selected by the chaplain. For the first time, prison authorities allowed women "outmates" to participate.

The group meets every other week for about two hours. A typical meeting includes: 15–20 minutes of sharing by each person about his or her life since the last meeting; discussion of a topic suggested by the inmates and introduced with a relevant section of Scripture; 15 minutes of one-to-one contact with particular inmates; and a closing circle of brief, honest prayers.

Inmates have found that there are Christians who care, an idea contrary to their negative impressions of Christianity. Changes of behavior through commitment to Christ are evident inside and outside the prison.

Church involvement has extended beyond the prison walls to help find housing for inmates on furlough and permanent housing and jobs for those being released.

"Outmates" have a new understanding of their faith and of the dark forces at work in society and in prisons, which can destroy hope in a person's life.

After beginning the group, it was discovered that the method was similar to that of the Yokefellow Prison Ministry, a national program which has worked effectively in prisons through committed Christians. When Yokefellows was discovered, the Royersford Baptist Church established a tie and began to use Yokefellow resources and support.

Rev. Paul D. Schoonmaker, Royersford Baptist Church, 452 South Lewis Rd., Royersford, PA 19468, tel.: (215) 948-4170; or National Yokefellow Ministry, 112 Old Trail North, Shamokin, PA 17876.

Community Service by Prisoners

How can the creative energies and talents of prisoners be encouraged, while at the same time meeting needs in the community?

Why not work with prison officials to develop small groups of 4–6 prisoners to work with a Christian "boss" to perform needed functions in the community?

—painting and carpentry in homes of seniors and other poor folk

—learning and doing other skilled trades

—working within existing community organizations to learn office and other business skills

—working with/for city and governmental agencies, performing needed tasks that would otherwise have to be paid for.

Some of these have been done with juveniles in rehabilitating housing (see page 84).

In a time of decreasing governmental revenues and a sagging economy, taxpayers are paying an average of $30,000 per year to maintain each prisoner. Why not use that as an investment in the community at the same time?

Death-Row Prison Ministries

The Open Door Community of Atlanta, Georgia, is committed to working with 1,500–3,000 homeless persons and with more than one hundred inmates on death row in the state prison.

The prison is about 120 miles southeast of Atlanta. Community members visit prison inmates and their families and also provide transportation for the families to the prison.

Rob Johnson, Open Door Community, 910 Ponce de Leon Avenue NE, Atlanta, GA 30306. Tel.: (404) 874-9652.

Juvenile Detention Center Ministry

The Youth Detention Center of Jefferson County, Colorado, is a temporary facility for juveniles, 80–85% of whom are boys. An average of 18–25 residents are there at any one time.

Youth and adults from Arvada Central Baptist Church,

under the direction of Rev. Walt Parsons, felt called to minister to the youth, hoping that while inside the detention center, the youth would be more open to hearing God's Good News for their lives than they would have been while outside on the street.

First contact was with the supervisor at the center when the church sought permission for a visitation program. The facility had had a number of prior experiences with groups wanting to come and do Bible study, but there had been a lack of consistency and commitment.

The goals of the Arvada church group were to establish friendship as the basis for helping youth become more aware of the forces at work in their lives and then to discuss alternative ways of behaving as the opportunities arose.

Three to seven youth over eighteen years of age go each week—state law forbids younger visitors. They attempt to follow up, after the release of the youth, visiting the youth in their homes or in group or foster homes, making phone calls, driving them to church, etc.

For a time, Walt tried to train the volunteers in advance of their going, but he eventually found that what is most important is for him to be aware of where the volunteers are, spiritually, prior to going and then to train them during the visiting process by reflecting with them on their visits.

Despite the limitations of the short contacts, the youth are making meaningful decisions; it is "God's love pouring out on these kids which works here and anywhere. Kids today have very low levels of self-worth . . . we just love them where they are and tell them that God loves them and wants to help."

Rev. Walt Parsons, Arvada Central Baptist, 7500 West 57th Avenue, Arvada, CO 80002. Tel.: (303) 422-1174.

Network for Ex-Prisoners

In 1980 a high school group from First Baptist Church of White Plains, New York, went on a one-time mission experience to nearby Taconic Correctional Facility. As a result of their encounter with the pain of loneliness felt by the inmates there, they insisted that a continuing ministry be developed.

Volunteers of all ages were trained in leading discussion groups with inmates approaching parole. Now more than twenty volunteers, ranging in age from 16–60, go twice a month for a 90-minute discussion group. The focus is on the reality of getting out and preparing to face the outside world.

The next stage of development came as some inmates on parole came to worship with the congregation. Continuing contacts revealed the difficulties of finding housing, jobs, and new friends.

An ex-inmate, Eddie Newton, was hired, after training in psychology and transactional analysis, to direct a ministry called the Prison Network, a continuing support group of

AFTER PRISON WHAT?

THE PRISON NETWORK, First Baptist Church, 456 North St. White Plains, N.Y. 10605 914 949-5207

ex-inmates, which meets at the church regularly. State laws forbid ex-prisoners to form organizations, but because of the church sponsorship and the positive focus of the program, this ministry is allowed.

The members of the group continue to counsel and support one another in facing the transition to a new life. Walk-in hours at the network office are advertised for one evening a week; other special sessions are by appointment.

The Prison Network, Rev. Ed Gunther and Rev. Elizabeth Emrey, First Baptist Church, 456 North Street, White Plains, NY 10605.

Tutoring Prisoners

Prison ministry, to be effective, does not have to be large. One concerned person can have a real impact.

Two people have begun to tutor prisoners at the Ventura County, California, Sheriff's Department Honor Farm. A young man whose wife is a member of First Baptist Church of Oak View went into jail for a 6-month term. He did not know how to read or write, but he was motivated to learn—following months of being told "no" in job interviews.

The Sheriff's Department was approached, through the Department of Inmate Services, with the request to begin a simple tutoring program in reading and writing, using two retired schoolteachers.

While it turned out that the young man was not eligible, two other young men did receive tutoring for four hours a week. One has made a commitment to Christ, while still in jail, and has begun to share his faith with others.

Edna Poole, who has been the key coordinator, is excited about getting other tutors from her congregation (First Baptist Church, Ojai, California) and from other churches and community groups. There are more than sixty prisoners interested in receiving tutoring help. Write to Edna Poole, % First Baptist Church, 930 Grand Avenue, Ojai, CA 93023.

Crime Prevention and Prison Ministry

East Oakland, California, is the location of Allen Temple

Baptist congregation under the energetic leadership of Dr. A. J. Alfred Smith, Sr. Says Dr. Smith, "We celebrate with high spiritual ecstasy on Sunday, but the other six days of the week, we're in the community. What we are trying to do is to come onto this 'turf' and to make some dramatic changes." And changes are being made!

The congregation is addressing the issue that in the city more blacks than any other group are victimized by other blacks. It has a variety of *crime prevention* programs including: education, a year-round *tutoring* program for children and youth in conjuction with a nearby school, a *Big Brother* program for boys who live in a home without a father, a counseling center, a senior adult activity center, and a specific prison ministry.

Prison Ministry: While only 12% of Oakland's population is black, 80% of the prison population is black. Malvina Stephens, an ordained seminary graduate, is working with the prisoners and prison leadership in the development of a ministry *within* the prison walls and *beyond* the walls, in the community.

The church is catalytic in other areas of ministry as well; it has begun a credit union, a seniors' housing facility, and a ministry with Spanish-speaking residents of the area. Efforts to clean up drug traffic in the area have continued, despite the fire-bombing of the church building.

What attracts new members? "It is because of our servant ministry concept, and not our homogeneity." People of all classes feel at home, from Ph.D.s to uneducated garbage collectors. "We have Ph.D.s and people with no 'D's'; people who teach English at Stanford and a deacon who doesn't know that the subject and the verb should agree."

Sharing the "living water of life" on the street for twelve years has filled the Allen Temple Church with grateful people who are moving back out in service to others.

Allen Temple Baptist Church, Dr. A. J. Alfred Smith, Sr., 8500 "A" Street, Oakland, CA 94621.

Clergy Cops

He's a cop who works the swing shift, patrolling the streets of Glendale, California, from 3–11 P.M. In his dark blue uniform he has the appearance of an airline pilot, but in reality, he's John Lane, a retired American Baptist minister who, at the age of 70, has been a chaplain on the Glendale Police Department for over two years.

One day a week Chaplain Lane serves as a volunteer, riding in a patrol car with one of his younger colleagues. John was, for thirty-four years, pastor of First Baptist Church of Sunland, California.

"I'm chaplain to police department personnel. . . . When you ride a squad car for eight hours with someone . . . you

101

get to know them pretty well. . . . And I'm a minister to the community, where there are crisis situations: rape, death notifications, and suicides. These are places I can minister, and, of course, I've done this all my life. . . .''

Resources for Prison Ministries

1. *How to Establish a Jail and Prison Ministry,* by Duane Pederson, Nelson, 1979.

The previously cited statistics were taken from this excellent study and training guide on prison ministry. The volume is designed for both individual and group use and has reflective questions throughout.

Contents include sections on scriptural mandates, Christian volunteers in local jails, prison chaplain and volunteer ministries, the relationship between inmate and volunteer, how to be an effective volunteer, answering questions about prison ministry, and *how to plan and involve the local congregation in prison ministry.*

The book also includes important resources, including a list of organizations that can support you in establishing and maintaining effective ministries and a major list of organizations involved in ongoing prison ministries, some with denominational affiliations and many that are independent. Duane Pederson has established one of those organizations himself: Christian Prison Volunteers, P.O. Box 1949, Hollywood, CA 90028. The book and other information are available, as well as a one-day workshop, ''Prison Volunteer Training,'' which is held throughout the nation.

2. Creativity in shared urban prison ministries and prison reform is demonstrated by the Genesee Ecumenical Ministries Judicial Process Commission, 121 North Fitzhugh Street, Rochester, NY 14614.

Their activities include direct services to prisoners and their families, as well as workshops/seminars on court processes and justice issues, statewide concerns about parole systems, violence, police practices and other criminal justice issues.

While some issues are local, the cooperation of the Genesee group and their process for addressing issues could be adapted in most communities. *Justicia,* a newsletter, $5 yearly from the above address.

The group also developed a workbook for use by local congregations or other groups wanting to study the whole area of criminal justice from a Christian perspective. The workbook, *Crime and Community in Biblical Perspective,* by Kathleen E. Madigan and William J. Sullivan, is published by Judson Press, 1980.

Global Concerns

We are World Christians! We put God's love for *all people* first. No race is superior to another, no government is more loved than another, no country is dearer than another. We don't put our nation's economy before God's economy. He tells us to seek *first His* Kingdom. He will then meet our needs.

We are driven to action daily with the knowledge that three billion people do not know our Savior. Our passion in life, our unquenchable desire, is to take God's love to them.

No task is too small for us. All that limits us is our unwillingness to believe God can enable us to do it.

We are sold out to Jesus Christ our Savior and Lord. Nothing less. We understand following Him means *absolute* death to ourselves. It costs *everything* to be His desciple [sic].

Don't give us blessings—give us grace to be unquestionably obedient to Your every last command and desire.

Don't give us status—give us a place to serve.

Don't give us things for our use—use *us*.

Don't give us a mansion to live in—give us a springboard to take Christ's love to the whole world.

Don't give us good jobs—put us to work.

Don't give us comfort—command us.

Don't give us pleasure—give us perspective.

Don't give us satisfaction—teach us sacrifice.

Don't give us entertainment—enable us.

Don't give us good salaries—give us strength to do Your will.

Our great joy in life is in pleasing our Lord—and there is *no other joy* comparable. (Copyright, Today's Mission. Reprinted by permission.)

This underlying perspective forms the basis for an exciting network of Christians who share their struggles with faithfulness through the magazine *World Christian*. Gordon Aeschliman, editor of the magazine and author of the preceding quotation, is seeking to call Christians back to the basic perspective of God, who gave everything in order to give us life (incarnation in the birth of Jesus) and calls us to follow that path of wholehearted and radical commitment to redeem *all* people.

World Christian magazine, P.O. Box 40010, Pasadena, CA 91104 ($11 cash, $12 if billed, 8 issues a year).

See also:

The Mustard Seed Conspiracy, by Tom Sine, Word Books, 1981 ($5.95). As a Christian "futurist," Tom shares the

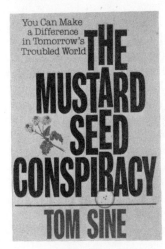

exciting news that God has always been at work changing the world through the *conspiracy of the insignificant*.

Sine clearly spells out the unprecedented problems that face the world in the next two decades. He sees as "the Mustard Seed Conspiracy" those Christians who are rediscovering the truths that greed and acquiring things do not bring satisfaction in life and that, on the contrary, meaning comes in the life given away. Questions for discussion and action are included at the end of each chapter, making it ideal for group use.

Two additional books critical for examining the relationships between biblical faith and political/economic action are:

1. *The Politics of Jesus,* by John H. Yoder, Eerdmans, 1972 ($4.95).

2. *Jesus and the Nonviolent Revolution,* by André Trocme, translated from French by Michel Shenk, Herald Press, 1974 ($8.95).

Both of these substantive works provide ample grist for thought, prayer, and discussion.

Global Concerns: Resources and Perspectives

1. *The Global Two Thousand Report to the President of the U.S.: Entering the 21st Century,* a three-volume report ordered by President Carter in 1977, released in 1980, United States Printing Office, Washington, DC 20402 ($4).

Volume 1, a summary of data, conclusions and recommendations, is the most useful for the average person to read. Fourteen government agencies cooperated in covering long-range projections in such areas as population, income, food, fisheries, forests, water, nonfuel minerals, and energy.

What does tomorrow hold? The prophets of old were able to discern what would happen if present behaviors continued, and in this sense the *Global 2000 Report* is clearly *prophetic.* The conclusions are sobering. Picture a world with almost two billion more people and only a tiny increase in arable land: a world with three times more malnourished people, twice as much desert, one-quarter of the population continuing to use three-quarters of the world's mineral production, health problems and climatic changes resulting from damage to the ozone layer, and severe water shortages.

The most dramatic impact will be felt in the less developed countries. For example, Mexico and Africa will more than double their populations; China will reach 1.3 billion and India, 1 billion. The total world population is estimated at 6.35 billion in the year 2000.

The disparity between the haves and the have-nots will continue to widen. For every $1 increase in the gross national product (GNP) in the less developed countries, a $20 increase is projected for the industrialized countries.

A commission led by the Secretary of State studied ways the United States could respond. Their report, *Global Future: Time to Act,* emphasized the absolute necessity of international cooperation involving a concerted attack on the socio-economic and political roots of extreme poverty. Economic and redevelopment reforms were urged, along with wise resource management and conservation.

To bring this into reality will take a commitment to development assistance by the richer nations.

2. *North-South: A Program for Survival* (The Brandt Report), the report of the Independent Commission on International Development Issues, edited by Willy Brandt and Anthony Sampson, MIT Press, 1980 ($4.95).

This volume, in a sense, is a companion to *The Global 2000 Report* in that it deals with the broader issues of the economic and political relationships among the nations of the planet.

Traditional and conventional wisdom of the past has told us that our greatest concern involves East-West relationships. The Brandt Commission Report calls for a dramatic change of perspective and indicates that the biggest, long-term, planetary survival issue is North-South related, involving the industrialized nations of the Northern Hemisphere and the southern, technologically less developed nations. Unless we see ourselves in common with the U.S.S.R. and other northern nations, we will continue to ignore the widening rift with the countries of the Southern Hemisphere.

Eighteen persons from five continents researched and compiled the report, which makes bold recommendations regarding short- and long-range reforms in international finance and the development of economic and monetary systems. Emergency actions are proposed to avoid imminent crises. There are priorities set for the 1980s and long-term reforms for implementation *before* the year 2000.

3. Ending World Political Oppression.

Amnesty International (304 West 58th St., New York, NY 10019) is committed to the fair treatment and the release of all prisoners of conscience—those imprisoned for their

beliefs, color, ethnic origin, or religion. It also opposes the death penalty and the use of torture in all cases.

In-depth investigations are conducted, reports published on individual countries and their treatment of prisoners, and contacts made with political structures on behalf of individual prisoners. Members of Amnesty International are encouraged to adopt a prisoner and write to him/her directly, as well as *to the authorities* on behalf of his/her release. Others commit themselves to participate in "prisoner of the month" letter-writing campaigns.

The Amnesty International newsletter is *Matchbox,* which is published three times a year for a contribution of any amount. Membership is $20 a year and includes *Matchbox* and *Amnesty Action* (published eight times a year).

4. Audiovisuals on Global Concerns.

Mennonite Central Committee (MCC) Audiovisual Library, 21 South 12th St., Akron, PA 17501.

*This is a *free* loan audiovisual library. Only the costs for mailings are required. Subjects include:

Africa	Disaster Service
Appalachia	Middle East
Asia	Multinationals
Children's Resources	Native North Americans
Europe	North America
East-West	Peace/Peacemaking
Food and Hunger	Poverty
Justice/Conflict	Refugees
Latin America	Relationships
Life-Style	Weapons/Arms Race
MCC Mission	World Development.

This is one of the best current resources for audiovisuals anywhere in the United States.

5. Fides/Claretian (221 W. Madison St., Chicago, IL 60606; tel.: [312] 236-3057) is an exciting new resource ministry within the Catholic community that examines the issue of social justice in the United States. Written for the grass roots, this group holds the premise that no one person can do everything, but it is our Christian duty as individuals to *do something*.

Some titles:

Homemade Social Justice: Teaching Peace and Justice in the Home

Christian Feminism: Completing the Subtotal Woman

Christian Business Ethics

Doing Good While Doing Well

Racism in America

Salt, a social justice magazine, $10 a year

Theology of Liberation

Consultations have been held worldwide on this theme, and many schools, seminaries, and local congregations have zeroed in on this focus in light of world needs.

Four major theme areas that are regularly addressed include—

Third World theology, especially relative to Latin America, Africa, and Asia;

Black theology and the U.S.A.;

Feminist theology and the U.S.A;

The relationship between Marxism and Christianity.

Several key books will get a group started in the study of this area:

1. *Cry of the People: The Struggle for Human Rights in Latin America—the Catholic Church in Conflict with US Policy,* by Penny Lernoux, Penguin, 1982, 552 pp. ($6.95). Best basic document on the struggle for human rights in Central America, according to Rev. Bill Phillippe, Chairperson of the Civil and Religious Liberty Committee of the World Alliance of Reformed Churches.

2. *A Theology of Liberation,* by Gustavo Gutierrez, Orbis Books, 1973 ($5.95).

3. *The God of the Oppressed,* by James Cone, Seabury, 1975. Powerfully stated themes by one of the best-known representatives of Black theology.

Additional resources:

1. Dr. Lenore Dowling, Immaculate Heart College, Suite 2021, 10951 West Pico Blvd., Los Angeles, CA 90064. Information about the Catholic church's struggle in Los Angeles.

2. *Lucha-Struggle,* bimonthly, $10 a year, P.O. Box 37, Times Square Station, New York, NY 10108. Forty pages of specific background information on individual countries, overview perspectives and networks of people around the world.

Commitment to a New Life-Style

Those interested in covenanting with others to live more simply so that others may simply live would do well to join with thousands of people who have signed the Shakertown Pledge.

The Shakertown Pledge group is a movement committed to simple living and to education and communication with people around the world who are interested in radical simplicity in response to God's call to faithfulness.

The pledge group is a loosely-knit association of people who hold the principles of the pledge in common and who, by attempting to redirect their lives toward creative simplicity, are working for a more just global society.

The Shakertown Pledge
(excerpts of nine points)

Recognizing that the earth and the fullness thereof are gifts from our gracious God and that we are called to cherish, nurture, and provide loving stewardship for the earth's resources, and recognizing that life itself is a gift and a call to responsibility, joy, and celebration, I make the following declarations:

1. I declare myself to be a world citizen.
2. I commit myself to lead an ecologically sound life.
3. I commit myself to lead a life of creative simplicity and to share my personal wealth with the world's poor.
4. I commit myself to . . . reshaping institutions. . . .

5. I commit myself to occupational accountability. . . .

6. I affirm the gift of my body . . . and its proper care.

7. I commit myself to examine . . . my relations with others. . . .

8. I commit myself to personal renewal through prayer, meditation, and study.

9. I commit myself to responsible participation in a community of faith.

The Shakertown Pledge group has resource persons for workshops, seminars, retreats; publishes a monthly newsletter, *Creative Simplicity;* and has a variety of other literature on the issues facing our world. (Copies of the pledge and background information sheet are 20 cents.)

Shakertown Pledge Group, West 44th Street and York Avenue South, Minneapolis, MN 55410.

Environment/Energy Future

Lester R. Brown, in his provocative book *Building a Sustainable Society* (Norton, 1981), includes the following quote on the cover: "We have not inherited the earth from our fathers; we are borrowing it from our children."

Aldo Leopold has written, "We abuse the land because we regard it as a commodity belonging to us. When we see land as a community to which we belong, we may begin to use it with love and respect."

Ron Sider, in *Rich Christians in an Age of Hunger: A Biblical Study,* says,

An Age of Hunger summons affluent people to a lower standard of living. But a general assent to this statement will not be enough to escape the daily seductions of Madison Avenue. Each of us needs some *specific, concrete* plan . . . . By all means avoid legalism and self-righteousness. But have the courage to commit your self to some *specific method* for moving toward a just personal lifestyle.

Will we dare to measure our living standards by the needs of the poor rather than by the lifestyle of our neighbors?

Saving Energy in the Local Congregation

Stewardship of the financial/energy resources of the local congregation is imperative. A January gas bill up by 33% from $192 to $299 a month made our small congregation stop and think.

1. *Reducing Energy Costs in Religious Buildings,* Massachusetts Energy Office, a 52-page handbook recommended by American Baptist Churches National Ministries' Facility Planning Services. Minimum order, two copies for $4.90 (total) from Center for Information Sharing, 77 North Washington Street, Boston, MA 02114.

2. *Energy Conservation Manual for Congregations,* by the Joint Strategy and Action Committee. Includes congregational worksheets to record and monitor energy use by degree days and to examine various conservation measures for their cost effectiveness. Joint Strategy and Action Committee, 475 Riverside Drive, Room 1700-A, New York, NY 10115-0099 ($2.50, including postage and handling; make checks payable to "JSAC").

Energy Task Group in Local Church

The construction of a 3-billion-dollar, 2,000-megawatt nuclear power plant within five miles of this church precipitated concerned laywomen in Royersford, Pennsylvania, to begin an Energy-Awareness Task Group. This group has been the catalyst for a variety of activities.

1. They have studied conservation, less wasteful lifestyles, and God's stewardship plan for the planet Earth. One theme has been that energy is a gift of God to be used wisely and with regard for the generations that will follow.

2. Articles have been written for sharing in a church newsletter, and a legislative focus has kept people alert on hearings on local and national energy use/abuse. Theological bases for action for use in study groups have also been developed.

3. An Energy Fair was held with exhibits of wind and solar devices, alternative furnaces, electric cars, and diesel engines. Workshops were held on home energy auditing, life-styles, and transportation. Open to the entire community, the fair drew many people into the life of the congregation and revealed many people interested in mutual survival on this planet.

Write to Rev. Paul Schoonmaker, Royersford Baptist Church, 452 South Lewis Road, Royersford, PA 19468.

Sharing Volunteers and Staff Worldwide

Intercristo

Intercristo is a job-recruitment clearinghouse for more than one thousand Christian organizations working worldwide in mission. It was founded as an information link between organizations needing Christian volunteers and individuals seeking places to serve.

An interested person fills out the Intermatch Personal Profile, giving specific information about his or her work and educational background and vocational perferences. It is an in-depth resumé in a simplified, systematic format.

The profile is compared by computer to the specific job criteria provided by the organizations that need help. A summary report is prepared on all the positions that meet the person's criteria and is sent to the individual. Organizations receive the names of the individuals who have received information on their positions.

Over 4,600 different job descriptions are included in the files; over 28,000 actual jobs are available throughout the world.

Cost: $31.50, which covers only 90% of actual expenses in serving individuals and agencies. Services available to organizations at no charge.

Write: Intercristo, P.O. Box 33487, Seattle, WA 98133. Toll-free telephone number: (800) 426-1342.

Mennonite Central Committee—Service Opportunities

The Mennonite Central Committee (MCC) regularly publishes *Service Opportunities,* a pamphlet describing personnel needs in the United States and around the world in such areas as rural development and agriculture, nutrition, economic and technical development, health services, teaching services, and social services.

The MCC welcomes persons of any Christian denomination who qualify. A complete copy of faith, service philosophy, and personal qualifications is available on request. The MCC is trying to select people who—

—are committed to the Christian faith and philosophy of service and have membership in a Christian church;
—are ready to identify with and participate in the life and activity of the Christian church in the community where they are assigned;
—possess personal, emotional, and vocational resources needed for creative work in demanding frontier situations; and
—are willing to be responsible to a group. . . .

Write Mennonite Central Committee, 21 South 12th Street, Akron, PA 17501.

Summer Service in Latin America

Participants must be 18 years of age; Spanish required. American Friends Service Committee: 980 North Fair Oaks Avenue, Pasadena, CA 91103. Tel.: (213) 791-1978.

World Hunger

"Let justice roll down like waters and righteousness like an everflowing stream" (Amos 5:24, RSV).

"[People] shall not live by bread alone (Matthew 4:4, RSV).

The physical survival of the people on this planetary "spaceship" demands that we have a certain minimum protein and caloric input each day, as well as essential vitamins and minerals. The fact that a full quarter of a billion persons of the passengers on spaceship earth do not have enough calories going into their bodies each day to survive is a horrendous reality, especially in light of the fact that, *worldwide, there is no scarcity of food.* In 1980,

without even counting all the beans, fruits, nuts, root crops, vegetables and non-grain-fed meat, there was enough *grain alone* to provide everyone in the world with 3,000 calories a day.

Is there scarcity of land? Our world's arable land is shrinking dramatically because of inappropriate technology and greedy ignorance of ecological realities. In Iowa during 1980, for every bushel of corn grown, two bushels of topsoil was lost through erosion. It takes *2,000 years to create one inch of topsoil.* Yet topsoil in California is being *lost* at the rate of *one inch every fifteen years,* according to a recent study by the California State Department of Agriculture (statewide average).

These realities constitute a serious challenge to the survival of the human race. However, even with the loss of one-half of the earth's arable land since the days of Solomon, there is *still* enough land to feed the people of the planet.

Bangladesh has half as many people per cultivated acre as Taiwan. Yet Taiwan has no starvation. China has *twice* as many people per cultivated acre as India; yet in China people are not starving.

The problem lies, not in the *amount* of arable land, but in *what is grown* on that land and *who controls this.* For example, in Central America and the Caribbean, where nearly 70% of the children are undernourished, at least *half* of the agricultural land is used for growing crops for *export and not for food* for the native people.

"I believe that God will punish our indifference to the poor. Our wealth, instead of being evidence of our blessedness, will be the cause of our judgment," says Anthony Campolo in his book *Success Fantasy* (Victor Books, 1980, p. 144).

Study Resources on World Hunger

1. *Rich Christians in an Age of Hunger: A Biblical Study,* by Ronald J. Sider, Inter-Varsity Press, 1977 ($4.95).

This book is a basic starting point for those becoming aware of world hunger as an ongoing reality in the global community. The book is filled with specific factual information on the magnitude of human suffering and the factors which perpetuate it, as well as a clear study of the scriptural call to involvement in the plight of the world. It is a basic study book, ideal for church school classes, study groups, youth fellowships, women's circles, and the like. A Leader's Guide may be ordered from the Judson Book Store, P.O. Box 851, Valley Forge, PA 19482-0851 (LS 14-209).

2. *Cry Justice: The Bible Speaks on Hunger and Poverty,* by Ronald J. Sider, Paulist Press, 1980 ($2.45).

This volume is a collection of biblical passages, quoted

in full, with the themes of justice, hunger, and poverty. In the first section the focus is on God's gracious gift of salvation as the basic source of grateful service to our neighbor. The second section highlights passages on the character and extent of God's concern for the poor. The third section examines the nature of the redemptive economic relationships God desires for God's people. Section four includes passages on the issues of property and possessions. A study guide of discussion questions is included.

3. *Christian Responsibility in a Hungry World,* by C. Dean Freudenberger and Paul M. Minus, Jr., Abingdon Press, 1976 ($2.50).

After identifying clearly the ten basic causes of world hunger, the authors focus on "deeds required for a time of crisis." Topics discussed include clear vision, increased awareness, mobilization of resources, development of responsible life-styles, and the reordering of public priorities. Excellent book for group use.

4. *Diet for a Small Planet,* by Frances M. Lappé, Ballantine, rev. ed, 1975 ($2.75).

This is not an ordinary cookbook. It is a manual on family and world nutrition, plus hundreds of high-protein vegetarian recipes for use in home and church kitchens. The first three parts provide an analysis of protein use and sources, and ratings of the protein value in common foods. The protein "drain" of converting grain into beef, as an example, is striking: eight pounds of grain and soy protein yield one pound of beef protein! The conversion factor for chickens, on the other hand, is three pounds of grain for one pound of protein (p. 11). Protein can also be multiplied when it is properly combined with complementary proteins.

What difference does this make? Globally, there is enough grain grown for each person on the planet to have three thousand calories a day, if the grain were all used for human consumption. Incredible quantities of meat are used to meet the expensive tastes of consumptive societies.

5. *Food First,* by Frances Moore Lappé and Joseph Collins, Houghton Mifflin, 1977.

This volume includes extensive documentation which dispels many of our myths about the causes of world hunger and what we can do about the problem.

a. The basic cause of hunger is not too many people.

b. The cause of hunger is not just a scarcity of arable land.

c. The cause of hunger is not lack of technology.

d. The cause of hunger is not overconsumption by greedy Americans.

e. Americans cannot solve the hunger problems of the world. The nation is not, and should not be, the breadbasket of the world.

f. Food wars and enforced birth control are not inevitable. Solutions are not easy. They involve the long hard process of democratization of our own and other societies and the redistribution of basic resources so that food is the first priority in the productive economy of each nation. This is a basic volume for those beginning to examine world hunger issues.

6. Institute for Food and Development Policy (1885 Mission Street, San Francisco, CA 94103) was founded by Frances Moore Lappé and Joseph Collins. The institute has a wide range of published books and articles on our global food resources and policies affecting these vital resources. Write to get a catalog and to be placed on a free-newsletter mailing list.

Program Resources

1. *Hunger Awareness Dinners,* by Aileen Van Bellen, Herald Press, 1978 ($1.00). This small volume gives specific ideas on how to use mealtime as an educational awareness experience in helping participants understand various aspects of the world hunger crisis and alternative solutions.

Recipes are also included, along with background data in summary form.

2. The *Lunchless Monday Group* is one of the many creative ministries of the First Baptist Church, 538 Carolina St., Vallejo, CA 94590. Each week, the group meets, with coffee and tea being the only items on the menu and the cost of lunch going to an offering for world hunger. Some of the offering recipients have included Church World Service, Heifer Project, American Friends Service Committee, Salvation Army, Meals on Wheels, and American Baptist Churches in the U.S.A. hunger projects.

How about your congregation? It only takes a commitment from two persons to get started. Meet for "lunch" anywhere—a restaurant, a park, a shopping mall near work, a home.

3. *Planned Famine* is a thirty-hour fasting/educational experience designed by World Vision, World Vision International, P.O. Box O, Pasadena, CA 91109.

Thirty Lutheran youth planned a "famine" for themselves during 1982, learned a lot experientially about the realities of world hunger, and at the same time raised funds from sponsors who pledged a certain amount of money per hour for the time the young people went without eating.

The thirty hours are not spent just sitting around. A complete packet of scriptural, educational, film, and other resources is available from World Vision. The experience is packed with opportunity for study, reflection, sharing, and planning for further involvement in hunger concerns. Write to Rev. Luther Tolo, Trinity Lutheran Church, 196

North Ashwood, Ventura, CA 93003.

The youth of First Baptist Church of Greenacres, California (10011 Rosedale Highway, Bakersfield, CA 93308), a small congregation near Bakersfield, raised $524 during their planned famine. The funds were divided between denominational hunger programs ($315) and World Vision hunger programs ($209). Participants urged their congregation to join in and become part of the solution to world hunger.

4. *Love Loaf.* World Vision also developed the "Love Loaf" program, using a small plastic bank shaped like a loaf of bread, which is placed on the family table. Sixty percent of funds collected in these banks go to World Vision for world hunger programs, and 40% go to local or denominational programs chosen by the local group.

5. *Skip a Lunch; Feed a Bunch.* The international relief and development arm of the National Association of Evangelicals has developed the World Relief Organization, which has produced educational and program materials and fundraising tools for addressing world hunger needs. "Skip a lunch, feed a bunch" is their theme. They use a simple black plastic lunch pail as a bank for the kitchen table and contribute $3 for worldwide use for each lunch skipped. Write National Association of Evangelicals, Box WRC, Wheaton, IL 60187.

6. *Wheel of Birth.* The hunger task force of American Baptist Churches of the Pacific Southwest made a "wheel of birth" out of plywood and used it as a roulette wheel to raise people's consciousness regarding the odds of being born on the various continents of our planet.

People were asked to step up and spin the wheel to see *where* they would be born if they were born today. The wheel was spun, and a color came up—coded by continent in proportion to birth rates and numbers worldwide. A pamphlet was given to them to help them become aware of what their life would be like if they were born on that continent.

Here are directions for making your own wheel:
Plywood Wheel, 2½ ft. in diameter, is mounted on metal stand to spin vertically. Nails mark divisions of 64 "slices." Slices are painted in colors by percentages re chances of

birth—42 yellow, Asia; 8 black, Africa; 7 tan, Middle East; 5 brown, Latin America; and 2 red, North America. Intermix colors around wheel. (Permission is granted to reproduce these materials for use in local congregations and judicatories, as long as no profit is involved and credit is given.)

(Pamphlet for Distribution)

Wheel of Birth

WE HAD *NO CONTROL* OVER WHICH CONTINENT WE WERE BORN ON . . . .

Most of us just happened to be born in a country which was blessed with human and natural resources almost beyond measure.

GOD CALLS US TO LOVING COMPASSION AND JUSTICE in caring for this human creation here on spaceship earth.

SOME FACTS AND ASSUMPTIONS:

1. As U.S. citizens we are barely 5% of the world's population, yet we have over half of the total income and consume nearly half the nonrenewable energy and resources of the earth.

2. Over $9 million worth of edible food was discarded in the city of Tucson, Arizona, in household trash in one year.

3. *Guilt* does not motivate long-range changes in our life-style. We are not "personally" responsible for hunger in the world. *Gratitude* can motivate compassion and long-range change.

4. There is no scarcity of food. In 1978 there was enough *grain alone* to provide every person in the world with 3,000 calories a day, and that's not counting beans, fruits, nuts, or vegetables.

5. Many food-poor nations are using prime farmland for food and nonfood crops to export to wealthy nations. At the height of the Sahelian drought in the early 1970s the *exports of cotton and peanuts* from those nations to Europe *actually increased!*

PERCENTAGES OF ALL CHILDREN BORN ON THE PLANET THIS YEAR:

(Yellow—64%) You are one of 82,800,000 [Asian] children born this year. Over 7 million of you died as infants. Millions more will die before age 5. As an adult you will live to an average age of 48 and will earn $475 income per year.

(Black—13%) You are one of 16,700,000 [African] children born this year. Over 2 million of you will die as infants. You can expect to live to the age of 45 and will earn an average of $190 per year.

(Brown—8%) You are one of 11,500,000 [Hispanic] children born this year. Over 600,000 of your brothers and sisters will die as infants. You can expect to live to an average age of 55 years and will earn, as an adult, an average of $450 each year.

(Tan—12%) You are one of 15,800,000 [Middle Eastern] children born this year. Over 400,000 of you will die as infants. You will live an average of 71 years and will earn $2,200 yearly.

(Red—3%) You are one of 4 million children born this year in the modern industrial nations. About 76,000 of your brothers and sisters will die as infants. You can expect to live to an age of 70 years and will earn an average of $5,200 yearly.

*Calculations based on figures from the United Nations World Health Organization and other compiled resources. All are reasonable approximations.

6. Sending food, alone, is not the answer. People must have appropriate technology and access to land and markets so they can be food self-sufficient. Arable land must also be used to produce *food first*.

WE CAN DO SOMETHING ABOUT WORLD HUNGER:

1. *Read* and *study* the facts regarding ongoing causes and alternative actions:
- *Bread for the World,* by Arthur Simon, Eerdmans, 1975.
- *Food First: Beyond the Myth of Scarcity,* by Frances M. Lappé and Joseph Collins, Houghton Mifflin, 1977.
- *Rich Christians in an Age of Hunger: A Biblical Study,* by Ronald J. Sider, Inter-Varsity Press, 1977.
- Resource packet: Hunger Task Force, American Baptist Churches of the Pacific Southwest, 970 Village Oaks Dr., Covina, CA 91724 ($1 for postage and handling).

2. *Examine* your life-styles for waste and over-consumption and *commit* to conserve and share the value of what would have been wasted with organizations working on the root causes of hunger.

3. *Begin a Bible study group* looking at the Scriptures and hunger/poverty. Or use this focus in your women/men/youth/church school group.

4. *Consider special projects and actions* aimed at dealing with long-range causes of hunger here in America and abroad. Christians and concerned persons around the world must join hands and hearts to deal with this world's most solvable problem. Where there is a will, there is a way.

Will you help bring God's will?

7. This is a wraparound for an aluminum soda can that becomes a bank. Place it on the kitchen table and make an offering before each meal. . . . The offering is collected each time Communion is served in the church and sent to alleviate world hunger. This idea comes from Rev. Richard Poteet, Preston Hills Presbyterian Church, 6224 Beltline Road, Dallas, TX 75240.

8. *Roots of Hope, Miss-a-Meal Meditations,* edited by the staff of *Seeds,* with a chapter by E. Glenn Hinson. Available for $1.95, plus 25 cents postage, from *Seeds,* Oakhurst Baptist Church, 222 East Lake Drive, Decatur, GA 30030.

This volume includes fifty-two meditations for an individual or family choosing to fast one meal a week for a year. Each meditation includes a Scripture passage and several paragraphs of "food for thought."

9. Excellent record albums:

"That There May Be Bread," The Monks of Western Priory, Weston, VT 05161 ($8.95). Male choir with unique instrumental accompaniment. Title song and several others.

"Take Off Your Shoes: Earth Songs and Other Celebrations," by Jim Manley, New Wine Productions, P.O. Box 544, Lomita, CA 90717 ($6.95). Particularly appropriate: "The Gifts That You Gave Me," "Lord of All Hopefulness," "Sunday Dinner," and the title song.

10. The spending and budgets of thirty-four popular organizations were analyzed in depth by the editors of *The Other Side* magazine in their March 1983 issue. This survey includes data on: costs of fund-raising, salaries of top administrators/executives, percentage of income spent on administration, cash financial reserves, and charts listing size of paid staff, significant affiliations, government and corporate influences, and a summary of annual income and expenses.

Organizations include everything from those focusing on relief and development to domestic parachurch organizations—for example, Intervarsity and Prison fellowship—to some denominational and secular groups. (A sampling: World Vision, Food for the Hungry, Christian Children's Fund, Covenant House, American Bible Society, Wycliffe, Lutheran and Mennonite agencies, and more.)

Check your library or write *The Other Side,* 300 W. Apsley St., Philadelphia, PA 19144.

Advocacy Groups

1. *Bread for the World,* 6411 Chillum Place, NW, Washington, DC 20012.

Bread for the World (BFW) is a Christian citizens' movement seeking government policies that will address the basic causes of hunger, both domestic and worldwide. Chapters are organized within congressional districts around the country. Members receive a monthly newsletter advising them of pending legislation, and options/alternatives. Members are encouraged to contact their congresspersons regularly regarding the issues at hand.

BFW has had an impact worldwide. Its people drafted the legislation for the U.S. grain reserve program. They have also drafted and mobilized support for the "right-to-food resolutions."

While all the efforts of a given denomination for world hunger might add up to several million dollars in a year, a *single vote* by Congress can have the effect of multiplying or erasing whatever churches do for hunger relief.

2. *Impact* is an interreligious network sponsored by national Protestant, Roman Catholic, and Jewish agencies, 110 Maryland Avenue, NE, Washington, DC 20002 ($15). Some states have local Impact groups covering state legislatures.

Impact seeks to monitor legislation pending before Congress in nine basic categories: U.S. food policy, U.S. foreign policy and military spending, health care, human services, employment, criminal justice, civil rights and liberties, energy and ecology, and issues affecting women. Members are kept aware through: *Action,* a two-page bulletin providing timely information on specific bills; *Update,* brief reports on a wide range of bills of concern to the religious community; and *Prepare,* major background and study papers on major policy issues about which there is concern in the religious community.

Members are encouraged not only to learn but also to act, by contacting legislators regarding their feelings on pending legislation and priorities.

Resource Organizations for Information and Action

Most religious bodies have their own "in-house" hunger relief and development agencies, which usually have an *excellent* ratio of administrative costs to funds used in actual program services.

Following is a list of organizations that can provide educational resources as well as action opportunities for individuals and groups.

1. The American Jewish Joint Distribution Committee, 60 E. 42nd St., New York, NY 10017.
2. Church World Service—CROP. 475 Riverside Drive, New York, NY 10115-0099.
3. World Relief Commission (overseas relief arm of the National Association of Evangelicals): write, World Relief, Box WRC, Wheaton, IL 60187.
4. Catholic Relief Services, 1011 First Ave., New York, NY 10022.
5. Baptists World Alliance, 1628 Sixteenth St. NW, Washington, DC 20009.
6. American Friends' Service Committee, 1501 Cherry St., Philadelphia, PA 19102.
7. World Vision, P.O. Box 0, Pasadena, CA 91109.
8. Heifer Project International, P.O. Box 808, Little Rock, AR 72203.
9. Mennonite Central Committee, 21 S. 12th St., Akron, PA 17501.
10. Food for the Hungry, P.O. Box 200, Los Angeles, CA 90041.
11. Oxfam-America, 115 Broadway, Boston, MA 02116.
12. UNICEF, 866 United Nations Plaza, New York, NY 10017.

Population

Another major area of concern in the global community is the rapidly increasing rate of population growth. One good resource is *Ethics for a Crowded World,* Seminar Series, 1977; prepared by the Center for Ethics and Social Policy, Graduate Theological Union, 2465 LeConte Avenue, Berkeley, CA 94709. Tel.: (415) 841-9811. ($5). This workbook also has leaders' guides available.

The workbook includes background papers on:

1. ethical analysis
2. world population
3. world income distribution
4. world agriculture
5. international development
6. nurtrition and health
7. women in development
8. energy and development
9. case studies in development.

This is an excellent resource on the big issues of ethics and the future.

A *simulation game* was created by Robert Herron of First Presbyterian Church, Clay Center, Kansas, as a result of Bible study and discussion of the book *The Population Bomb,* by Paul R. Ehrlich. Bible passages studied included Genesis 1:26-32, Psalm 8, and others. The game is based on Don Griggs's "Teacher Survival Game." It stimulated great discussion and sharing.

To play the game, begin by describing the setting to the group: Our world is facing an international crisis in 1990. There simply is not enough food to feed everyone even in the United States. You have been appointed by the president to serve on an emergency committee that will set priorities for our nation for the next decade. You must decide what action will be most useful in stemming the crisis in our nation and the world.

1. Ask each individual, in no more than five minutes, to rank the following items in priority order:

a. Large grants of aid to only the people with children
b. Opportunity to breathe clean air and drink fresh water
c. Opportunity to live without fear of pesticides
d. Voluntary family planning with suggested limit of two children
e. National parks with a chance to hunt/fish
f. A chance to have space for your own home
g. Enough food in world so no one is hungry
h. Required sterilization of every male after he has fathered two children
i. Freedom from nuclear war
j. Individual right to have unlimited numbers of children
k. Ability to move about freely

2. Form groups of eight to ten persons and have each group, in forty-five minutes or less, develop a priority list that reflects group consensus.

3. Report back to the entire group feelings/processes/reflections.

4. Close with worship and prayer.

Reconcilers and Peacemakers

"There is no way to peace; peace is the way." This quote, attributed to A. J. Muste, is appropriately reflected in the Scriptures: Jesus said, "I am 'the Way,' the truth and the life." There is no "way" to Jesus; Jesus is "the way."

"Blessed are the peacemakers, for theirs is the kingdom of heaven." All of us need guides for the implementation of a life-style of peace.

Peace is a life-style. The journal of two persons in search for a new way of life is *Things That Make for Peace: A Personal Search for a New Way of Life,* by John and Mary Schramm, Augsburg, 1976 ($3.25). This volume of notes and quotes along the path documents the Schramms's involvement as members of the body of Christ in seeking a life-style that makes for peace.

Explored are issues of nonviolence, ecology, world hunger, contemplation, and personal relationships.

Peacemaking: Structure and Strategies

Gordon Cosby and Bill Price, *Handbook for World Peacemaker Groups,* World Peacemakers, 2852 Ontario Road, NW, Washington, DC 20009. Tel.: (202) 265-7852. ($1.25).

A world peacemaker group is a small gathering of concerned people, from two to ten or twelve, who, conscious of the action of the Holy Spirit in their lives, offer the gift of their corporate life for the world's healing and unity through peacemaking. The group has both an "inward" and "outward" journey. The inward allows for the nurture of the spirit, and the outward, empowered by the inward, engages in activities aimed at national and international peacemaking.

An excellent process of study and prayer for helping a group come together and function as God's people around this concern is offered in this handbook. It includes a listing of resources with key Scripture passages relating to peace.

Peacemaking: Shalom Congregations

The Disciples of Christ (Christian churches) have begun a challenging program of calling individual congregations to covenant together as Shalom Congregations.

In deciding to enter the shalom covenant, a congregation makes a one-year commitment. Congregations that join the shalom congregation promise the following:

1. An official board action must be taken authenticating a minimum one-year commitment.

2. A representative(s) of the congregation will attend a training event to facilitate the local congregation in planning specific strategies and programs in their program relating to peace.

3. The congregation will plan, as an integral part of their individual lives, involvement in worship, study, and action experiences that lift up the vision of God's shalom.

4. Progress reports will be submitted each six months.

Here are some suggestions that are given for those getting started:

1. Establish a special task force or committee for planning and implementing programs within the congregation.

2. Include specific concerns and input in the worship setting, through sermons, drama, skits, slide presentations. Have a Peace Sunday annually.

3. Organize Bible studies and other regular study groups on peacemaking.

4. Use creativity in communicating with the congregation by means of bulletins, newsletters, and special mailings.

5. Consider providing counseling to those who face decisions regarding military service.

6. Encourage members to join a National Peace Fellowship made up of disciples who work ecumenically for peace.

Write to: Robert Steffer, Christian Churches (Disciples of Christ), Division of Homeland Ministries, P.O. Box 1986, Indianapolis, IN 46206.

Peacemaking: Nonviolent Alternatives

Hundreds of volumes have been written on the strategies of military conflict through the centuries. Few have explored the history of the effective use of a nonviolent national defense.

Many people denounce nonviolence as a cop-out or as

unrealistic and ineffectual in today's violence-prone world. For others, there is limited commitment or an unwillingness to try nonviolence because it is too difficult. For most of us, nonviolence is new, uncharted territory—aside from reading about Jesus' nonviolence in the face of Herod and Caesar.

In his volume *Exploring Nonviolent Alternatives,* Porter Sargent, 1971 ($3.25), Dr. Gene Sharp provides basic information on the concept and technique of nonviolent action and civilian defense *without armaments.*

Dr. Sharp also has published a classic, three-volume series on nonviolence, all published by Porter Sargent:

Part One: Power and Struggle (127 pp).

Part Two: The Methods of Nonviolent Action (336 pp).

Part Three: The Dynamics of Nonviolent Action (455 pp).

In Part One, theories of political power and the use of nonviolent techniques of struggle are documented historically and in current world situations.

The second volume documents 198 specific methods of nonviolence, an expanded list of possibilities in any situation.

Part Three shows how nonviolent action can be a form of political "jujitsu" to overcome violent repression—turning the energy of the oppressors back upon themselves.

Detailed and clear, these volumes are basic resources to the religious community in exploring the pragmatics of nonviolent action in a violent world.

These volumes and others on related subjects are available from the Life Center Association—Visionworks, 4722 Baltimore Avenue, Philadelphia, PA 19143. Write for a catalog of resources.

Movement for a New Society

The Movement for a New Society envisions a new society based on maximum decentralization, democracy, and local control in political and economic sectors; no rich and no poor; guaranteed social services; minimizing of material indulgence while maximizing social and personal relations; production based on human needs rather than on personal profit; sophisticated methods of nonviolent conflict resolution; no war; and concern for ecological and biological posterity.

For more information about nonviolence, grass-roots community organizing, and the Movement for a New Society, write to 4722 Baltimore Avenue, Philadelphia, PA 19143.

Prayer Chain for Peace

A simple Christmas message of hope for the world was shared with all by the Monkton United Methodist Church.

If everyone lit just one candle, what a bright world this would be. . . . If everyone stopped for a few minutes to remember each day why we celebrate Christmas, what a significant holiday this would be.

If everyone offered just one little prayer for peace on Earth, good will to all men, how much more compassionate this world would be.

. . . At 12 o'clock will you join our family in lighting a little candle, reading the Christmas story from the Bible and saying a little prayer for peace among all nations?

We hope you will, and may the joy of Christmas remain with you throughout the New Year.

Begun as a practice *within* the church fellowship, hundreds of other churches and thousands of people have "caught the light" and committed themselves and their families to this simple, powerfully symbolic beginning of the Christmas Day.

For cards, music, and resources write to: Rev. Steve Bowman and Bill Clawson, layleader, Monkton United Methodist Church, 1930 Monkton Road, Monkton, MD 21111.

Peacemaking: Action Alternatives

1. World Peace Tax Fund, 2121 Decatur Place, NW, Washington, DC 20008. Tel.: (202) 483-3751.

The World Peace Tax Fund is seeking to create a legal alternative to paying taxes in support of war. If passed, such a law would allow individuals to designate that the percentage of their taxes which go for military expenditures should go, instead, to a world peace fund aimed at peaceful action and education worldwide.

Why would Christians want to do this?

a. A conscientious objection to the payment of military taxes is a civil rights and human rights issue.

b. The World Peace Tax Fund will provide legislative relief for those Americans whose religious, moral, or ethical beliefs prohibit their participation in war or preparation for war.

c. Opposition to war taxes is substantially *different* from opposition to payment of taxes for nonmilitary social programs.

d. Funds will be increasingly available for social programs, since the military portion of taxes by conscientious objectors would be transferred into them and into peacemaking activities.

For more information, write to the World Peace Tax Fund and receive its newsletter.

2. Evangelicals for Social Action (ESA), 25 Commerce Street, SW, Grand Rapids, MI 49503.

This organization is a network of evangelical Christians committed to living out their faith in the world, bringing about the realities of justice, liberty and peace, even as Jesus prayed, "Thy Kingdom come . . . on earth as it is in heaven."

A newsletter is published regularly, and local chapters have sprung up around the country. Research and educational workshops are among the activities of the various local groups.

3. Fellowship of Reconciliation (FOR), Box 271, Nyack, NY 10960.

The FOR is working within the United States and globally in the process of seeking reconciliation at all levels of society. The global FOR network develops innovative nonviolent initiatives that are on the cutting edge of human survival.

For example, working in South Africa for nonviolent change, they work with political prisoners. They also work with minorities in southeast Asia in such countries as Bangladesh, Sri Lanka, Thailand, and India.

The Fellowship of Reconciliation helped to originate The New Abolitionist Covenant, a covenant by committed Christians to abolish all nuclear weapons in the name of God. Copies are available for 30 cents each by writing FOR. A resource guide is also available.

4. Clergy and Laity Concerned, *CALC Report,* 198 Broadway, Room 302, New York, NY 10038 ($10/year).

CALC is an action-oriented, interfaith peace and justice organization consisting of forty-nine chapters, action groups, and affiliates in thirty-two states.

Founded originally to mobilize opposition to the Southeast-Asian War (1965), the organization now has programs that have broadened to include other peace and justice concerns. The goal is to inspire people to challenge government and corporate policies that oppress people personally, politically, or economically.

They publish *CALC Report* monthly, which includes background articles, reviews of resources and films, networking information, theological perspectives, and worldwide reports on peace and justice actions.

5. The Institute for Policy Studies, 1901 Q Street, NW, Washington, DC 20009. Tel.: (202) 234-9382.

The Institute for Policy Studies was formed in 1963, and the Transnational Institute formed in 1973. They are committed to research, education, social invention, and the examination of the fundamental disparity between the rich and poor of the world, seeking democratic and just solutions.

The work of the institutions is devoted to national security, international economy, the Third World, domestic policy and cultural critique.

Publications of books and resources are categorized in several ways:

a. Disarmament
   1) Alternatives to the arms race
   2) Intervention
   3) Nuclear war
   4) Arms and security
   5) The new cold war
b. The Third World
   1) Latin America
   2) Africa
   3) The Middle East
c. Global Economy
   1) Food and resources
   2) Corporate power
d. America
   1) Politics in crisis
   2) Work and welfare

In each category there are a variety of titles. While the studies are not religious, they do present data, facts, background, and perspectives that are essential if we are to be serious about peace and global matters.

6. Physicians for Social Responsibility, 639 Massachusetts Avenue, Cambridge, MA 02139. Tel.: (617) 491-2754.

Physicians as a group have tended to be politically conservative in their approach to life, and yet they have bonded together to speak out as a group in response to the requests by the federal government to prepare treatment plans for health care survival services in the wake of an atomic nuclear exchange.

Their research has led them to some startling conclusions:

a. The explosion of a single 20-megaton bomb (small by today's standards, and yet 1600 times larger than the single Hiroshima bomb) dropped in the Los Angeles metropolitan area (a likely target, with its military-related industries) would immediately kill nearly 2 million people. That is more than twice as many as killed in *all* the United States wars in the entire history of our nation.

b. Completely discounting the impossibility of getting adequate medical treatment (there are only about 1,000 beds in the entire United States for treatment of severely burned victims), the lack of clean water, no communication systems, etc., if all the physicians in the entire United States were able to come to Los Angeles and if they each worked 20 hours a day, 7 days a week, it would take all of them 14 days to see each surviving victim *only once*—for a maximum of ten minutes.

c. The United States and the U.S.S.R. combined have over 50,000 nuclear warheads.

d. The conclusion of the physicians was that *there is no preparation for nuclear war,* short of guaranteeing that it can never happen. Guaranteeing that it can never happen means a *complete dismantling of all nuclear weapons on the planet.*

e. The chances of a nuclear war beginning by accident are increasing at an astounding rate, with our complete dependence upon fallible technological systems and fallible human beings.

1) A 1982 House Committee reported that in 1977, a typical year, 100,000 American military personnel had some form of access to or responsibility for nuclear weapons. During that year, 1,219 of that 100,000 were removed from duty because of mental disorders, 256 for alcoholism, and 1,365 for drug abuse.

2) The potential of computer or equipment malfunction is even scarier. During an 18-month period, the North American Defense Command reported 151 computer false alarms. One had American forces on alert for a full six minutes.

f. Recovery from an all-out nuclear exchange would be impossible. The economic, ecological, and social fabric on which human life depends would be destroyed both in the U.S.S.R. and the U.S.A.—and in much of the rest of the world as well.

Audiovisual materials and resources on the nuclear threat which have been produced by the Physicians for Social Responsibility are:
- *The Last Slide Show*
- *The Race Nobody Wins*
- *The Last Epidemic*
- *8-Minutes to Midnight*

Currently Physicians for Social Responsibility has 105 chapters and 16,000 members. Write to them for more information.

Peacemaking: Resources

1. *World Military and Social Expenditure*, by Ruth Sivard, 1981, World Priorities, Inc., Box 1003, Leesburg, VA 22075. Tel.: (703) 777-6444. ($4).

This book is an extensive documentation of the military and social expenditures by the nations of the world. Sections include the documentation of military growth, increasing expenditures, arms imports and exports, and military training. A whole section is devoted to describing the spread of the nuclear industry and the future capability of nuclear weapon production for these nations.

In addition, treaties to control nuclear weapons are documented, as well as inflation, productivity, unemployment, and basic needs worldwide. The social and economic side is explored, with statistics on horizontal and vertical proliferation. Tables document comparative resources for over 141 countries!

In the Appendix are maps of the nuclear world and diagrams of Moscow and Washington, showing the effects of a small, one-megaton nuclear explosion on them.

This is an indespensible tool for study and comparison of the world's nations.

2. *Military Budget Manual:* How to Cut Arms Spending Without Harming National Security, National SANE Education Fund, 711 G Street, SE, Washington, DC 20003. Tel.: (202) 546-7100. ($1.50).

This is a comprehensive overview of weapons and systems, their cost, and their effectiveness, as analyzed by the Department of Defense and other advisors. It contains background data on definitions of national security, an analysis of the threat of nuclear war, and information on conventional weapons and general purpose forces. The Summary Table has budget proposals, realities, and proposed reductions, which could be made *without* harming national security.

SANE, a citizens movement for a sane world, also has a wide variety of resource materials on issues of war and peace. Write them for more information.

3. *The Fate of the Earth*, by Jonathan Schell, A. Knopf, 1982 ($11.95).

This excellent resource includes three essays on the physical, moral, and political significance of nuclear weapons.

In the first section Schell describes in detail the consequences for the several layers of the ecosphere—social, biological, geological—showing their intricate interrelationships. The real potential is that all that might remain of America following a nuclear exchange might be a "republic of insects and grass."

In the second section of the book, Schell presents an extended meditation on the morality of extinction. How can we in our finitude understand the end of all consciousness? Schnell helps us to begin to comprehend the incomprehensibility of human extinction and, he hopes, come to our senses and act on behalf of the future of the human race.

Appropriate actions, after we come to our senses, are the subject of the third section.

4. *Waging Peace: A Handbook for the Struggle Against Nuclear Arms,* edited by Jim Wallis, Harper and Row, 1982,

304 pp. ($4.95). Order from Sojourners, 1809 L Street, NW, Washington, DC 20005.

The Sojourner community has compiled this excellent twelve-session study guide for use within the local congregation, college/seminary settings, and prayer and Bible study groups. It is arranged in three major sections: a thorough assessment of the present state of the arms race, biblical and theological responses to it, and a discussion of what can be done.

5. *Militarism, Security, and Peace Education:* a Guide for Concerned Citizens, by Betty Reardon, UME Communication Office, %Educational Ministries, American Baptist Churches in the U.S.A., P.O. Box 851, Valley Forge, PA 19482-0851 ($4.50).

This guide is divided into six sections. Session 1 explains the "how-to's" of organizing and conducting a study group. Sections 2 through 5 deal with specific issues: human security, national security, the goals and tools for peace education, and preparation for action as peacemakers.

A supplemental learning packet of four paperback books and numerous documents and brochures is also available. The set costs $12. Write Educational Ministries for more information.

6. *Kill? For Peace?* by Richard McSorley, S.M., Center for Peace Studies, 1977. Room #2, O'Gara Building, Georgetown University, Washington, DC 20057 ($4).

Richard McSorley, a Catholic priest, is professor of theology at Georgetown University. He paints a sobering picture of the destructive power of nuclear weapons, documents the history of the just-war theory, and applies its tenets to the realities of nuclear weapons and finds it sadly wanting. Other chapters deal with "The Example of Christ and Today's Conventional Wisdom" and "A Look at Conventional War Today." More important are the later chapters "The Process of Peace" and "Hopes and Fears in Our Future."

The Center for Peace Studies is working to integrate faith, action, and research into the process of peace. Resources include: printed materials, slide shows, tapes, taped lectures, and speakers.

7. *Faith, Justice, and Our Nation's Budget* by Ronald D. Pasquariello, Judson Press, 1982 ($6.95). Ronald Pasquariello is a fellow of the Church's Center for Theology and Public Policy in Washington, D.C. This book is a guide to understanding how the priorities of the national budget are set. Specific guidelines are given for citizens to affect the process.

8. *Seek Peace and Pursue It,* by Kenneth L. Maxwell, Judson Press, 1983 ($9.50). This book by Kenneth L. Maxwell, who has long been a leader in church activities for peace, defines peace in its various aspects and tells church people how they can take specific steps to work for peace.

9. *Peace Be with You,* by Cornelia Lehn, Faith and Life Press, Newton, Kans., 1980. We have war heroes galore. But do we have peace heroes? Yes! They are there, but many of the peace stories coming out of our biblical heritage have gone begging for someone to document them for us.

This resource book is ideal for parents and teachers and can help us all to appreciate the Christian way of peace. The project was initiated by the Mennonite Central Committee.

The nearly sixty stories told here in understandable language are about those whose lives have been committed to peace. Arranged chronologically starting with the first century, selections include: "If Your Enemy Is Hungry, Feed Him" (Servitor); "God Uses the Weak" (St. Francis of Assisi); "Blessed Are the Merciful" (Menno Simons); "I Cannot Forgive Him" (Corrie ten Boom); "It Must Not Happen Again" (Keiko Hatta).

Many of the stories rendered in dialogue form can be adapted for brief dramatic presentations for use in worship and other settings.

There *is* a strong legacy of peace heroes!

10. *An Educational Exhibit About the Effects and Dangers of Nuclear War,* jointly produced by United Nations Association, American Friends Service Committee, Union of Concerned Scientists, United Presbyterian Church in U.S.A., and other groups concerned about the future of the world.

This 16-page, 8½-by-11-inch pamphlet is a reduced version of a series of educational posters (originally 38 in. by 25

For Better or For Worse   **by Lynn Johnston**

in.) for use in workshops and educational settings regarding the use and effects of nuclear weapons in Hiroshima and Nagasaki and the potential use of such weapons in the future as the major (and now minor) powers of the world continue to produce and stockpile new and better models.

Thermal effects of nuclear explosions in Hiroshima are shown pictorially, as are the blast effects of nuclear explosions from tests in Nevada. The first 110 seconds after a hypothetical one-megaton air burst are diagramed and superimposed on a map of New York City.

This booklet is available from Helen Redding, Wilmington College Peace Center, Pyle Center, Box 1183, Wilmington, OH 45177. Tel.: (513) 382-5338.

11. *The Hundredth Monkey,* by Ken Keyes, Jr., Vision Books, 1982 ($2), 790 Commercial Avenue, Coos Bay, OR 97420.

In this fascinating book Keyes describes a phenomenon noticed by scientists observing the monkeys on the Japanese island of Koshima. The scientists had been providing the monkeys with sweet potatoes dropped in the sand. The monkeys liked the taste of the potatoes, but they did not like the sand.

One young female monkey began to solve the problem by washing the sweet potatoes in the water. She taught this trick to her mother and a number of playmates, who taught their mothers also.

Between 1952 and 1958, all of the young monkeys learned to wash the sand off of their sweet potatoes, and only adults who learned this habit from their children practiced it. The other adults were still eating sandy sweet potatoes.

In late 1958 something startling happened. The number of monkeys who knew how to wash the potatoes reached a critical number, let us say ninety-nine for the sake of discussion. Then *one more monkey learned* the trick, and by that evening *almost every monkey* in the tribe *was washing* the sweet potatoes before eating them!

The most surprising thing was that this practice jumped spontaneously over the sea to other colonies on other islands isolated from the main colony. Ken Keyes concludes that when a certain critical number achieves a particular awareness, this new awareness may be communicated from mind to mind.

You may be the ''hundredth monkey'' needed to save the world from nuclear destruction.

Nuclear War Would Cause Unprecedented Deaths

The immediate costs in lives and property are incalculable. Whereas few
U.S. civilians have been killed in recent wars, most U.S. casualties in
a nuclear war would be civilians. For the first time, an international war
would devastate the U.S. homeland.

AMERICAN DEATHS

| IN PAST WARS | ♦ = 200,000 people | IN A NUCLEAR WAR* |

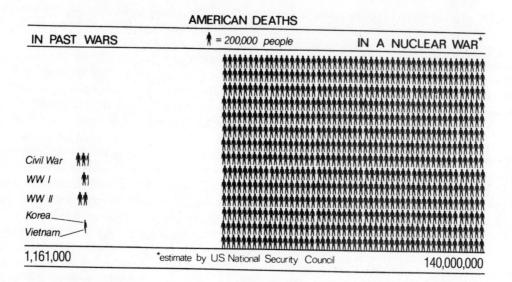

Civil War
WW I
WW II
Korea
Vietnam

1,161,000   *estimate by U.S. National Security Council   140,000,000

SOVIET DEATHS

| IN PAST WARS | ♦ = 200,000 people | IN A NUCLEAR WAR* |

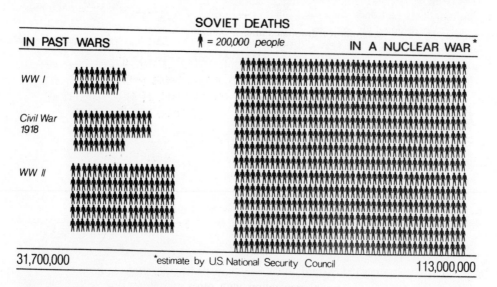

WW I

Civil War
1918

WW II

31,700,000   *estimate by U.S. National Security Council   113,000,000

"Effects and Dangers of Nuclear War," Wilmington College Peace Resource Center. Reprinted with permission.

From *An Educational Exhibit About the Effects and Dangers of Nuclear
War,* produced by the United Nations Association.

Appendix A

Check Lists of Some Whos and Whens of Needs Ministry

Groupings by strategies of ministry: around passages of persons' lives or stages of maturity;

Special groupings: around common crisis/issue/needs—homogeneous characteristics;

Groupings by ages/stages: infants; toddlers; early elementary, middler, junior, junior high, and high school students; young adults in college/trade-school or working/unemployed; older singles; young married persons with children/no children; married persons with older children, teenagers, or children leaving home; divorced and single parents, with/without children; remarried persons without children, with children of the "new" parents, or with children from prior marriages; persons in midlife crisis, including male/female menopause and other issues; the aging; and the homebound.

Groupings by life events: opportunities for entrances/celebrations and/or intervention-friendship/support, etc.:

EVENT	POSSIBLE FOCUS FOR MAKING A CONTACT OR STRUCTURING A GROUP
Birth of a baby	infant baptism/dedication, study of childbirth in advance of birth, child care, parenting from practical and scriptural perspectives, marriage issues; child abuse
Educational stages	graduations, special celebrations, "what next" sessions for graduates and/or parents
Vocational focus	career choice/changes, skill preparation, job search process, unemployment stress/crisis, family budgeting/finances, getting back into job world, career changes, underemployment, discrimination in job setting
Moving	structures for saying hello and good-bye, acknowledgment of growth and changes
Friendships	nature of nurture, boy-girl friendships, dating, homosexual and heterosexual relationships, fears/misinformation/myths
Preparation for marriage	individual/couple counseling, wedding preparations, group preparation with other couples and already-marrieds, parenting skills, budgeting, household-management skills such as cooking and maintenance, spiritual disciplines, health care, etc.

Divorce	prior discussion, marriage counseling, contact with children, extended family, jobs/child care, housing, transportation, guilt/forgiveness
Commitment to Christ and preparation for church membership	*youth:* inquirer's class, definitions and calls to commitment, beginning disciplines of growth, adult sponsors in 'the way'; *adults:* inquirer's class, discipleship for new members, clarification of covenant/commitment, formal rituals/celebration of the step, opportunities to meet others in congregation, sponsorship or one-on-one sharing *inactive members:* opportunity for creative contact, listening, exploration of perceptions and needs, call to recommitment and service
Illness/hospitalization	all ages, potential contact; all health care problems/issues opportunity for bringing people together; ministry; *healing* ministries
Health	care of body, prevention of disease, exercise, diet, care for spirit and mind, rest/sleep, life-style, stress awareness and management, drug abuse, Alcoholics Anonymous, Al-Anon, Agape groups, Weight Watchers/TOPS, yoga, jazzercise, hunger/food, economic independence/job
Spiritual growth	Bible study, prayer, study, action, meditation, retreats, workshops, spiritual disciplines, covenants and commitments to growth by individuals and groups, appropriating forgiveness, reconciliation, gifts of Spirit, repentance, commitment, love
Housing	search, deposit, cleaning, moving, locating services in new area, furniture and other needs
Prison	family member in prison, direct contact with prisoner, family needs/concerns
Wealth/poverty	life-style issues, persons with common concerns, increased self-awareness and options
Aging	individuals, families dealing with aging parents, needs/options, energy, meaning, purpose, housing, family, interpersonal relationships, relationships with children/grandchildren
Death	of child, of parent(s), of young person, from illness, from violence or suicide, from natural causes, grieving, understanding, sharing

Grist for the mill can also come from issues within the community that affect various people. (Most of these involve the systems of our society and their impact on individuals/groups.)

Some issues have both local and global ramifications and provide the potential for bringing people together, using either or both of those foci. Another working perspective might be those who are directly affected vs. those who are concerned but not directly affected. Some significant areas are:

education   sexism   energy

housing   poverty   natural resources—uses and abuses of air/water/soil

hunger   unemployment

racism   employment

control: use/abuse of resources by agencies/business/governments;

transportation and public safety;

war, defense, peace;

economy;

population: location, density, control;

justice: legal system, control, legislation, problem solving vs. violence;

health and health care: costs/service, doctors, pharmacies, manufacturers, hospitals, resources; inoculation;

abortion and care for pregnant women: access to resources; counseling, finances;

censorship/pornography;

civil rights;

mobility of population;

media: purposes, control, uses, abuses;

threat of nuclear destruction;

land: control—use for food/nonfood;

oceans—use

sanitation, disease control

Appendix B

Mission Groups of the Church of the Saviour

From *Handbook for Mission Groups,* by Gordon Cosby, Church of the Saviour, 1658 Columbia Road, NW, Washington, DC 20009 (see p. 44).

In 1982 the ministry of the current missions groups of the Church of the Saviour was as follows:

1. *Alabaster Jar:* Focus on the serious pursuit of an art, such as painting, sculpture, poetry—all to God's glory and the mutual edification of God's church.

2. *FLOC* (For the Love of Children): An ecumenical group serving abandoned, abused, and neglected children. Develops foster homes for over one hundred children. Refers volunteers to families seeking help in preventing their children from becoming wards of the court. Advocates on behalf of neglected children. Acts as a watchdog of the public system.

3. *FLOC Wilderness School:* Provides a year-round residential therapeutic camping program designed as an alternative to public correctional (and other) institutions for boys with serious social and behavioral problems.

4. *FLOC Learning Center:* An alternative school for foster (and other) children with emotional and learning disabilities that hinder their development in public schools.

5. *Gateway:* A group called to welcome and provide for the needs of newcomers and visitors to the Church of the Saviour. A regular Sunday lunch is sponsored, as well as other fellowship experiences.

6. *Children's Education:* Children over six years of age meet in mission groups that they choose themselves. Like adult groups, the children's mission groups have an inward and outward journey. Younger children are cared for and led in their spiritual growth by other leaders in the group.

7. *Cluster 70:* A support and counseling outreach to those in the community who are in crisis and are hurting, through a counseling center opened near the Potter's House.

8. *The Potter's House:* A rustic coffee house/restaurant in the inner city. Walls are available to local artists who wish to exhibit their works and a bookshop carries books for those looking inward and outward. Each evening except Tuesday there is a special group presentation on a rotating series of themes. Tables are served by members and intern members of the group.

9. *Dunamis:* A call to be the church to those in positions of political power. Members seek to build positive relationships with those in the nation's capital who carry responsibilities for decision making regarding the future of our nation. They believe that "Dunamis power," the power of the Holy Spirit, can break open the systems of death and oppression and allow our citizens to be fully human.

10. *Jubilee Housing:* Purchasing and renovating houses and apartment buildings in the inner city. Over 213 units now in operation. The residents of the units are being integrally involved in the rehabilitation, with each building having a management committee. Ultimately, the residents will own the buildings cooperatively.

11. *Jubilee Neighbors:* Five hundred families live in one square block in which the two Jubilee apartment houses are located. This group is seeking to develop a sense of community among these families through developing a number of mini-institutions. Examples include a basement-room coffee house, a "good as new" store for clothes and household items, a tutoring education program for children, and a health-care program. The goal, of course, is to bring God's hope into reality for each person.

12. *Literacy Action Mission:* This group is working with individuals and groups, training groups of tutors and helping coordinate education programs for adults throughout the city. In the District of Columbia alone there are over 100,000 functionally illiterate adults, not counting youth. As soon as students master material, each is set up to help another. In one year, over two hundred tutors were trained.

13. *Mustard Seed:* Those concerned with improving the play life of children in the inner city. They operate a toy-lending library, among other programs.

14. *New Life:* A team of facilitators available to other mission groups to help them deal with blocks that come up within their groups and to facilitate the confession of problems and feelings.

15. *Polycultural Institute Mission:* Provides low-cost housing in the D.C. area for students from around the world. Students work to help renovate the apartments in exchange for their rent and food. Twelve students were accepted to begin the program.

16. *Potter's House Senior Communities:* For those seniors who are alone, without family or community. Provides meals, educational opportunities, friendship, classes, trips to concerts and the theatre, picnics, and exercise classes. Help in finding jobs is provided also.

17. *Retreat Mission:* Operates a retreat center and program called Dayspring. Each mission group in the church plans an annual silent retreat. There are also retreats open to folk from around the world.

18. *Shepherd Groups:* These are responsible for the three nights of classes of the School of Christian Living. The school has three 11-week semesters each year and offers basic courses to understand the Christian faith: Old Testament, New Testament, Christian doctrine, Christian growth, and Christian ethics. Many other elective classes are offered.

19. *Threshhold:* Corporate Sunday services are planned by this group for all the mission groups. (Group meetings and worship happen at other times.)

20. *Wellspring:* This group provides an in-depth, three-year experience for twenty to thirty participants around the country who come to the Church of the Saviour for brief times each year. A spiritual director is assigned for each person, and close contact makes year-round learning and growing possible.

21. *World Peacemakers:* These are committed to the practice of peacemaking among individuals and in the global community. They lead retreats and produce materials for study and action.

22. *Cosign:* A group involved in the resettlement of refugees in the greater Washington, DC, area—primarily folk from Thailand.